The Ethics of Cyberspace

The Ethics of Cyberspace

Cees J. Hamelink

SAGE Publications
London • Thousand Oaks • New Delhi

This work was originally published as *Digitaal Fatsoen*
© Uitgeverij Boom 1999, Holland
This translation © Cees J. Hamelink 2000

First published 2000

Reprinted 2002

SAGE Publications Ltd
6 Bonhill Street
London EC2A 4PU

SAGE Publications Inc
2455 Teller Road
Thousand Oaks, California 91320

SAGE Publications India Pvt Ltd
32, M-Block Market
Greater Kailash – I
New Delhi 110 048

British Library Cataloguing in Publication Data
A catalogue record for this book is
available from the British Library

ISBN 0 7619 6668 4
ISBN 0 7619 6669 2 (pbk)

Library of Congress catalog card number available

Typeset by Keystroke, Jacaranda Lodge, Wolverhampton.
Printed and bound in Great Britain by Biddles Ltd., Guildford and King's Lynn

Contents

Preface

This book is about the governance of CyberSpace. CyberSpace is the virtual communicative space created by digital technologies. It is not limited to the operation of computer networks, but also encompasses all social activities in which digital information and communication technologies (ICTs) are deployed. It thus ranges from computerized reservation systems to automated teller systems and smart cards. With the 'embedding' of digital facilities in more and more objects (from microwave ovens to jogging shoes), these acquire intelligent functions and communicative capacities and begin to create a permanent virtual life-space.

The issue of the governance of CyberSpace emerges in many current ICT debates at different levels. There is the staunch anarchistic position that considers CyberSpace a totally new territory where conventional rules do not apply. As the CyberSpace Declaration of Independence (1996) states: 'We have no elected government, nor are likely to have one, so I address you with no greater authority than that with which liberty itself always speaks. I declare the global social space we are building to be naturally independent of the tyrannies you seek to impose on us . . . CyberSpace does not lie within your borders . . . It is an act of nature and it grows itself through our collective actions.' For those holding this cyber-libertarian view (represented by visionaries like John Perry Barlow) no governance is the best governance.

But, however attractive this approach may seem, if more people are to use CyberSpace this is likely to need public and corporate policy-making. This is equally the case if CyberSpace is to be protected against unprecedented opportunities for criminal activity. Moreover, CyberSpace technology does create a virtual reality, but this is not altogether de-linked from politics in the real world.

Opposed to cyber-anarchy are those governments who want a strict regime for activities in CyberSpace in order to control not only the pornographers and neo-Nazis but also the copyright pirates or just anybody who holds politically subversive aspirations. Then there are the CyberSpace citizens who feel they can best police themselves and who discuss among themselves a variety of forms of self-regulation ranging from Parent Control software to CyberAngels, codes of conduct and netiquettes.

CyberSpace is perceived by the digital settlers as the last 'electronic' frontier, but CyberSpace also colonizes our non-virtual reality and lest it totally controls daily life it needs to be governed by norms and rules. A recurrent question is whether CyberSpace gives rise to new forms of democratic (electronic) governance, which are less territory based, less hierarchical, more participatory, and demand new rules for political practice.

Whatever position one may take regarding future governance of CyberSpace, it cannot be denied that in any case (moral) choices have to be made and are actually being made since inevitably the proliferation of CyberSpace technologies implies like all technological development a confrontation with moral issues on different levels. These relate to – among others – choices about the way the technology will be designed; choices among possible applications and the responsibility for certain applications; choices about the introduction and the use of applications. They also address issues such as the unequal distribution of harm and benefit of applications among social actors; the control over technology and its administration; and the uncertainty about the future impacts of technology.

At present, the prevailing practices and institutions of global governance are ill-suited to shape future information societies in a humanitarian way. The kind of global governance that is required needs the active intervention of civic movements. In spite of encouraging initiatives around the world, this is a slow-moving process at a time of great urgency. Citizens are at the crossroads: but can they decide where to go? This needs reflection and consultation. However, time is limited and risks are real.

The specific question that concerns me in this book here is whether international human rights standards can provide us with meaningful moral guidance for the governance of CyberSpace. It is my moral prejudice that the governance of CyberSpace should be driven by compassion for humanitarian concerns.

This book follows an earlier publication, *The Politics of World Communication* (1994). To some extent the text is a reworked version of a book in Dutch that came out in 1999 and was entitled *Digitaal Fatsoen* which translates as 'Digital Decency'. In the process it turned out that the Dutch text provided much documentation and inspiration, but in important ways the present book contains different materials and arguments.

I am grateful to Julia Hall of Sage Publications for her confidence and good spirits and to Carola Hageman of Boom Publishing for her encouragement to write the book on digital decency and her cooperation in using parts of this for *The Ethics of CyberSpace*. I would also like to thank Dominique van der Elst (University of Amsterdam) for invaluable research assistance, and Cynthia Hewitt (United Nations Research Institute for Social Development) for asking me to join the UNRISD project on ICTs and Social Development and providing some background papers.

As always – against her will – it is important for me to recognize the critical questions, the discussions and the support a special partner has provided.

Finally, the book is dedicated to a life-long friend and comrade in the struggle for a different world, the late Gerrit Huizer.

Cees J. Hamelink
Amsterdam

Prometheus in CyberSpace 1

Moral choice

The audacious Prometheus, according to Greek mythology, stole the fire from the Olympic Gods. When Zeus saw the glow of fire on earth, he became very angry and punished humanity by sending Pandora. She carried a mysterious box and when she could not control her curiosity, she opened it. All the disasters and plagues that were in the box escaped and spread around the world. Prometheus' theft is essential for human progress. Yet, the myth warns us that progress exacts a price: the anger of Zeus. Whatever breathtaking advances technological innovations offer, they are never without trouble. Technology inevitably brings great benefits and awesome risks. This essential ambivalence raises the challenging question about human governance of technological development. Can a balance be struck between progress and plague? What choices should be made to shape technology towards humanitarian aspirations?

Choices have to be made about the design, development and innovation of technology. Choices have to be made among ranges of possible applications. Choices have to be made about the use of such applications. These choices have far-reaching and long-lasting effects upon individual lives, societies, and even the sustainability of all life on earth. They confront the human being with an almost unbearable moral responsibility. How can we cope with moral choices about technology?

Throughout our lives we make choices. Often such choices are part of easy, almost trivial, daily routines. Sometimes they are different and have moral implications. This happens when we have to make choices among conflicting moral principles or when our choices have significant consequences for others. Most difficult are those situations that demand choices between two or more basic moral principles that are equally valid but demand different and conflicting courses of action. These are real dilemmas since any course of action violates a fundamental moral value. If we violate principle A by doing X we commit a wrong. Equally if we violate principle B by doing Y we commit a wrong. The dilemma challenges us to choose between two wrongs. Sometimes these dilemmas are 'made in Hell'. Such is *Sophie's Choice*. In this movie Meryl Streep features as Sophie, a mother, who in Nazi-Germany faces the ultimate dilemma when a German officer gives her the choice to save either her little son or her little daughter from deportation and subsequent death. Sophie is morally obliged to save both her children. Yet, she can save only one.

It is a common observation in most human communities that people make distinctions between forms of conduct they find morally justified and behaviour they condemn as morally unacceptable. There are most probably no genuinely amoral societies and very few absolutely amoral individuals. Usually we find in communities and individuals some form of collective or personal moral consciousness. Most people seem capable of a moral account of the choices they make with regard to themselves, their peers, or the collective they belong to. They can reflect on the perennial question: What is the right thing to do? In search of a satisfactory response, another question arises: Can ethics provide guidance in moral choice? Can ethical theory provide arguments that justify choice A versus choice B in specific situations? Without conducting a comprehensive analysis of all available approaches to moral choice, even a brief survey indicates that the conventional methods cannot satisfactorily resolve how people should come to justifiable decisions. Conventional ethical theories are usually divided into duty-based (deontological) and effect-based (utilitarian-consequentialist) approaches.

Duty-based approaches to moral choice

Act-deontology: This method is largely determined by the assumption that most people intuitively know how to choose in moral dilemmas. This implies that the crucial factor in moral choice is personal moral intuition. Professionals often claim that they instinctively know what is the right thing to do. Their moral feelings guide them flawlessly to responsible moral choices. The problem with this approach is the enormous latitude it offers for shady moral trickery which basically serves self-interest only. The method implies a large degree of arbitrariness and moral arguments based upon intuition are difficult to justify particularly when people use different definitions of what intuition is.

Rule-deontology: This method takes the position that rules based upon moral principles can provide guidance in moral choices. In essence the method searches in concrete situations of moral choice for the moral rule that applies. For the professional practice such rules may be articulated in a so-called code of conduct. However, given the great variety of choice situations and the inevitable general nature of the rules embedded in codes, these moral rules are not likely to provide concrete moral guidance. Moral prescriptions in codes suggest an almost universal applicability which is not realistic since actors, situations and interests differ greatly over time and place.

The rules of a code may prescribe that professionals should be truthful but they will not explain how this general principle should be applied in concrete situations. Or the code may not tell its users when justifiable exceptions to its rules can and must be made. Also, the different rules in a code may conflict with each other and the code does not explain how choices should be made when basic moral principles clash.

A problem is also that no single moral rule has validity for all the different circumstances of its application in real life. Codes can be useful as instruments to identify an autonomous professional group. They provide a common set of rules for the members of a profession which contribute to the credibility and accountability of their professional performance. A code of conduct tells the clients of professionals what quality they may expect from the professional conduct. Although codes of conduct can certainly provide a starting point for ethical enquiry and debate, they fail to provide concrete moral guidance.

The gravest problem however with deontological methods is their neglect of the consequences of moral choices. This does create a peculiar tension when codes of conduct are used. The rules in codes suggest that those who use the code will act in responsible ways. However, since the code prescribes conduct in accordance with its general rules and principles, this does not necessarily imply a responsible attitude towards the consequences of such conduct.

Effects-based approaches to moral choice

Act-utilitarianism: This method is casuistic, meaning that from case to case it must be considered what type of conduct has the best consequences. This casuistry is necessary since general rules and principles are of little use in the great variety of choice-situations that real life confronts us with. However attractive this may seem, the approach has certain drawbacks. Firstly, who defines what optimal consequences of certain choices are? Secondly, it is extremely difficult to establish what optimal consequences are under different conditions for different actors.

Rule-utilitarianism: This method assumes that one finds sufficient similarity between choice-situations for general rules to be useful. In this sense this method resembles rule-deontology. Both methods propose that general rules should define what moral acts are. However, because of the large variety of real choice situations rule-utilitarianism is bound to fail. Moreover – as in the case of act-utilitarianism – there is no unequivocal understanding of what constitutes the best consequence (effect) for the largest number of people.

An important attraction of utilitarian methods is that they take the consequences of moral choices seriously. A complex problem, however, is that most of the time people cannot know the consequences of their acts. Moreover, consequentialist type approaches imply the risk that beneficial ends justify immoral means. In the professional practice the optimal consequences of moral decision-making are often identified as the effects that serve the 'common good'. This suggests a societal consensus about the notion of 'common good'. In reality, this is a highly evasive concept that has many different interpretations. In all societies opinions about what constitutes the 'common good' are divided. Actually, its meaning is often defined by the most powerful groups in society and rarely coincides with the needs of the less powerful.

The application of classical moral theories of deontological or utilitarian signature provides little or no help in the resolution of concrete moral dilemmas in real-life situations. Moral principles – in difficult choice situations – do not provide guidance to unequivocal, consensual decisions. Examples can be found in choices about euthanasia, abortion, suicide, armed conflict, social security, immigration and drugs policy. Concrete experiences in such fields as medical and business ethics have led 'to a serious if not widespread erosion of confidence in the power of normative theory to decisively guide the resolution of real practical problems' (Winkler and Coombs, 1993: 3). In the quest for a more adequate approach it has been proposed to conceive of morality as 'an evolving social instrument' that is part of a specific cultural context (Winkler and Coombs, 1993: 3). This suggests a contextual approach to moral decision-making which 'adopts the general idea that moral problems must be resolved within the interpretive complexities of concrete circumstances, by appeal to relevant historical and cultural traditions, with reference to critical institutional and professional norms and virtues, and by relying primarily upon the method of comparative case analysis' (Winkler and Coombs, 1993: 4).

The contextualist approach rejects the deductive model of moral problem-solving and prefers an inductive model of moral argument. This does not imply the wholesale dumping of moral theory or moral principles, but it does position theory and principles differently in the course of reasoning. From the contextualist perspective, a primary task in the situation of choice is the precise interpretation of the moral issue at stake. The first step is the attempt to understand in detail what the basic choice is in a concrete case. This differs from the deductive approach where one begins with a general moral theory or with general moral principles and applies these to the concrete case. The contextualist approach proposes a comparative case analysis through which resolutions to new choices are sought by reasoning from solutions that were preferred in similar situations. In the course of the inductive moral argument, questions are asked about the institutional and cultural settings and their value orientations in which choice situations are located. In this light questions are also asked about the consequences of choice and the interests involved: 'Where does the choice lead to?', and 'Is this desirable?' 'How are benefits versus damages of choice distributed?' And 'Whose interests are served with a particular choice?' 'Who gains and who loses?'

Ethical dialogue

The deductive approach to moral choice is increasingly problematic as societies become more democratic, pluralist and multicultural. Moral standards cannot any longer be authoritatively imposed upon all the members of such societies. Under these conditions ethics can evolve in a legitimate fashion only through the dialogue among all those concerned. As German social philosopher Jürgen Habermas proposes, moral standards are valid only when all those concerned would give their consent following their common deliberations (Habermas, 1993: 66). Herewith the basis is given of what has been termed a communicative or discursive ethics (Apel, 1988). In the dialogue it is explored upon which 'minima moralia' societies can find basic and common agreement. Since there are never ideal solutions for moral choices and since any moral choice is essentially contestable, the ethical dialogue does not automatically lead to the only acceptable moral choice, but renders moral choices communicative acts that are transparent for all those affected by them. The proposal for an ethical dialogue assumes there are always various plausible solutions to moral choice-situations. Therefore, ethical reflection should not focus on identifying the single correct solution, but should rather concentrate on the due process of the moral argumentation.

The ethical dialogue does not depart from a consensus on fundamental moral values, but seeks those solutions to moral dispute that optimally accommodate the parties' interests and principles. In the dialogue moral choice is conceived as a reiterative and dynamic process since situations and moral standards change over time and space.

Technology and ethical dialogue

How realistic is it to expect that societies would conduct an ethical dialogue about technology choices? This is a pertinent question since ethics tends to be assigned to an alibi role vis-à-vis technological development. The philosopher Goffi has compared the role of ethics with the use of bicycle brakes in a jumbojet (Achterhuis, 1992: 149). Whatever moral philosophers may say and whatever warnings they may hand out, 'progress' just goes on. Usually, the technological decisions are taken first and ethics may reflect on them after the event. Thus ethics becomes the agreeable topic of interesting seminars about norms and values. The developments with cloning are a telling illustration. According to biologist Lee M. Silver of Princeton University (USA) we cannot stop the cloning of human beings. Expert in the cloning of mice Laith Reynolds says that human cloning is not practised because there is not yet a market for it. But this will change, thinks Brigitte Boisselier, scientific director of 'Clonaid' on the Bahamas, and shortly human clones will be with us.

Whatever the case may be, the ethicists will not be asked and they will develop fascinating philosophical thoughts in the social margin. The prevailing trend is to think that all possible problems can be fixed by technological means that do not require ethical reflection. All social problems are technological problems. In this frame of mind their solutions do not need any ethical reflection.

Throughout the history of technological innovation its main architects have often denied their moral responsibility. This is the 'Frankenstein syndrome' that Mary Shelley describes in her famous novel (Shelley, 1818). Shelley tells how the scientist runs away from the laboratory when his creation comes to life. Doctor Frankenstein wants to escape from the monster he invented. In Shelley's story Frankenstein symbolizes the refusal of science and technology to accept moral restrictions, the inclination to be guided by considerations of 'engineerability' only, and the tendency to reject liability when undesirable effects occur. This amoral attitude on the part of the inventors is ever more problematic as more and more people – given the complexity of modern technologies – tend to delegate responsibility for technology choices to the experts.

The historical emergence of a 'technological culture' has made the issue of moral responsibility for technological development increasingly urgent.

Since the late European Middle Ages a bourgeois class of traders emerges that demonstrates a strong confidence in its capacity to control nature and master society. This is inspired by an almost unlimited belief in technological progress and in the perfectibility of the human species. This expansive mood is not hindered by moral considerations. There are always new targets and new tools to achieve them. The moral quality of technological aspirations is not questioned and their premises are never seriously tested. In the development of a 'technological culture' the human being liberates itself from the forces of nature, and at the same time it subjects itself to the power of technical instruments. In a sense human beings lose out against their own 'tricks'. In this process technology acquires human features. Even destructive tools, such as missiles, bombs and rockets get endearing names. They may be baptized 'Fat John', for example. And in the TV series *Star Trek* the man-computer Data wrestles with the question about his consciousness. The android considers that although he has human curiosity, he may never know what it means to cry or to laugh.

It is increasingly clear that human beings adapt to artificial environments and are equipped (through regenerative surgery) with artificial limbs, blood vessels, hearts, livers and bones. This in fact renders the question whether robots resemble human beings as intriguing as whether humans resemble robots. In science fiction the borderlines between human beings and their technology have already disappeared in the manifestation of the 'cyborg'. The cyborg is a combination of cybernetic technology and biological organism. This bionic creature is more than a fiction since so many cybernetic tools can already be constructed within the human organism (pacemakers, for example).

In any case the distinctions between human beings and technological products begin to blur. A shadowy domain evolves where robots learn from their mistakes and people talk to intelligent ovens. Appliances have begun to run parts of our daily lives, from self-learning microwave ovens, through to light switches that can be programmed, cruise controls in automobiles and alarm clocks that inform coffeemakers. These tools demonstrate a certain behaviour and we increasingly trust them to carry out our instructions with a high degree of precision and reliability. In principle we could program such appliances to realize that they fail in their performance and make them offer their apologies to their masters!

In general the relations between human beings and technological developments are characterized by the following features:

- a complete trust in technological solutions to personal and social problems;

- the belief that social developments are determined by technological progress;
- the tendency to jump on any technological opportunity;
- the thought that technological progress equates to the progress of human civilization.

These characteristics of the 'technological culture' are not conducive to the critical questioning of technological developments. The obsession to engineer what is engineerable – whether genetically manipulated tomatoes or cloned sheep – leaves no space for moral restrictions.

There seems to be in many countries an anxiety not to miss the next technological revolution. Consequently, most public policy decisions relate to the spending of public funds on the acquisition of the latest in information and communication technologies (ICTs). The overriding moving force in much public policy-making is the syndrome of 'technology opportunity'. Because the technologies are available, they should be purchased and utilized. Thus, policy-making is driven by technological development and fails to adapt technology to social needs. This is corroborated by the fact that in most countries technology choice is a highly undemocratic process, not involving even minimal accountability to the public. There is often no proper assessment, no public consultation or even minimal comparative 'shopping'. Very seldom is there a comprehensive analysis of needs and of alternative choices to meet those needs. There is often no serious discussion on the possibility of negative social impacts. Choices are more inspired by the risk of not joining the 'revolution' (the competitive risk) than by the costs of using the new technologies (the social risk).

The state of most policy-making is characterized by more emphasis on operational choices (procurement and deployment) than on strategic choices (the direction of technological development). Most public policies tend to be reactive and restricted to incremental adaptations within an already defined technological environment.

Although prospects for critical, ethical reflection on technology choice may not augur well, it should also be observed that there is today in many societies a renewed interest in moral issues generally. There is considerable public attention for such moral matters as genetic manipulation, in vitro fertilization, euthanasia, environmental pollution, or pornography involving children. There is also a widening debate on the social impact of new information and communication technologies in such domains as privacy, cryptography, digital democracy and cyberporn. It seems therefore worthwhile to explore the combination of ethics and CyberSpace.

CyberSpace

Science fiction author William Gibson invented the term CyberSpace in 1981 to describe a new, virtual world: 'A consensual hallucination experienced daily by billions of legitimate operators, in every nation, by children being taught mathematical concepts. . . . A graphic representation of data abstracted from the banks of every computer in the human system' (Whittle, 1997: 4).[1] John Perry Barlow, one of the founders of the Electronic Frontier Foundation, and lyrics writer for the popgroup Grateful Dead, referred to CyberSpace as: 'that place you are in when you are talking on the telephone' (Whittle, 1997: 6).

CyberSpace is a geographically unlimited, non-physical space, in which – independent of time, distance and location – transactions take place between people, between computers and between people and computers. Characteristic of CyberSpace is the impossibility to point to the precise place and time where an activity occurs or where information traffic happens to be. We participate in CyberSpace whenever we surf on the Web, but also when our personal data get stored in a databank, when we pay with a credit card, reserve a seat on a flight, or when neurologists make a three-dimensional computer scan of our brains. It is important to note that there is no single CyberSpace. There are 'cyberspaces'. People live, love, play and work in multiple virtual spaces that are sometimes complementary and sometimes conflicting.

CyberSpace encompasses all forms of computer-mediated communications and is thus composed of six components:

- digital computers (from laptops to expert systems);
- networks that connect telephones, fax machines through digital electronics;
- digitally-operated transportation systems (such as cars, trains, aeroplanes, elevators);
- digitally-operated control systems, such as are applied in chemical processes, health care or energy provision;
- digitally-operated appliances such as watches, microwave ovens and videorecorders;
- digitally-operated robots that independently run automated systems.

CyberSpace creates the fictional world in which most of today's financing takes place. Through CyberSpace flow daily $2 trillion in a complex money game.

Since more and more objects are provided with digital facilities, they acquire forms of intelligence, can communicate with each other (the toaster with the microwave oven, for example), and thus create a permanent virtual space in which time and space lose their absolute significance. Business is done in the off-office hours and off the physical premises, prisoners can be surveilled from outside the prison and without the prisoners ever knowing what happens to them.

The spaces of the physical and the virtual world are closely inter-connected. The social relations that obtain in the physical world do not disappear in the virtual world. Features and qualities of people do not dissolve as they enter the virtual world. It needs to be noted that expectations about the different and totally new nature, the openness and equality of life in CyberSpace tend to be exaggerated and require considerable qualification. Unequal gender relations, for example, do not go away as men and women sit down in front of their computer screens. Misogynist macho types will most likely just be 'digi-machos' in virtual reality.

When more transactions occur in the virtual world, this does not mean one can begin to ignore the realities of the physical world. Electronic commerce in particular nicely demonstrates the interconnectedness of the two worlds. Its growth implies that more people will buy and sell goods and services in virtual space. These virtual transactions affect the physical world. Among other reasons because the products people buy in Cyber-Space need to be delivered in the real world through physical means of transportation. As a result, increases in CyberSpace traffic lead to increases in the usage of the infrastructures of the real world.

Information and communication technologies: features

The virtual world of CyberSpace is largely created by the development and application of digital ICTs. These encompass all the technologies that enable the electronic handling of information in a variety of ways and that facilitate different forms of communication among human actors, between human actors and electronic systems, and among electronic systems. They can be subdivided into:

- Capturing technologies that gather data and information; these include a variety of sensing technologies e.g. bar code scanners, image scanners, remote resource sensing satellites; and related software tools.
- Storing technologies that store and retrieve data and information; these include such devices as magnetic tapes and disks, hard disk technology

for microcomputers, optical disks such as CD-ROMs, videodiscs; special
devices such as smart cards, and related software.

- Processing technologies: these include computers in different formats; mainframes, supercomputers, PCs, laptop computers; microprocessor chips, semiconductors; related system and application software tools.
- Communication technologies that include broadcasting, various audiovisual devices, local area networks, cellular phones, fax machines and electronic mail applications.

State-of-the-art ICTs are characterized relative to earlier generations by an increase in connectivity (most ICTs function in networks, as with the Internet), interactivity (as in CDi-ROMS and interactive TV), mobility (cellular telephones or smart briefcases), and intelligence (smart missiles, thinking telephones, expert systems).

A most salient characteristic of ICTs is their pervasiveness. ICTs are found in an increasingly large number of applications. They are everywhere: in the home from kitchen to toilet; in the office from electronic badge to smart phones; in health services for administrative and diagnostic services; in defence systems (smart missiles); in government; in education; in manufacturing; in an increasing range of service activities (banking, finance, travel, insurance). Increasingly computers are adapted to specialized environments and are built into desks, sneakers, walls and wristwatches.

Basic to the features of ICTs is their digitization. This means that technologies for the processing and transmission of information have begun to use the same language. This is the computer language of the binary code. This digital language facilitates the convergence of computers, telecommunications, office technologies and assorted audiovisual consumer electronics. Digital integration offers speed, flexibility, reliability, and low costs. Digitization means better technical quality at lower prices. Channels greatly expand their capacity, the electromagnetic spectrum can be more efficiently used, there is more consumer choice and more possibilities for interactive systems. Economic efficiency is achieved as conversion to digital forms of storage, retrieval and editing imply savings in time and labour. Digitization considerably improves the quality of voice and video transmission. In the process of digitization earlier analogue modes of information transmission and storage begin to be replaced by more powerful, reliable, and flexible digital systems.

The most important trend in ICTs – resulting from their digitization – is convergence. As all signals – whether they carry sound, data, or pictures – converge into the digital format, they become, however different in substance, identical in the technical sense. As a result, telecommunications and broadcasting integrate – that is, telecommunications services can be provided by TV cable networks or TV signals can be carried by telecommunications operators. This raises complex regulatory problems (what kind of legislation?) and institutional issues (what kind of jurisdiction?), but also consumer questions about the quality of services on offer. Although today it is still feasible to distinguish computer manufacturers, telephone service companies, publishing houses, broadcasters and film producers as separate industrial actors, they are rapidly converging into one industrial activity.

The technical convergence leads to institutional convergence and to the consolidation of national and international provision of information (and culture) into the hands of a few mega-providers.

ICTs are designed, developed and deployed by a transnational industry that generates worldwide approximately US$1.5 trillion annually. The leading companies in this industry belong to the world's largest manufacturing and service conglomerates (see Table 1.1).

Digitization facilitates a growing scale of information-related activities. Information has always been a crucial factor in social processes. Always, people have produced, collected, duplicated, or stolen information. Recent economic and technological developments have, however, significantly changed the scope of these activities. Digitization reinforces a social process in which the production and distribution of information evolves into the most important economic activity in a society, in which information technology begins to function as the key infrastructure for all industrial production and service provision, and in which information itself becomes a commodity tradable on a global scale. Digital technology is a 'synergetic' technology. Its growth leads to growth in other sectors of the economy. It creates an infrastructure around its products and services, similar to the car technology earlier in the twentieth century. As with the transition from manual power to mechanization techniques and later to electro-mechanical innovations, today's shift towards the pervasive application of electronic information techniques spawns a scala of new industries, such as software production, processing services, time-sharing facilities, semiconductor manufacturing, database management, or electronic publishing. As a result, issues that in themselves may not be new are confronted with the necessity to find new policy responses as many of the current solutions (in, for example, criminal law or intellectual property protection) are no longer sufficient.

Digitization is largely a response to the demand of the very big users for advanced Digital Information Technology (DIT) applications and DIT-based services. To meet this demand exceedingly large investments are needed. Such investments are prohibitively expensive for most operators

TABLE 1.1 *The 50 leading companies in CyberSpace industry, 1998*

Position	Company	Revenues in $000,000
1.	General Electric (USA) (Electronics)	100,469
2.	International Business Machines (USA) (Computers)	81,667
3.	Nippon T&T (Japan) (Telecom)	76,119
4.	Siemens (Germany) (Electronics)	66,038
5.	Hitachi (Japan) (Electronics)	62,410
6.	Matsushita (Japan) (Electronics)	59,771
7.	Sony (Japan) (Electronics)	53,157
8.	AT&T (USA) (Telecom)	53,588
9.	Hewlett-Packard (USA) (Computers)	47,061
10.	Toshiba (Japan) (Electronics)	41,471
11.	Fujitsu (Japan) (Computers)	41,018
12.	Deutsche Telekom (Germany) (Telecom)	39,710
13.	Philips (Netherlands) (Electronics)	38,456
14.	NEC (Japan) (Electronics)	37,235
15.	Bell Atlantic (USA) (Telecom)	31,566
16.	Compaq Computer (USA) (Computers)	31,169
17.	Lucent Technologies (USA) (Electronics)	30,147
18.	Motorola (USA) (Electronics)	29,398
19.	SBC Communications (USA) (Telecom)	28,777
20.	BT (Britain) (Telecom)	28,324
21.	France Télécom (France) (Telecom)	27,409
22.	Intel (USA) (Electronics)	26,273
23.	Telecom Italia (Italy) (Telecom)	26,164
24.	GTE (USA) (Telecom)	25,473
25.	Alcatel (France) (Telecom)	23,641
26.	LM Ericsson (Sweden) (Telecom)	23,190
27.	BellSouth (USA) (Telecom)	23,123
28.	Walt Disney (USA) (Entertainment)	22,976
29.	Canon (Japan) (Computers)	21,616
30.	Xerox (USA) (Computers)	20,019
31.	Telefónica (Spain) (Telecom)	19,457
32.	BCE (Canada) (Telecom)	18,507
33.	Dell Computer (USA) (Computers)	18,243
34.	MCI WorldCom (USA) (Telecom)	17,678
35.	Northern Telecom (Canada) (Electronics)	17,575
36.	Electronic Data Systems (USA) (Software)	16,891
37.	Nokia (Finland) (Electronics)	14,543
38.	Ameritech (USA) (Telecom)	17,154
39.	Sprint (USA) (Telecom)	17,134
40.	Time Warner (USA) (Entertainment)	14,582
41.	Microsoft (USA) (Software)	14,848
42.	Cable & Wireless (Britain) (Telecom)	13,142
43.	News Corp (Australia) (Entertainment)	12,995
44.	Bertelsmann (Germany) (Publishing)	12,803
45.	Viacom (USA) (Entertainment)	12,096
46.	Ricoh (Japan) (Computers)	11,156
47.	Seagram (Canada) (Entertainment)	10,743
48.	Sun MicroSystems (USA) (Computers)	9,791
49.	Apple Computers (USA) (Computers)	5,941
50.	America Online (USA) (Services)	3,052

Sources: *Fortune, Business Week,* Company reports

except the very powerful and resource-rich. The risks of these investments in a deregulated, competitive environment are of staggering proportions. One of the inevitable consequences of this configuration is that only a limited number of firms will eventually survive. Large investments in high-risk contexts tend to restrict the number of players in the marketplace.

Information and communication technologies: importance

> If all computers in 1960 stopped functioning, few people would have noticed ... Circa 1999 is another matter. If all computers stopped functioning, society would grind to a halt. (Kurzweil, 1999: 157)

The increasing economic importance of ICTs can among others be derived from the growth of electronic commerce. This kind of commerce results from the application of ICTs to the commercial transactions that take place among businesses and between business and consumers. The OECD defines electronic commerce as all commercial transactions that take place through open networks (like the Internet).[2] The growing number of people around the world that are connected with the Internet (some 140 million in 1998 and probably over 200 million by 2002) have begun to develop a digital economy. In CyberSpace they purchase flowers, shirts, jeans, books, CDs, tickets, hotel reservations, skin care products, pornography, kitchen equipment and household consumer goods.

Market analysts generally expect that e-commerce will exceed the trillion dollar mark early in the twenty-first century. A note of caution is due since it is difficult to precisely measure the economic significance of electronic commerce. Several of its important features such as easy access to data cannot be quantified. Moreover, reliable and comprehensive statistics are not yet available. Precise quantification is difficult and estimates vary widely. Overall increase of World Wide Web sales can be approximately put at a growth from US$8 billion in 1994 to US$19 billion in 1997 and US$251 billion in 2000. According to Forrester Research (in *Business Week*, 4 October 1999) digital trade could grow further to US$1.4 trillion by 2003. The Forrester forecasters see increases of online revenues as shown in Table 1.2.

An important development is the electronic sales of software. This implies that software is traded across the Internet. The scope is still limited but there is enormous growth potential. Some estimates expect that by 2000 50 per cent of packaged software may be downloaded and its sales may represent some 5 per cent of total world software sales (OECD,

TABLE 1.2 *Growth of on-line trading*

Industry sector	1999 (US$ billion)	2003 (US$ billion)	Percentage of overall trade
Travel	12.8	67.4	17
Retailing	18.2	108.0	6
Financial	14.0	80.0	6
Telecommunication	1.5	15.0	5
Electronics	52.8	410.3	37
Energy	11.0	170.1	12

Source: Forrester Research, *Business Week*, 4 October 1999

1998a). Sales of pre-packaged software reached US$109 billion in 1996, and this is generally expected to double by 2002 (OECD, 1998a: 4).

Whatever the precise significance and validity of all these forecasts may be, the general expectation is formidable growth of this sector in the global economy. It should be observed however, that even the expected US$1.4 trillion represents little more than 0.5 per cent of total retail sales in OECD countries (Dryden, 1999: 25). Most of this trade consists of business-to-business transactions. Expectations of the growth of business-to-consumers trade are based on the estimate that online trading will lower costs of production and thus of distribution up to 10 per cent of total sales. Some 50 per cent of this may be used to decrease consumer prices thus stimulating more purchases by consumers.

At present it should be noted that even a successful enterprise such as online bookseller Amazon.Com still makes losses. In the third quarter of 1999 these amounted to US$197 million. This reflects a not uncommon experience of online traders: the numbers of customers increase, the sales figures grow and the financial losses get bigger as successful operations demand more investments.

One reason for the growth of CyberSpace trading may be that a new generation that grows up with ICT enters the marketplace. For them there is nothing mysterious or uncommon about online transactions. A generation that spends much of its time in MUDs and MOOs will have little difficulty with cybershopping. They are used to what sociologist Sherry Turkle calls 'life on the screen' (Turkle, 1995). For the 16-year-old who tells us that 'Before I was on the net, I used to masturbate with *Playboy*; now I do netsex on DinoMUD with a woman in another state', the digital ordering of a pizza poses no problems.

Online trading raises governance issues in such fields as taxation. Should customs duties in the trading of ICT products be eliminated?[3] Another question is the feasibility of executing regulations of taxation on digital trading as its monitoring is almost impossible. Conventional taxation is linked to the place of residency of the taxpayer and Internet technology renders it possible to have floating residences so that it becomes difficult to link the potential taxpayer to any precise residency at a given point in time. Other questions concern policy principles for cryptography policies,[4] the assignment of domain names to host computers on the Internet (such as .com or .org), and how disputes should be resolved,[5] the question how laws should be harmonized to ensure that public confidence in electronic trading systems is promoted, the measures that are needed to ensure that proprietary standards do not create entry barriers to electronic commerce,[6] the problems of authentication and the agreement on techniques that establish security and trust in digital commerce, such as the validation of electronic signatures across borders, and the questions of jurisdiction and liability: which laws are applicable, where does an Internet Service Provider (ISP) reside, who is liable in cases of errors (in the event of telemedical diagnosis, for example)?

Obstacles in CyberSpace

Expectations about the success of digital trading have to be qualified as long as problems of security (of payments) have not been satisfactorily resolved, there are queues on digital highways, and the consumer has not yet decided to like virtual shopping on a sufficiently grand scale.[7] In many countries consumer unions have warned that many virtual shops do not meet requirements in matters of privacy protection, product quality, warranties, or methods and schedules of delivery. Irritating delays and slow-downs in virtual supermarkets are most likely when the numbers of virtual shoppers grow to possibly over one billion by 2010 (according to International Data Corporation in *Business Week*, 22 June 1998: 86). Moreover, traffic jams will be caused by the increasing number of appliances that will be connected to the Net, such as TV sets with a link to the World Wide Web and dishwashers that warn maintenance services through telephone lines about the replacement of parts.

The problems of failing security need urgent solutions. 'Net security is practically a contradiction in terms', says Jack Danahy, chief of security at GTE Internetworking Services (*Business Week*, 22 June 1998: 86). It would seem that a large number of potential users still hesitates to communicate financial information through the Internet as they are afraid of misuse, fraud and violations of their privacy. Using credit card numbers on the Net is still a somewhat risky business. Interception is fairly easy for the average hacker. However, to some extent the risks are not much greater than when using credit cards in the real world.

The greatest inconvenience of digital payments is their user-unfriendliness. They should be as simple as paying the person who delivers the goods at the front door. Not only is it necessary to install special software and know how to operate this but the money is paid before the goods are delivered. It is much more attractive to pay upon delivery or even with some delay as in the case of credit card use. In the present situation CyberSpace banking is more beneficial to the banks than to the average consumer.

For some it may come as a delight that CyberSpace finance makes control over tax payments more difficult. Digital money traffic makes tax evasion much easier. The tricks used by large international firms are now also available to the ordinary taxpayer. As cyberspace pioneer John Perry Barlow sees it there are bad times ahead for fiscal authorities. Taxation is based upon knowledge about flows of money and their proprietors and on the principle of territoriality. This is all changing. With digital capital it becomes increasingly difficult if not impossible to know who owns what money. Moreover, national territories are no longer of any importance. The taxpayers can live anywhere in the virtual world. The difficulty to identify and control transactions on the Internet because of their anonymity, speed and large volume renders chances of being caught very slim indeed and thus increases the attraction of fraudulent behaviour.

Information and communication technologies: impact

In connection with the use of ICTs the most frequently asked questions address their socioeconomic, political and cultural implications. The possible answers to such questions are essential for those private and public policies at national and international levels that seek to optimize positive impact and to minimize negative impact. A rapidly growing body of literature provides scores of claims, expectations, hopes and fears about the impacts the ICTs have. Since this concerns largely the social effects that ICT applications may have in the future, the various positions in the debate are all mainly speculative. This is also due to the fact that most of the empirical findings on current implications are ambivalent.

The economy

Most studies and discussions on ICT implications have focused on the relationship between the introduction of ICTs and the level of economic productivity and on issues of employment, job displacement, deskilling and reskilling. ICTs are applied by some 50 per cent of the workforce in the industrial nations, and their capacity doubles every two years. Of the world's total investment in capital goods 50 per cent goes to ICTs. There is empirical evidence that automation eliminates jobs. There is also evidence to conclude that automation creates new jobs. What remains uncertain is what the eventual balance will be. What we do know is that the notion of a single standard impact is very inadequate. We should rather think about plural impacts. Skills implications of ICTs are varied and flexible and are related to differences in socioeconomic, cultural and political environments.

It is puzzling that the widely expected growth in productivity as a result of ICT deployment did not happen until now. It is uncertain what causes this paradox between ICT investments and their outcome. It could be caused by problems with organizational adaptation. It could also be that what looks like an unexplainable delay is in fact the normal timespan needed before new technologies lead to higher levels of productivity.

In recent years it has become clear that the information economy is no solution to worsening trade deficits. In the USA, for example, the large-scale investments in ICT have not led to a decrease in its trade deficit. One factor here may be that the growth of ICT-type industries (software, entertainment, Internet, financial services) is not matched by their export value. Actually, the so-called post-industrial services export far less than the old-time manufacturing industries. As Fingleton reports in the *International Herald Tribune* (24 September 1999) information-based products have a hard time in export markets. They face theft of intellectual property and linguistic and other cultural barriers. They also tend to have a high service content and require a strong local component, among others for direct interaction with clients.

Politics

There is a strong claim in the literature that ICTs will enhance democratic decision-making. The lack of citizen involvement in democratic processes is common in most democratic societies as demonstrated by the low voter turn-out at elections and the even lower membership in political parties and cadres. The claim states that the utilization of ICTs will bridge the gap between governors and governed. This is a utopian scenario in which representative democracy is replaced by direct democracy and citizens directly consult or challenge politicians, and contribute to decision-making. There is, however, also an anti-utopian scenario in which ICTs reinforce state surveillance by massive data files and digital citizen profiles. In this scenario public decision-making is limited to the pushing of buttons.

A variety of current experiments (in so-called digital cities) demonstrate there is potential for improvement of decision-making, exchange of information and debate. It remains uncertain how this potential can be realized. ICTs can facilitate ways to consult citizens about political choices. But it is uncertain whether the political system will use this facility, when it will use it, and what it will do with the data it collects. It is uncertain how far ICTs improve the efficiency, the effectiveness and responsiveness of local or national government. In the fashionable 'information society' scenario ICTs are heralded as a democratizing, equalizing force due to their revolutionary features in providing information and establishing communication. This expectation is largely based upon the projection of a future in which unprecedented numbers of people have more access to information and have more capability to communicate with each other than ever before. There is ample empirical evidence that digital ICTs can spread information more widely than conventional technologies could and as a result allow more people to participate in public decision-making. They can support public deliberation in democratic processes. The problem with emphasizing the democratizing impact of ICTs is that they work just as hard against democracy. ICTs are equally effectively used by those who advocate the protection of democratic rights for all people as by those who vigorously promote genocide. Just as one can sing the praises of the democratic impact of ICTs, one can point to their potential for mind management.

ICTs make impressive volumes of information available to people. However, this capacity to inform does not necessarily equate to the capacity to empower. It is uncertain whether more access to information leads to the social empowerment of disenfranchised individuals and to the creation of a more egalitarian society. Through ICTs information reaches poor farmers in rural areas. It is, however, uncertain whether they can use the information to change the quality of their lives.

Culture

In terms of ICT cultural impact different scenarios are offered in the debate.

The Disneyfication scenario In this scenario a specific brand of Western modernity becomes the dominant 'way of life' around the globe and local cultures are assimilated by it. A very common concern in many developing countries is that the global proliferation of ICTs reinforces the colonial patterns of cultural 'synchronization' (Hamelink, 1983). Facilitated by technological innovations, the enormous growth of international trade, and a very supportive liberal political climate, we can see the rapid transnational proliferation of mass-market advertising and electronic entertainment produced by a handful of mega-conglomerates. There is a worldwide spread of commercially packaged cultural products. A uniform consumerist lifestyle is aggressively marketed across the globe. America's hottest export item today is pop culture. There is worldwide a clear trend towards an increasing demand for the American-brand entertainment. However, with the globalization of informational and cultural production, no longer US transnational companies only, but equally German and Japanese firms use information and culture to sell consumerism across the globe. Maintaining American style and production values, media products have now become 'the generic material for all transnationals, whatever their ownership base' (Schiller, 1993: 29). Fusing different sources of capital, the global transnational information and cultural producers are 'turning the world into a shopping mall for those with sufficient disposable income' (Schiller, 1993: 40).

It is obviously possible to argue that this 'Disneyfication' of the world does not yet create a uniform, global culture. And – correctly – one may point to the forcefully distinct cultural entities in the world to which the manifold inter-ethnic conflicts are so many dramatic testimonies. Or, one could cite the fact that non-Western values are by no means extinct and that an impressive volume of local customs is very much alive around the world. One could also claim that the project of a global culture is inherently weak as it has no historical and spatial location. A basic ingredient is missing for a global culture. Culture provides people with a sense of identity, a past, destiny and dignity. Culture is bound to time and space. Disneyfication is ahistorical and spatially non-located. It is hard to see that people can identify with it or derive dignity from it. But even if 'global culture' is not an adequate category of analysis, there is undoubtedly a process of 'cultural globalization' at work. A lively expression of this cultural globalization are the Disney amusement parks, whether in Tokyo Disneyland or Paris Disneyland.

The Disney-type cultural conquest has an important impact on economic development patterns and may well raise serious obstacles for self-reliant economies. Its greatest success is the worldwide emergence of consumer societies. Disneyfication sells very persuasively a consumerist, resource-intensive lifestyle that this world's ecology can ill afford. What matters most is that Disneyfication reduces local cultural space. The process of cultural globalization is engineered by forces that are intent on reducing local cultural space. The aggressive around-the-clock marketing, the controlled information flows that do not confront people with the long-term effects of an ecologically detrimental lifestyle, the competitive advantage against local cultural providers, the obstruction of local initiative, all converge into a reduction of local cultural space.

The dual-track scenario Even if the ICTs as vehicles for the proliferation of modern values and institutions affect the cultures of importing countries, the impact may be limited to those cultures' peripheral layers. All cultures consist of different layers and an impact on their outer layers (fashions in clothing, music styles, food tastes) does not imply an equally strong impact on their core layers (such as world view and cosmology) (Sogolo, 1994: 127). Local cultures may well maintain their core values and assimilate only in their peripheral layers. Local cultures may also define their own specific responses to cultural globalization modernization and may use ICTs in this process. Local cultures may also be commercially packaged and sold as exotic produce with the help of ICTs.

The hostility scenario Partly in response to cultural globalization, aggressive forms of rejection of the imposition of modernity have emerged in several parts of the world. This suggests that the poor may not always emulate the example of the rich and learn how to consume. They may rather entrench themselves into forms of 'tribalism', such as nationalism or religious fundamentalism. This tribalism not only rejects the values of modernity it also promotes the primacy of the values of collective belonging, racial and ethnic identity, national chauvinism, and religious and moralistic revival. At its core, tribalism is driven by the 'tribal instinct', a powerful force that has shown its devastating potential throughout human history and in recent times in former Yugoslavia, the Russian Federation and Rwanda.

The 'tribal instinct' represents the strong belief in the superiority of the value-system of the clan to which one belongs and the dedication to defend if not expand this by physical force. Its ultimate scenario is the total refusal of social cooperation with the outsiders, the fragmentation of the world into separate local communities that have no common ground unless one of them manages to impose its set of supreme values upon all others and locks all up in the oppressive irrationality of 'Holy Terror' (Conway and Siegelman, 1984). An ironic element is that also Holy Terror increasingly deploys advanced ICTs (such as cellular phones and websites) in its resistance.

Information and communication technologies: boom versus doom

The 'boom' scenario

This scenario couches its support for the deployment of ICTs in such terms as 'new civilization', 'information revolution', or 'knowledge society'. This reflects an emphasis on historical discontinuity as a major consequence of technological developments. New social values will evolve, new social relations will develop, and the widespread access to the crucial resource information will bring the 'zero sum society' to a definite end. The 'boom' scenario forecasts radical changes in economics, politics and culture.

In the economy ICTs will expand productivity and improve chances for employment. It will upgrade the quality of work in many occupations. It will also offer myriad opportunities for small-scale, independent and decentralized forms of production. In politics decentralized and increased access to unprecedented volumes of information will improve the process of democratization; all people will be empowered to participate in public decision-making. In culture new and creative lifestyles will emerge as well as vastly extended opportunities for different cultures to meet and understand each other, new virtual communities will be created that easily cross all the traditional boundaries of age, gender, race and religion.

The 'doom' scenario

Critical analysts reject the idea of discontinuity and stress the incorporation of ICT deployment in the historical continuity of socioeconomic disparities, inequalities in political power, and gaps between knowledge élites and the knowledge-disenfranchised. On the economic level this scenario forecasts a perpetuation of the capitalist mode of production with a further refinement of managerial control over production processes. It foresees in most countries massive job displacement and deskilling.

In politics the expectation is that a pseudo-democracy emerges that allows all people to participate in marginal decisions only. ICTs enable governments to keep their citizens under surveillance more effectively than before. The proliferation of ICTs in the home will individualize information consumption to the extent where the formation of a democratic, public opinion becomes an illusion. Cultural developments will be characterized by the divergent and antagonistic processes of a forceful cultural 'global- ization' (homogenizing the world's ways of life into the mould of global

Disneyfication) versus an aggressive cultural 'tribalization' (fragmenting cultural communities into fundamentalist cells with little or no understanding of different 'tribes').

Surveying the current literature and policy papers of many public and private institutions, it is obvious that the utopian and discontinuity claims generally have more support than the anti-utopian, continuity counterclaims. The prevailing scenarios are based upon the claim that a fundamental technological revolution is taking place which inevitably entails a radical social transformation. The conventional framework suggests that changes in ICTs (labelled as revolutionary) cause changes in society (also labelled as revolutionary). These changes provide the basis for claims to utopian versus anti-utopian scenarios.

The key assumption is that there is an Information Revolution! Basic to this social revolution is a technological revolution which is unlike all previous technological developments. The Information Revolution will lead to the creation of the Global Information Society. This society is fundamentally different from earlier societies. It is a post-industrial society and the implication is that the way we live, work, play, organize our societies and define ourselves will be transformed.

The technological revolution

Technical developments can hardly ever be described as radical breakthroughs since they usually have long histories of earlier technical discoveries and applications. Studies on technological inventions usually demonstrate that innovations have (often long) pre-histories of conceptual and technical developments. Also today's ICTs evolve quite logically from earlier technological generations. Size diminishes, speed increases, and capacity expands. But this is hardly revolutionary. Almost all developments today are just further refinements of what is there already.

New ICTs are often old ICTs provided with gradual upgrading and enhancement. Most of today's developments are gradual innovations that fuse existing technologies such as computing and consumer electronics by adding high-quality audio and video features to the PC, or making it possible to surf the WWW on the TV screen. The ICT industry promises to deliver shortly more powerful videogame players, cable TV set-top boxes for interactive and on-demand television, digital TV sets, digital videodiscs, intelligent home systems in alarm clocks, wireless telephones with computing capability and so on. Most of these developments are new but hardly revolutionary. Most of them add more processing power to the already existing tools such as television sets, home videorecorders and telephones.

It can be argued that the really dramatic changes took place much earlier in the twentieth century. The transition from a telephone, computer and TV set to the PC/TV is not as revolutionary as the shift from horse to auto. The latter represented a fundamentally new concept of transportation. So was the transition from card file boxes to computing. The transition from TV plus computers to the Information Highway is hardly a revolution. Once telecommunications, broadcast and computing technologies were in place the long phase (as in all technologies) of upgrading and extending began. Technical innovations can only be called totally new or revolutionary if the world is conceived from an ahistorical perspective.

The social transformation

Some two hundred years ago, in some parts of the world, mechanical techniques began to be used increasingly in the production and distribution of industrial goods. This mechanization process – largely motivated by considerations of cost efficiency – logically evolved in several stages of upgrading, such as rationalization (Taylorism) and conveyor belt automation (Fordism). Technical developments, for example in the field of energy utilization, assisted this process of refinement. Mechanical techniques, however, required capital-intensive energy in the form of manual labour or fossil fuel. The logic of cost efficiency supports their replacement by semi-independent systems that have minimal energy requirements and yield better cost–benefit ratios. Thus, electronic systems utilizing information rather than energy input came to substitute for machines. This process can be called informatization: mechanical techniques are increasingly replaced by information techniques in the production and distribution of industrial goods.

On the surface, this suggests the transition to a totally new type of economy: the service economy. Informatization implies the disappearance of industry, and it is certainly true that in many developed countries (as well as in some of the industrializing ones) the service sector contributes considerably to the national economy. However, many services are integrally related to industrial production and distribution and could not survive in a deindustrialized economy. There is little indication that the significance of industrial production is fundamentally withering away. The post-industrial thesis states that the numbers of so-called 'information workers' have dramatically increased. Apart from the problem of defining who these 'information workers' are and measuring their increase, the key question is whether this change implies a radical shift of power in labour relations? What kind of revolution does the information society imply for female workers or the ethnic minority workforce?

The question arises whether the historical process in which informatization evolves from mechanization implies fundamental changes in the social structures in which it takes place. It is usually argued that, in the transition from an agricultural society to an industrial society, and from an industrial society to an information society, the sources of social power shift. It may be that the sources of power changed from land ownership to capital ownership, and from capital ownership to information ownership; but what fundamental difference does this make when, after every shift, there is a new élite (usually evolving from the old one) that controls access to the source of power? The 'Information Society' scenario claims that, whereas access to land and capital was restricted, everyone can own information. A number of factors militate against this simplistic statement:

- In certain social sectors information is becoming increasingly complex and specialist. In general this implies that, despite an increased volume of available information, more people know less.
- The resource 'information' is far more difficult to exploit than land or capital. It demands highly developed intellectual and managerial skills which are very unevenly distributed in all societies.
- Advanced hardware and software for information processing are expensive and can be afforded only by land owners or capital owners. The rest will have to try to catch up using obsolete instruments.
- Information becomes a source of power only if the necessary infrastructure for its production, processing, storing, retrieval and transportation is accessible.
- The scenario assumes that people were never able to exert power because they were ill-informed. However, too often people knew precisely what was wrong and unjust, and were very well informed about the misconduct of their rulers. Yet their information did not become a source of power, because they lacked the material and strategic means for revolt.
- Control over and access to advances in ICTs are very unevenly distributed in the world, and the fact that millions of individuals can fiddle with their home computers does not change this. The management structure of the information industry is not affected by the proliferation

of electronic gadgets. If anything, it is considerably strengthened by the widespread use of its products.

This section of history may upon reflection turn out to be more a continuous process than the 'watershed' prophets want us to believe. What we experience in our era can often be explained as a mere continuation of the historical process. Rather than thinking in terms of a revolutionary change from the past, or a radically new 'paradigm', the 'information society' can be described as a logical sequence to previous historical phases.

The gravest problem with the prevailing scenario is that it ignores the social origins of the ICTs. It suggests that they originate in a socioeconomic vacuum. Their generation and development is, however, always led by specific interests, usually of a commercial and military nature. The information society scenario refers to ICTs as disembodied, independent factors. It takes a 'tool-centric' perspective that abstracts from concrete institutional settings. It ignores that the actual social use of ICTs is a constituent element of the existing social order. It bypasses the reality that ICTs are embedded in institutional arrangements that determine its social applications.

Although probably most participants in the ICT-debates would agree that institutional arrangements are important, in actual writings and decision-making most of them manifest a conception of technology as a force that drives social developments. Also, when ICTs are perceived as an 'enabling tool', there is usually more emphasis on technology as a disembodied variable than on the institutional arrangements within which it functions. It seems very difficult to move away from the notion that ICTs by themselves would create social impacts.

In the information society scenario there is the common assumption that social development is technology-driven. The real moving causes of social development however are élite decisions. As Went convincingly argues, the internationalization and deregulation of financial markets is not technology-driven but the result of political decisions (Went, 1996: 53–5). Following the current trends of deregulation, privatization, concentration, conglomeration and globalization (Hamelink, 1995) the information-communication infrastructures and their provision of information are increasingly privately owned and have almost completely moved out of the public realm. The current institutional arrangements are market-driven, corporate-directed and profit-oriented. This is supported by most national governments and by the international financial institutions.

A key feature of the current institutional formats is shaped by an important structural transformation of the past 50 years: the ascendancy of private power over state power with the establishment of the primacy of market economics over politics. One of the consequences of this development is the de facto administration of the world economy by social actors who refuse to accept public accountability for their decisions although they affect the lives of millions of people around the world. We have entered an era in which 'corporations rule the world' (Korten, 1995), the global reach of whom is not matched by their acceptance of global responsibility.

Technological innovations do not in and by themselves create the institutional arrangements in which they function. These are the result of processes of political decision-making that are strongly influenced by the world's leading economic actors. The world's current institutional arrangements for international (and national) telecommunications were more shaped by the decisions in the GATT Uruguay Round of Trade Negotiations than by the developments in telecommunications technology. These decisions reflect unequivocally the interests of the large transnational corporations that buy and sell telecommunications goods and services.

The actual social uses of ICTs are to a large extent guided by the political-institutional arrangements within which they are embedded. Whether the ICT potential will be realized to support human development, depends much more on the institutional organization of the technology than on its technical features per se. Given the growing demand for digital technologies, policy-makers will need to make policy choices about the deployment of these technologies in processes of human development: 'For all our ignorance of the overall impact of IT on jobs, general agreement exists that the impact is real, pervasive and occurs at an increasing pace. . . . Social choice, as well as technological potential, is clearly crucial to whatever pattern eventually emerges' (Lyon, 1988: 72). The critical implication of this situation is that policy-makers will have to make social choices that adjust the technological potential to the needs of human development.

A major problem policy-makers encounter here is that the general tendency today is to adopt and deploy ICTs within the social and institutional (conceptual and organizational) frameworks and routines of yesterday. ICTs can link industrial design, manufacturing, testing, marketing, distribution, repair and innovation. This facilitates new modes of custom-tailored and on-demand industrial production. As the UNESCO *World Science Report* argues,

> The benefits expected to accrue from these developments are enormous. New forms of management have already made it possible to shorten manufacturing lead times for existing and new products while reducing the volume of stock and improving the organization and performance of services.

> At the same time, the management and use made of equipment are becoming more efficient, as is the control of both production and quality. All these improvements can lead to reductions in overhead costs. (Ferné, 1996: 272)

However, if the organizational structures of industrial companies that deploy digital technologies do not adapt, this potential will not be realized:

> The integrated application of IT by business firms requires a radical reorganization of their working methods, as most organizations still apply a highly specialized and differentiated division of labour with the de-skilling of many tasks, inflexible production procedures and controls, a many-tiered, hierarchical management structure based on bureaucratic decision-making procedures and a mechanistic approach to performance. (Ferné, 1996: 273)

ICTs will not by themselves change existing institutional settings. This will need processes of political decision-making that are guided by the genuine aspiration to bring about sustainable and democratic human development. Once it is accepted that the digital technologies should be (re)-shaped to suit scenarios of preferred futures (for example, increased productivity with reduced resource consumption, full employment, direct democracy, cultural diversity), then the social and institutional changes required to realize the potential of the technologies to achieve this have to be identified and ways to bring about these changes have to be proposed. This is an urgent matter, because as the UNESCO *World Science Report* warns the use of ICTs within conventional social and institutional frameworks may not only hamper the realization of possible benefits, but may also reinforce the possible social risks (Ferné, 1996: 273).

The common ahistorical approach to ICTs leads to the 'muddling through' of reactive policies. It can be argued that a clearer view on implications emerges if one understands how technological innovations came about. This understanding could, for example, help to see that a given undesirable impact could have been avoided if the technological design had been altered. This makes proactive policy possible.

It is essential to note that possible benefits from ICT applications (in public administration, education, health or business) depend on how the technology is used in the production and distribution of products and services and whether the necessary skills and institutional settings have been developed for their effective use. It is also realistic to expect that the materialization of potential benefits will take considerable time. The acquisition of the necessary skills and the design of adequate institutional structures are time-consuming processes. Moreover, these processes demand considerable investments in both material (finance, technology) and human resources. Mansell and Wehn use the example of ICT applications in health care and write, 'The successful implementation of tele-medicine is not only reliant on the availability of the necessary technology but also upon the willingness and ability of health care professionals to adopt ICTs' (Mansell and Wehn, 1998: 85).

A sober assessment of ICT efforts in different areas of application teaches us that at the present time we do not yet have unequivocal empirical evidence to demonstrate success stories. In view of the prevailing euphoric claims, it should be asked why the new ICTs would lead to a more equitable distribution of benefits. There are no convincing responses to this question in the present literature.

There are obvious benefits: educational facilities can be improved by providing distant learning and online library access; resource sensing satellites in combination with data processing capacity can provide early warning to sites vulnerable to seismic disturbances, or can identify suitable land for crop cultivation; government administration can be improved; health care can be enhanced by remote access to the best diagnostic and healing practices; ICT utilization can improve the competitive position of local manufacturing and service industries. There is however also sufficient evidence to suggest that the utilization of ICTs implies costs (and indeed in some cases increasing costs; in many countries many people have to pay today for information that used to be available for free!) and in most countries around the world income inequalities are on the rise. The simple but awkward question is whether ICT benefits can be equitably distributed in a world where over 2 billion people live on less than $300 a year, where more than 1 billion people are illiterate; and where there are no schools for some 500 million children.

The conclusion then is that as with all technologies, the ICTs offer both potential for positive social change and heavy social risks.

The tall order for the governance of CyberSpace is to make social choices that adjust the technological potential to the needs of human development. The immediate question this raises is what analytical perspective could guide the search for these choices. This is particularly important since the 'digital landscape' is kaleidoscopic. There are strong expectations that the social and economic implications of digital technologies create a very bright future. There are also very negative and pessimistic projections that point to serious social and economic problems. These scenarios are compounded by the fact that empirical reality appears to neither completely confirm the utopian nor the dystopian projections. The question is thus how can we prepare for justifiable moral choices in this confusing panorama?

Notes

1. William Gibson says he borrows the term CyberSpace from the work by John Brunner (*The Shockwave Rider*, 1975) who attributes the notion to Alvin Toffler. Toffler did indeed in *Future Shock* (1971) popularize the term 'cyborgs'. In the chapter 'The cyborgs are among us' he wonders what will happen when we increasingly replace human components by electronics. How will we cope with the human/machine symbiosis? The term 'cyborg' was invented by space scientist Manfred Clynes and psychiatrist Nathan Kline in 1960 for an article on 'Cyborgs and Space'. They called the man-machine systems they considered essential to the development of space cyborgs. This term has been used more and more after the publication of Donna Haraway's *Manifesto for Cyborgs* (1985).

2. Electronic trading via the Internet is in fact the successor to the Electronic Data Interchange (EDI) that is already deployed by many companies. EDI is the exchange of electronic documents in goods trading and financial services. EDI usually operates within closed networks (so-called Value Added Networks, VANs). EDI is expensive and rather inflexible. The costs are incurred because complicated software applications have to be installed for each new trading partner. Flexibility is constrained because invoices and orders must be exchanged in fixed standard formats. The Internet facilitates the exchange of electronic data in many different formats. However, many of the big EDI users see EDI as more reliable than current Internet traffic. In the USA at present EDI traffic volumes exceed Internet traffic some fourteen times (*Business Week*, 22 June 1998: 83). Many analysts expect that in the years ahead this ratio will change. First to a more equal distribution between EDI and Internet transactions and later to a definite advance for the Net. This will be reinforced by the rate at which companies begin to share their 'intranets' (internal networks for authorized users) with more trading partners and thus create 'extranets'.

3. By way of illustration: The Information Technology Agreement, December 1996 (Singapore, Ministerial Declaration on Trade in Information Technology Products), elimination of customs duties on IT products signed by 28 governments.

4. By way of illustration: OECD Council Guidelines for Cryptography Policy, adopted 27 March 1997. A set of non-binding recommendations on policy principles; among others market-driven development; protection of personal data, liability; international cooperation; and standards.

5. By way of illustration: The Memorandum of Understanding on the Generic Top Level Domain Name Space of the Internet Domain Name system, WIPO, March 1997; OECD Working Party on Telecommunications and Information Services Policies, April 1997: Internet Domain Names: Allocation Policies. ITU Memorandum of Understanding on Internet Domain Names, 1997.

6. By way of illustration: The Model Law on Electronic Commerce developed by the United Nations Commission on International Trade Law (UNCITRAL), addressing the matter of contracts concluded for electronic commerce; OECD Recommendations on Electronic Commerce: Opportunities and Challenges for Government, 1997.

7. It is unclear how consumers will react to growing volumes of commercial messages. As there will be more trading in CyberSpace the interest of marketing

managers to reach virtual markets will inevitably increase. In January 1998 The US National Organization of Internet Commerce (NOIC) threatened to publish five million e-mail addresses of America OnLine (AOL) subscribers. NOIC wanted to force AOL to participate in direct marketing through e-mail. AOL reacted by stating that it constantly tries to stop the mailing of advertising and marketing messages, sometimes up to 2.5 million commercials per day.

Morality in CyberSpace 2

Old issues and new issues

The growth of interactions in CyberSpace raises moral concerns and sometimes even moral panic. This is particularly the case in relation to the distribution of pornographic materials involving children, toddlers and even babies through the Internet. However, not only such extreme cases are causes for concern about sex in CyberSpace.

Virtual sex

Sex sells well, also in CyberSpace. Actually, sex is among the driving forces of Internet growth, as it was with cable television, videocassettes and camcorders. Naughty Linx (an online index of JMR Creations, Boston) reports in 1998 that there were over 28,000 sex sites on the World Wide Web ranging from the Playboy Cyberclub to the Masturbation Home Page. Estimated revenues of sex sites are between several hundred million dollars and over two billion dollars annually (Forrester Research (Cambridge, MA, and Naughty Linx).

The moral issues that are posed by the combination of sex and CyberSpace are the eternal 'usual suspects'. The old problems of adultery, infidelity and deception. The American John Goydan filed for divorce in 1996 on the ground that his wife Diane had been digitally unfaithful to him. She had virtual sex with someone she had never met physically.

Digital technology creates the ultimate safe sex. Making love with 'sexbots' is now possible: these are robots made of soft materials, with human features, a pleasant voice, various dildos and an Aroma Scanner producing the body odour one likes best. The sexbot never has periods or headaches, does not need a Viagra pill and demands no alimony. Once widely used, advertising for condoms becomes old-fashioned. Safe sex in the near future may well be sex without a condom, but with the Virtual Reality helmet and data-gloves.

The large-scale introduction of the digital sex provider will certainly cause moral commotion in conservative circles. Age-old questions will be asked about sex without love and sex with yourself.

Hacking

Computer hacking causes concern and sometimes a great deal of damage. Hackers try – without permission – to enter computer systems by breaking through security measures. Those who do this with evil purposes in mind are usually referred to as 'crackers'. The practice of hacking is growing as it has become simpler all the time to be a hacker. You no longer have to be a digital expert. There is now available on the Internet a vast range of easy hacking programs – Programs to scan weaknesses in computer systems and programs to break into systems can easily be downloaded.

In principle hacking does not raise new moral questions. Breaking into a computer system with criminal intentions is illegal and a case for criminal prosecution. Also the stealing or damaging of materials in a computer falls under acts punishable by law. It becomes more complicated when hackers contend to enter systems with constructive intentions: to demonstrate that the security is not foolproof. Or when the hacker justifies his or her operations with reference to the right to freedom of information or the efficient use of the overcapacity in computer memory. For Clifford Stoll, however, even when hackers want to convince people that CyberSpace is unsafe, their ethics is an ethics of vandalism. Stoll argues that the hacker who intrudes uninvited into a system violates the trust which is essential for electronic communities (Stoll, 1995). Contrary to this position, John Perry Barlow has stated that it is a moral obligation to hack professional systems as resistance against the paramilitary bureaucracy that runs the United States.

There are manifestations of vandalism in CyberSpace that are very much the same as destruction of buildings, telephone booths or bus shelters in the physical world. Digital vandalism can be carried out under the cloak of anonymity and the perpetrators are more difficult to find.

In CyberSpace all those moral issues that confront us in daily realities are again on the agenda. All the immoralities of physical life occur in virtual reality: censorship, lust for power, treason, stalking, lying, gossiping, peeping, stealing, cheating, seducing, breaking promises, insulting, and being unfaithful, unreliable, uncivilized or abusive.

Old issues, new dimensions

Old moral issues do, however, acquire a new dimension in a digital context. The specific features of ICTs like anonymity, speed, outreach and ease of manipulation give extra urgency to conventional problems.

Chance to get caught

Although pornography does not just appear on your screen, it is certainly easier to obtain through the Internet than in more traditional channels. Most Internet Service Providers (ISPs) provide access to tens of thousands of public discussion groups among which there are paedophiles. Pictures and films can be retrieved from such groups and search engines can inform subscribers about the topics under discussion. Child pornography can also be exchanged through chat rooms, websites and bulletin boards that operate separately from the Internet. Distributors can use false identities and often wipe their traces clean through respectable institutions. They are spread around the world in countries that all have different legal systems and catching them involves the assistance of the ISPs. However, the ISPs violate their clients' privacy if they collaborate with law enforcement agencies.

In CyberSpace it is relatively difficult to prohibit the distribution of illegal materials. All of this, however, does not imply that we face new moral problems. The problem has existed for a long time, but the chance to get caught on grounds of immoral behaviour has diminished considerably. This is partly related to the possibility to operate in CyberSpace anonymously.

Persona and anonymity

In the so-called Multi-User Domains (MUDs) people communicate with each other through a 'persona' that they have invented themselves. Often men take a female persona and in general people like to pretend to be a much younger person. The anonymity makes lying very easy and difficult to detect. Deceptive behaviour in CyberSpace is, however, not a new moral issue though it raises the problem of 'moral distance' with extra urgency. The greater the distance to potential victims, the easier it will be for people to inflict harm they would refrain from in face-to-face situations. The classical illustration is the bomber pilot who drops his lethal loads from such great distances that he never sees the consequences and may believe he is playing a computer game.

Scale and speed

ICTs tend to reinforce effects in exponential ways. Data can be copied, modified and distributed at a grand scale with much speed and very easily. The speed of digital communication does not create new forms of immorality, but makes it possible to commit immoral acts so fast one hardly notices. Moreover, whatever one wants to communicate, it is easy to reach an almost unlimited number of addressees.

New issues: challenges to a human-centric morality?

A special dimension of current technological developments is the design of artificial intelligence (AI) and its application in so-called expert systems. Here we may encounter completely new moral issues.

AI research not only attempts to replicate human brain capacity in digital systems, but also tries to find forms of man/machine symbiosis that enlarge the problem-solving capacities of both human beings and machines. It is remarkable that the literature on computer ethics hardly touches this. Present discussions focus on the possible effects of intelligent robotic systems on employment (Nilsson, 1990) and the use of expert systems in health care (Bynum and Fodor, 1998; Snapper, 1998). It is quite common to criticize or ridicule the pretentious forecasts of the AI community. According to Forester and Morrison many such forecasts are 'hype, hot air and bulldust' (1995: 191). It is indeed true that many excited claims by AI researchers never materialized. Critics argue against AI research that the nature of human intelligence and the limits of machine-thinking render it futile to reflect upon future forms of new and intelligent life. This criticism is, however, based upon the flawed assumption that certain developments will not occur, because we presently hold them to be unrealistic. This is not a very convincing argument against the possibility that what we perceive as fiction could be reality.

AI research raises moral issues that were not posed by other technologies. Let us assume that new types of human intelligence could be developed that would be superior to the capacities of the human species. The confrontation between the human being and the humanoid digital system (the 'cyborg') creates a fundamentally new situation for moral philosophy. The cyborg presupposes a development by which digital electronics is deployed within the human body and human brainpower is linked to cybernetic systems. This would seem to belong to the realm of science fiction and indeed it is not possible to predict with any certainty which forms of digital life this leads us to. Since there are no indications that human beings will be held back by moral considerations in the search for the possibility of 'virtual people', it is only reasonable not to discard the evolution of a new humanoid species, more intelligent than human beings. This would raise such new questions as: How should we coexist with cyborgs? Can we design new moral codes in consultation with them?

It is a fascinating thought experiment. For the first time in their history, human beings would have to cooperate with a different species. The relations between human beings and other species were never based upon cooperation. Whatever feelings people may have for animals, they never cooperate with them. People have never negotiated with other species about coexistence. The cyborg would force humans to do so. In this confrontation it may turn out that our moral rules are too human-centric. Many animals have suffered under this, but could not negotiate with humans about a change of the moral canon. The new species could do just this and challenge the human being to design a morality that takes all sentient beings seriously.

In moral philosophy as it has developed over centuries, the human being has always been the essential yardstick. Choices among alternatives for action are usually measured against their significance for the human species. There may be rules for moral conduct vis-à-vis other beings (such as animals) but the framework within which these rules are applied is decided by the human being. Animals will be decently treated, but within the frame of them being 'pets' or caged in zoos or circuses. The other species are excluded from the definition of these frameworks.

In the common ethical theories the essential moral categories, such as conscience, duty, responsibility, are typically related to the human psychology. Most moral rules apply only to relations among human beings. The prohibition of torture, for example, does not normally apply to animals. The rationale for many moral rules is based upon qualities of life among human beings. Not lying, for example, protects human societies from total chaos – when nobody trusts anybody – but why would this apply to societies made up of non-human intelligent beings?

If this reads more as 'fiction' than as 'science', one may want to think about today's achievements in science and technology:

- The replacement of biological organs with artificially produced organs ('regenerative medicine').
- The production of complete copies of human organisms ('cloning technology').
- Isolating and keeping alive human brains (neurophysiology).

- The implantation of technical systems in human organisms (pacemakers, hearing aids).
- The development of neural networks with extraordinary intelligence capacities.
- The temporary transfer of organic functions to technical systems (in kidney dialysis, for example).
- The production of humanoid robots that are capable of solid and creative forms of cooperation.
- The mapping of the human genetic blueprint to predict illnesses such as cancer or Alzheimer.

An important factor to take into account is also the increasing rapidity of technological development: if we put the emergence of the homo sapiens (the only humanoid species) at some 40,000 years ago, then the first signs of agricultural technology arose only 30,000 years later. However, whereas the first electronic computers arrived in the early 1940s, in 1994 there was the World Wide Web and in 1997 the software Deep Blue could beat the world chess champion Kasparov. There is reason to believe that the exponential growth of technological potential will continue. Technological development is an accelerating process (Kurzweil, 1999: 15). Also the time that is needed for large numbers of people to accept a technology decreases over time. It took almost 50 years before 50 million people used radio, 16 years for personal computers, 13 years for television, and only four years for the World Wide Web.

Whatever we may think of this, the current applications of intelligent systems already cause complicated moral choices. How should we deal with the issue of accountability when computers are used in decision-making processes? Who is to blame when digital systems fail to make the right decision? Should hospitals be insured against the accidents that decisions made by expert systems may cause? A digital defibrillation system regulates a patient's heartbeat and takes decisions just like the human medical practitioner would do. The digital system, like the human being, makes mistakes. It fails to ask for sufficient information, ignores warning signals, or dedicates too much valuable time to the wrong search (Snapper, 1998: 48). Under what conditions are medical doctors responsible for choices made by digital systems? As long as such systems function under their direct supervision, the question is easy to answer. However, the medical doctor is not responsible for the mistakes the nurse makes during the doctor's absence.

Possibly a similar reasoning applies to the digital assistant. Using intelligent digital systems for human tasks does not pose in itself new questions. As long as the tasks are formulated in relatively simple ways or systems have acquired high degrees of intelligence, there is hardly a problem. If tasks are delegated to systems that are inadequately equipped to perform them, the problem is similar to asking human assistants to carry out jobs for which they are not qualified. The issue of moral (ir)responsibility remains the same. The new problem occurs when responsibility is given to digital systems in situations where there is no direct liability of the human supervisor. This is the case of the nurse who acts during the doctor's absence. The nurse is now liable for the choices he or she makes. However, can an expert system be made liable for harmful choices? This is an important question because the issues of responsibility and liability are an integral part of moral reflection. There is a fundamental desire in human beings to know 'who did it', who is to blame and who will compensate for wrongs inflicted. Political scientist Allison Renteln did comparative research on the universality of human rights (Renteln, 1990). She found in all cultures the need to seek some form of retribution for evil deeds conducted by the members of a community.[1]

When people hand over responsibility for risky choices to digital systems, a new moral issue is at stake: How to cope with situations in which serious suffering is caused by the wrong choice for which no one is liable and for which no compensation can be given? The moral issues that CyberSpace raises occur at different levels. In most current discussions about ethics in CyberSpace these are the dimensions of personal, professional and corporate morality.

Personal morality

For the individual conduct of CyberSpace users there is an impressive volume of rules, prescriptions and commandments on the market. In most books on computer and ICT ethics the crucial question is how individuals (private and professional) should behave in CyberSpace. Interesting ideas are found in the publications of Baase (1997), Ermann et al. (1990), Forester and Morrison (1995), Johnson (1994), Kallman and Grillo (1996), and Kling (1996). These authors raise questions such as: Do CyberSpace interactions require the same rules as conventional mail? Can one remain anonymous? Is it acceptable to use pseudonyms? Can the choice of a fictive personality ('persona') do harm to other users? How decent is it to post a nude picture of your ex-partner on the Web? Can one gossip, lie or deceive in the virtual world? Are you responsible for decisions taken by your personal digital assistant? What about 'hacking', 'spamming', 'flaming'? How well should one protect one's privacy? Should your children's access to CyberSpace be guarded? What dangers threaten your children when they surf on the Internet? Should one arrange financial matters through CyberSpace? Is software piracy the same as theft? Is digital surveillance of employees morally acceptable? What should we do if we want free speech in CyberSpace but also want to rid the Net of child pornography and racism? As more and more schools begin to use the Internet questions come up such as: Should pupils be totally free in the use of the Internet? Can we design reasonable guidelines for children's use of CyberSpace? Does CyberSpace demand moral rules different from existing ethics? How adequate are the existing moral standards? Do we need a new morality for virtual reality?

Professional users confront complex questions about the reliability of test procedures, conflicts between employers and clients, responsibilities for system crashes or the balancing of systems security against users' privacy. How adequately are professional responsibilities and liabilities addressed in professional codes of conduct?

The conventional approach to these moral issues tends to follow a common pattern. Authors first provide an introduction to the most important ethical theories: Aristotelian virtue ethics, ethical relativism, Kantian deontology, utilitarianism (or consequentialism), and rights-based theories. This is followed by an overview of the key issues, often with scenarios and practical exercises. Most books have a chapter on professional ethics and provide examples of codes of conduct. Issues dealt with are usually intellectual property rights, piracy, privacy, cryptography, security, computer crime, liability, unreliability, censorship and free speech, artificial intelligence, and the effects of computers in the workplace, the school, health care, the home, electronic democracy and gender issues in CyberSpace. The solutions proposed by various authors are often based upon existing legislation, and where this fails reference is made to self-regulatory measures such as 'netiquette' rules and codes of conduct.

Self-regulation: rules and commandments

Increasingly Internet communities set their own norms and standards and define their own specific rules and duties. Early on in the development of electronic networks discussions arose on forms of self-regulation. In order to avoid external interference, network users have tried to develop norms for acceptable usage of digital technologies. Attempts at self-regulation dealt with the limits to the commercial use of academic networks, or with the restrictions to the distribution of pornographic materials and hate speech.

In 1985 Norman Z. Shapiro and Robert H. Anderson produced a report (funded by the National Science Foundation and the RAND Corporation) about ethics and etiquette in relation to sending and receiving e-mail messages. They were primarily interested in the effective and efficient use of the new communication technology. The report discussed among other topics 'flaming'. Flaming is the sending of messages with an explicit emotional, often aggressive content. The authors advise that recipients should not immediately respond but should wait some 24 hours and then react through another means of communication, for example the telephone. Such common-sense recommendations fall more in the domain of psychological insights than under the rubric of morality.

On the Internet one finds many examples of so-called 'acceptable use policies': guidelines for an acceptable use of CyberSpace. The University of Southern California, for example, proposes a 'Network Ethics Statement' that prohibits the deliberate disturbance of network traffic, the fraudulent use of university computers, theft of data, equipment and intellectual property, misconduct in rooms for common use of computers, forfeiting of electronic mail.

Internet Service Provider CompuServe concludes a Service Agreement with subscribers in which users accept 'not to publish on or over the Service any information, software or other content which violates or infringes upon the rights of any others or which would be abusive, profane or offensive to an average person'.

America Online operates with a Service Agreement that has among others the following rules: 'AOL Inc. reserves the right, but does not assume the responsibility, to restrict communication which AOL Inc. deems in its discretion to be harmful to individual Members, damaging to the communities which make up the AOL Service, or in violation of AOL Inc.'s or any third party's rights'. Among the activities that are prohibited are 'to harass, threaten, embarrass or cause distress, unwanted attention or discomfort upon another Member or user of AOL Inc. or other person or entity; post or transmit sexually explicit images or other content which is deemed by AOL Inc. to be offensive; to transmit any unlawful, harmful, threatening, abusive, harassing, defamatory, vulgar, obscene, hateful, racially, ethnically or otherwise objectionable Content'.

Some network providers go even beyond these restrictions. To be admitted to the US-based National Capital FreeNet (NCF) for example the aspiring member should agree to censorship exercised by the provider and a serious restriction of privacy. The contract reads in parts:

1. That the use of the System is a privilege which may be revoked by the Board of Directors of the System at any time for abusive conduct or

fraudulent use. Such conduct would include, but not be limited to, the placing of unlawful information on the system, the use of obscene, abusive or otherwise objectionable language in either public or private messages, or violation of this Agreement. The Board of the National Capital FreeNet will be the sole arbiter of what constitutes obscene, abusive, or objectionable language.

2. That the NCF reserves the right to review any material stored in files or programs to which other Members have access and will edit or remove any material which the Board, in its sole discretion, believes may be unlawful, obscene, abusive or otherwise objectionable. (Doheny-Farina, 1996: 146)

The well-known 'Guardian Angels' (volunteer vigilantes who among others patrol the New York subway) were in August 1996 complemented by their virtual colleagues, the CyberAngels.[2] The code of conduct for the CyberAngels is based upon the right to freedom of expression combined with the responsibility to use this freedom to the common good of the CyberSpace community. CyberAngels believe the Internet should regulate itself: 'We further believe that the best legislation and rules governing the Internet comes from the Internet community itself.' The CyberAngels pledge they will not hinder or intimidate other users. They hunt after paedophiles and software pirates and report problem cases to ISPs.

The American Ethical Hackers Against Paedophilia focuses on the distribution of child pornography on the Internet and its members search in chatrooms for illegal material that they hand over to the police authorities.

It is increasingly common for news groups or discussion groups to agree upon some basic rules of conduct. Many newsgroups and discussion groups have rules about handling personal mail, use of sarcasm, the reduction of flaming. Often these rules are based upon the Golden Rule not to treat others in ways one does not want to be treated oneself.[3]

A fairly comprehensive model of 'netiquette' has been developed by Arlene Rinaldi.[4] She points out that the users of electronic mail carry responsibility themselves for the contents of their e-mail traffic. She warns that users should consider the possibility that others read the electronic mail. Never think, Rinaldi says, 'your e-mail can be read by no one except yourself; others may be able to read or access your mail. Never send or keep anything that you would mind seeing on the evening news'. Confidential messages should never be sent via e-mail. Rinaldi also suggests: 'Avoid public "flames" – messages sent in anger. Messages sent in the heat of the moment generally only exacerbate the situation and are usually regretted later. Settle down and think about it for a while before starting a flame war.' She also gives recommendations for decent behaviour: 'If you're asking for something, don't forget to say "please".

Similarly, if someone does something for you, it never hurts to say "thank you". While this might sound trivial, or even insulting, it's astonishing how many people who are perfectly polite in everyday life seem to forget their manners in their e-mail.'

Netiquette addresses the issue of good manners in human interactions. Its rules offer no innovative moral insights. They are merely based upon commonly accepted moral rules. In fact they say that users should act with integrity and care. They reflect the standards that apply to human communication in civilized societies. Arlene Rinaldi's website offers the Ten Commandments for Computer Ethics developed by the Computer Ethics Institute.[5] They read:

1. Thou shalt not use a computer to harm other people.
2. Thou shalt not interfere with other people's computer work.
3. Thou shalt not snoop around in other people's files.
4. Thou shalt not use a computer to steal.
5. Thou shalt not use a computer to bear false witness.
6. Thou shalt not use or copy software for which you have not paid.
7. Thou shalt not use other people's computer resources without authorization.
8. Thou shalt not appropriate other people's intellectual output.
9. Thou shalt think about the social consequences of the program you write.
10. Thou shalt use a computer in ways that show consideration and respect.

These commandments reflect to a large degree the moral prescriptions that the Old Testament proposed at the time of Moses (Exodus 20: 1–17).

Professional morality

With the emergence of the middle classes in eighteenth- and nineteenth-century Europe, a professional culture developed in the struggle against the aristocracy. One of the middle class emancipatory symbols became professionalism, the independent performance of professionals as it developed towards the end of the nineteenth century in medicine, the law and the clergy. For these new professions the articulation of a code of conduct reinforced the autonomy of the professional. It meant recognition of its social status.

Related to the development of ICT new professions came into existence. For the design and development of ICT hardware, software and networks, there are programmers, system designers and operators, engineers, instructors and consultants. ICT professions are still fairly young as compared to such fields as medicine or the law. These conventional professions tend to be better organized and have a clearly recognizable public status. ICT specialists in general have an enormous advance in knowledge in relation to both their employers and their clients. This gives them a certain power base. Combined with the diffuse nature of their profession this has stirred up the interest in efforts to formulate professional rules (Forester and Morrison, 1995: 17).

Professionals face moral issues in their relations with their employers, clients, colleagues, competitors, and the societies within which they work. For the employer–employee relation there are usually various contractual rules in an agreement that binds both parties. A key issue here is the matter of employee loyalty to the employer. Deborah Johnson writes in *Computer Ethics* (1994: 43, 44): 'Organizations could probably not function unless individuals recognize that they owe something special to their employers. . . . Clearly employers cannot demand every form of behaviour that will serve the interests of the company.'

The classical problem arises when an employee discovers that something is wrong with the product the employer puts on the market. If he or she warns the employer and the criticism is ignored the difficult question of remaining silent out of loyalty to the company or going public as 'whistle-blower' poses itself. Either moral choice entails serious risks. Another important issue is whether employees can transfer knowledge to their new employers should they leave their earlier employment? For both employer and employee this raises the question of the balance between the protection of industrial secrets and the freedom of expression.

In relations with clients trust is a crucial issue. Can the client trust that the company he or she hires executes the assignment conscientiously and with competence? What happens if the contractor knows that a competitor could deliver to the client a better product? How to deal with conflicts of interest if an engineer recommends systems manufactured by a company of which he or she is a shareholder?

In relations among professionals the question of duties to colleagues arises. Should one openly criticize or even accuse one's co-professionals? Is it a moral obligation to expose those colleagues who damage public trust in the professional group by irresponsible behaviour? Is it better to keep the dirty linen within the family and avoid harm to the professional image?

With regard to competitors there are questions about industrial espionage. Specifically, the development of digital ICTs creates many chances to 'steal' information from competitors.

ICT professionals also have responsibilities to the larger communities within which they work. For example, when they are involved in the design, production and maintenance of computer systems in hospitals. Those who design high-risk technologies confront difficult issues of moral and legal responsibility and liability.

To deal with such moral issues more and more professional groups design their own professional rules. Professional codes can be divided into ethical codes and codes of conduct. The ethical code is in fact a 'mission statement': a public announcement about the moral position of a professional group. The code of conduct recommends specific rules for the performance of the professional. Some codes unite both dimensions in one document. Several organizations of professional informaticians have in recent years developed codes.

The American Association for Computing Machinery (ACM) has formulated an ethical code for its members. The ground rules are: 'Avoid harm to others. Honor property rights including copyrights and patents. Give proper credit for intellectual property. Respect the privacy of others. Honor Confidentiality.' For specific professional duties the ACM code states, 'Excellence is perhaps the most important obligation of a professional.' And,

> To minimize the possibility of indirectly harming others, computing professionals must minimize malfunctions by following generally accepted standards for system design and testing. Furthermore, it is often necessary to assess the social consequences of systems to project the likelihood of any serious harm to others. If system features are misrepresented to users, co-workers, or supervisors, the individual computing professional is responsible for any resulting injury.

In the work environment the computing professional has the additional obligation to report any signs of system dangers that might result in serious personal or social damage. If one's superiors do not act to curtail or mitigate such dangers, it may be necessary to 'blow the whistle' to help correct the problem or reduce the risk. However, capricious or misguided reporting of violations can, itself, be harmful. ACM members promise to respect and promote the principles of the Code and they will accept violations of the Code as incompatible with ACM membership: 'Adherence of professionals to a code of ethics is largely a voluntary matter. However, if a member does not follow this code by engaging in gross misconduct, membership in ACM may be terminated.'

The ethical code of the American Institute of Electrical and Electronics Engineering (IEEE) obliges its members 'to accept responsibility in making engineering decisions consistent with the safety, health, and welfare of the public, and to disclose promptly factors that might endanger the public or the environment'. In relations with employers members should 'avoid real or perceived conflicts of interest whenever possible, and to disclose them to affected parties when they do exist'. With regard to their colleagues, members are expected 'to assist colleagues and co-workers in their professional development and to support them in following this code of ethics'.

The members of the Australian Computer Society state in their Code that the professional person should uphold and advance the honour, dignity and effectiveness of the profession in the arts and sciences of information processing, and in keeping with high standards of competence and ethical conduct, will be honest, forthright and impartial, and will serve with loyalty employers, clients and the public, and will strive to increase the competence and prestige of the profession, and will use special knowledge and skill for the advancement of human welfare. The Code states that:

> I will act with professional responsibility and integrity in my dealing with clients, employers, employees, students and the community generally. By this I mean:
>
> 1. I will serve the interests of my clients and employers, my employees and students, and the community generally, as matters of no less priority than the interests of myself or my colleagues.
> 2. I will work competently and diligently for my clients and employers.
> 3. I will be honest in my representations of skills, knowledge, services and products.
> 4. I will strive to enhance the quality of life of those affected by my work.
> 5. I will enhance my own professional development, and that of my colleagues, employees and students.
> 6. I will enhance the integrity of the Computing Profession and the respect of its members for each other.

The Code of the Canadian Information Processing Society provides for the following professional duties. Due to the obligation to the profession:

> 1. I will not knowingly allow my competence to fall short of that necessary for reasonable execution of my duties.
> 2. I will conduct my professional affairs in such a manner as to cause no harm to the stature of the profession.
> 3. I will take appropriate action on reasonably certain knowledge of unethical conduct on the part of a colleague.

Due to the obligation to colleagues:

> 1. I will not unreasonably withhold information pertinent to my work or profession.
> 2. I will give full acknowledgement to the work of others.

Due to the obligation to the employer and to management:

1. I will accept responsibility for my work, and for informing others with a right and need to know of pertinent parts of my work.
2. I will not accept work that I do not feel competent to perform to a reasonable level of management satisfaction.
3. I will guard the legitimate confidentiality of my employer's private information.
4. I will respect and guard my employer's (and his supplier's) proprietary interest, particularly as regards data and software.
5. I will respect the commercial aspect of my obligation to my employer.

Due to the obligation to clients:

1. I will be careful to ensure that proper expertise and current professional knowledge is made available.
2. I will avoid conflicts of interest and give notice of potential conflicts of interest.
3. I acknowledge that the statements cast in the employee/employer context, are also applicable in the consultant/client context.

Due to the obligation to students:

1. I will maintain my knowledge of information processing in those areas that I teach to a level exceeding curriculum requirements. . . .
3. I will treat my students respectfully as junior scholars, worthy of significant effort on my part.

The British Computer Society sets the professional standards of competence, conduct and ethical practice for computing in the United Kingdom. The code of conduct states that:

Members shall in their professional practice safeguard public health and safety and have regard to protection of the environment. Members shall have due regard to the legitimate rights of third parties. Members shall ensure that within their chosen fields they have knowledge and understanding of relevant legislation, regulations and standards and that they comply with such requirements. Members shall in their professional practice have regard to basic human rights and shall avoid any actions that adversely affect such rights.

The professional organization of Italian informaticians (AICA, Associazione Italiana per l'Informatica ed il Calcolo Automatico) has adopted a code of conduct that recommends its members:

1. A constant personal engagement in keeping updated on the developments of informatics in the fields that are more directly connected to his activity.
2. To make full use of all his competence in carrying out his duties, at least up to the level that he declared to have when he accepted them, and not to declare to have a higher level of competence than the one he effectively has.

3. To maintain the most complete secrecy on the data and news concerning his employer or clients.
4. To be conscious of the possible social impact of his work.
5. Impartiality in the decisions he will take or suggest and to be frank in declaring his possible actual interests in the choices of solutions of problems he is dealing with.
6. To be conscious of the responsibility he has in consequence of the most technical aspects of his activity – beginning with those of analysis and programming – because they are unfamiliar to other people, and because they can cause severe negative consequences if improperly used.

The Japanese professional body JISA (Japanese Information Service Industry) uses a Code of Ethics and Professional Conduct that advises its members, among others, to 'realize the mission of the information service industry and fulfil its social responsibility not only to the region it belongs to, but also to society as a whole'; and to

understand that its prosperity could be inseparably linked to its clients and make every effort to win their confidence of partnership by:

1. entering into a contract with clear and exact terms and implementing them faithfully.
2. strictly adhering to the client's need to keep its project, its strategies, and any other related information confidential.
3. and constantly providing the clients with quality service.

The Computer Society of South Africa (CSSA) proposes to its members the following principles. They:

1. Will behave at all times with integrity. A member will not knowingly lay claim to a level of competence not possessed and will at all times exercise competence at least to the level claimed.
2. Will act with complete loyalty towards a client when entrusted with confidential information.
3. Will act with impartiality when purporting to give independent advice and must disclose any relevant interests.
4. Will accept full responsibility for any work undertaken and will construct and deliver that which has been agreed to.
5. Will not seek personal advantage to the detriment of the Society and will actively seek to enhance the image of the Society.
6. Will not engage in discriminatory practices in professional activities on any basis whatsoever.

The professionals of the Computer Society of Singapore (SCS) accept as general principles:

1. SCS members will act at all times with integrity.
2. SCS members will accept full responsibility for their work.
3. SCS members will always aim to increase their competence.

4. SCS members will act with professionalism to enhance the prestige of the profession and the Society.

In Sweden the Swedish Ethical Rules for Computer Professionals recommend that:

1. Computer professionals only perform tasks that acknowledge legitimate integrity claims and are in accordance with common understanding of law.
2. Computer professionals only participate in development tasks, the objectives and context of which have been made explicit.
3. Computer professionals only take part in projects with the time and resources assigned that make it possible to do a good job.
4. Computer professionals only develop systems in close collaboration with the user.
5. Computer professionals show respect for, and contribute to the development of, the professional competence of the users.
6. Computer professionals develop systems that use technology in such a way as to satisfy the interests of the users.
7. Computer professionals develop systems that bring about good work environments.
8. Computer professionals refrain from tasks aiming at control in ways that can be of harm to individuals.
9. Computer professionals keep themselves informed about laws and agreements related to their work and they participate actively in disseminating knowledge about computing activities violating such laws and agreements.
10. Computer professionals only access data required to perform their job.
11. Computer professionals feel responsible for ensuring that computer technology is not used in ways that harm people, the environment, or society.

In a general sense all these codes say that professionals should work with competence and integrity, that they should not harm the reputation of the profession, take the social effects of computer use into account and provide the general public with adequate information about computer technology. In most professional organizations there are, however, no procedures for the imposition of sanctions in case members violate the rules of the code. This may suggest that codes primarily serve the image of the group and its monopoly position: 'In other words, they are a bit of window dressing designed to improve the status and the income of members' (John Ladd quoted in Forester and Morrison, 1995: 19).

A serious flaw of professional codes is that they almost exclusively address the individual professional. However, the moral choices the professional makes take place within an institutional context. Most professional ICT workers are employed by or get assignments from large international corporations. The moral rules of the game that prevail in the company determine the autonomous space individual professionals have for moral choices. This space is more often than not seriously restricted. Moreover, often professional informaticians work on a small part of a much larger project and may not have a full view of all possible effects. In spite of the rising volume of studies on professional ethics, we still know very little about moral decision-making by professionals. Some of the following questions still need to be addressed: What is the impact of the political-economic context, the competitive position of the employing firm and their interaction between such variables and such personal factors as education, social class and gender? This implies that we need to go beyond the personal ethical reflection and look into the ethics of legal persons.

Corporate morality

Corporate morality addresses moral issues in relation to commercial enterprises, state institutions and non-governmental interest organizations. This is important because the role and significance of these entities is on the increase. In particular privately owned, commercial legal persons (like transnational corporations) are interesting. Often they have more power and influence than public social institutions (like governments). Their economic significance, for example, may exceed that of governments (see Table 2.1).

TABLE 2.1

Revenues	Gross Domestic Product
General Motors: $169 billion	
	Denmark: $146 billion
Shell: $110 billion	
	Norway: $109 billion
	Portugal: $92 billion

In 1994 The top five companies in the world had a combined income of over $870 billion. In the same year the countries of sub-Saharan Africa had a total GDP of less than $250 billion (UNDP, 1997: 92).

Since large international firms have faced in recent times demonstrations of public moral indignation about their conduct, they seem to have a growing interest in the moral quality of their performance. One finds more and more reports and debates about such topics as 'corporate governance'.

Self-regulation: business ethics and codes of conduct

Ethical reflection on social institutions is usually part of business ethics. This is a field that enjoys a growing interest as is demonstrated by the ever larger numbers of seminars, training courses and publications. Increasingly, consumers, political parties, shareholders and social movements (such as Amnesty International and Greenpeace International) mobilize pressure on corporations to take a position on their moral responsibility. Companies like Shell, Heineken and Nike, have shown a certain sensitivity to the moral lobbying of their clients, for example with regard to investments in countries where political regimes violate human rights. This interest for 'ethical business' is not altogether new. Already in the 1920s there were discussions in many European countries among Christian entrepreneurs about the moral dimensions of their operations.

A popular instrument to deal with the issues of business ethics is the code of conduct. More and more companies adopt a code or have at least 'mission statements' or 'business principles'. Shell, for example, has developed a code of conduct and has invited external agencies to audit its performance under the rules of the code. At Shell headquarters staff work on the company's 'Social Responsibility Measurement Systems'.

Companies that operate in CyberSpace have also begun to think about rules for responsible conduct. One illustration is the Nintendo company that prescribes for its computer games,

> No random, gratuitous and/or excessive violence. No subliminal or overt political messages. No domestic violence and/or abuse. No ethnic, racial, religious, nationalistic, or sexual stereotypes and language. No use of illegal drugs, smoking material, alcohol. No graphic illustration of death. No sexually suggestive or explicit conduct. No excessive force in sport games. No profanity or obscenity. No sexist language or depiction. (Whittle, 1997: 286)

Companies, such as IBM, have special rules for the handling of information. The IBM business rules state that there are limits to the use of information one acquires in the process of doing business with other companies. Negative information that serves no commercial purposes should not be kept in files. Information that is kept has to be handled with care and should only be transferred and made accessible to those who have a legitimate interest in this information (Kimman, 1991: 148, 149).

The International Chamber of Commerce has published a special Code for Ethical Conduct for advertising and marketing on the Internet.[6]

The weakness of most industrial codes – just like the professional codes – are the inadequate or totally absent mechanisms for enforcement. The lack of effective sanctions becomes particularly noticeable in situations where the principles of morality and the demands for profit-making collide. It is very unlikely that voluntary, self-regulatory codes can withstand commercial pressures. Companies may for example adopt the protection of their clients' privacy in their codes, but as the economic value of their personal data increases, the rule of the code is likely to remain a dead letter.

Even so, it may be that usefulness of a code can be found in its inspiration for creating a moral sensitivity. It may also be the case that a code provides guidelines for the relations between employers and employees. For example, in relation to the issue of electronic surveillance it is important to work out clear agreements. This is also true for situations in which employees blow the whistle. The code of conduct can also offer some help in defining the moral responsibility of a company vis-à-vis its clients. Clear standards on dealing with damage claims, acceptance of liability and honesty in advertising can only help to improve the clients' trust in companies.

Keeping up appearances?

It may well be that all the interest business shows for ethics is intended to give companies a good 'corporate image' – to outdo the competitor on moral grounds. The ethical enterprise may just be a response to scandals about fraud, bribery and pollution.

Companies may claim that they want to express to the public at large their responsible attitude regarding their choices and the claims that clients and others may make towards the quality and reliability of their products and services. It would seem, however, that particularly the big corporations have often launched codes as part of their 'issue management' strategy to counteract negative publicity by action groups. The classical illustration is the code that the baby food industry published in reaction to the publication of 'Nestlé Kills Babies' in the 1970s. Presenting a code can also serve to avoid public measures. An example is the code for pharmaceutical advertising (1981) by the joint international pharmaceutical industry in response to the intentions of the World Health Organization (WHO) to design regulation for this industry.

Even if codes were designed with honest intentions their contribution to the solution of moral dilemmas would be very limited. In the actual confrontation with real issues they usually are flawed. Solutions for moral dilemmas can only be found in the dialogue between those concerned and not by prescriptions and rules.

Social morality

Although personal, professional and corporate moral choices are of paramount importance, it can be argued that the most decisive questions are issues of social ethics. Even if all personal, professional and corporate users of CyberSpace were to behave in virtuous and decent ways, this would not automatically mean we would have a decent society. The combined moral acts of these actors does not necessarily create a moral society. They could, for example, make moral choices with regard to consumer behaviour that are in their own right morally acceptable. Yet, the cumulative effects of all these choices may be immoral because they may cause growing social inequality and serious environmental damage.

Critical reflection on the moral quality of personal, professional and corporate choices is undoubtedly a very pertinent matter. We need, however, also to reflect on the moral quality of social choices since these shape the general framework within which other choices will be made. This takes us into the domain of social ethics as the systematic and critical reflection on the moral choices that shape the ways in which societies organize themselves. Social ethics raises the fundamental question about the moral quality of societies.

The need to reflect on social morality can be illustrated with the example of the protection of the private sphere. Although this seems more than anything else an issue of personal morality, privacy is basically a social problem. Its major violations are caused by the way in which modern societies are organized: bureaucratic and market-oriented. A society in which commercial markets are essential requires the collection of vast amounts of data about consumers. The violation of individual privacy may also be necessary for the solution of collective problems, such as criminal conduct. Data-mining causes social problems because databanks will increasingly exclude certain social groups. Those whose data are not commercially interesting will be excluded from a range of social transactions.

Privacy as a social issue implies the need to balance individual autonomy and collective interests in a complex dialectical process. Extreme forms of individual autonomy create serious social disintegration. But equally, the sustainable social order requires individual autonomy in the sense of artistic creativity, technological inventiveness and cultural diversity.

Also the issue of intellectual property rights (IPRs) protection is foremost a social issue and is related to broader social developments. The strict enforcement of IPRs is linked with the expanding privatization of science and technology research, the related industrial concentration, the ensuing lack of competition and the drive towards the protection of private investments. IPRs also have far-reaching social consequences in relation to the social distribution of knowledge as, for example, their enforcement marginalizes the production of traditional knowledge in poor countries.

In the field of social ethics the questions tend to be more complex than in personal, professional or corporate ethics. The unit of reflection ('society') is very broad, complex, heterogeneous, internally divided and constantly changing. The key question for social ethics is: 'What is a decent society?', and social morality in relation to CyberSpace raises the question 'How should a decent society govern CyberSpace?'[7]

Notes

1. Almost always this retribution is guided by the principle of proportionality between crime and punishment. In different forms most cultures know the 'lex talionis' (the notion of an eye for an eye and a tooth for a tooth) which imposes certain limits on the retaliation against the wrongdoer if harm has been inflicted.
2. For the code of conduct of the CyberAngels see website: http://www.cyberangels.com.
3. *Towards an Ethics and Etiquette for Electronic Mail* at http://www.fau.edu/rinaldi/net/user.html. For more material on netiquette and other moral issues a good source is The Center for Applied Ethics' Home Page: http://www.ethics.ubc.ca/resources/computer.
4. See: http://www.fau.edu/rinaldi/net/dis.html. For a bibliography consult: http://www.fau.edu/rinaldi/net/bib.html.
5. See: http://www.fau.edu/rinaldi/net/ten.html.
6. From the ICC *Revised Guidelines on Advertising and Marketing on the Internet* (1998):

   These Guidelines apply to all marketing and advertising activities on the Internet for the promotion of any form of goods and services. The Guidelines set standards of ethical conduct to be observed by all involved with advertising and marketing activities on the Internet.

   Article 1: All advertising and marketing should be legal, decent, honest and truthful . . . Advertising and marketing messages should be sensitive to issues of social responsibility and should in addition conform to generally accepted principles as regards ethical marketing. . . .

   Advertising and marketing messages should not be designed or transmitted in such a way as to impair overall public confidence in the Internet as a medium and marketplace.

   Article 2: Advertisers and marketers of goods and services who post commercial messages via the Internet should always disclose their own identity . . . in such a way that the user can contact the advertiser or marketer without difficulty.

   Article 5:

   1. Collection and use of data. Advertisers and marketers should disclose the purpose(s) for collecting and using personal data to users and

should not use that data in a way incompatible with those purposes. Data files should be accurate, complete and kept up to date.

2. Data privacy. Advertisers and marketers should take reasonable precautions to safeguard the security of their data files.

3. Disclosure of data. The user should be given the opportunity to refuse the transfer of data to another advertiser or marketer.

4. Correction and blocking of data. Advertisers and marketers should give the user the right to obtain data relating to him and, where appropriate, to have such data corrected, completed, or blocked.

Article 6: Advertisers and marketers offering goods and services to children online should: not exploit the natural credulity of children or the lack of experience of young people; not contain any content which might result in harm to children; provide information to parents and/or guardians about ways to protect their children's privacy online.

Article 7: Given the global reach of electronic networks, and the variety and diversity of possible recipients of electronic messages, advertisers and marketers should be especially sensitive regarding the possibility that a particular message might be perceived as pornographic, violent, racist or sexist.

7 The notion of the decent society has been used by Avishai Margalit (1996) in his book on the foundation of social morality.

The Decent Society and CyberSpace 3

Everyone is entitled to a social and international order in which the rights
and freedoms set forth in this Declaration can be fully realized.
                    Universal Declaration of Human Rights, Article 28

The essential question for this chapter is: On which moral standards
should a decent society found its governance of CyberSpace?
Governance implies making political choices. Many of these have moral
implications. This raises the question about the basic moral principles that
should guide these choices. It also raises the question about the quality of
the social order within which these principles can be realized.

The foundation of morality

The debate on foundations for ethics has a long and complex history.
It reflects the perennial and puzzling question 'Why be moral?' The
philosophical search for foundations of human morality is already found
when Plato writes (in *The Republic*) about the discussion Socrates has with
Glaucon and Adeimantus. Glaucon wants to learn from Socrates why
people should be righteous. He wants to hear an argument that explains
why justice is superior to injustice. His brother Adeimantus points out that
the unjust often lives much more comfortably than the just person and
he adds that people will only act justly if they get something out of this
behaviour or if they will be punished for unjust conduct. The brothers
search for the foundation of moral obligations (Plato, *The Republic*:
43–55). This is no simple matter. Throughout history most philosophical
and theological efforts to find a legitimate foundation for norms and values
are flawed and it turns out that the validity of any argument to justify
moral principles can be essentially contested.

It is indeed a difficult challenge to identify a foundation for moral
judgements that can be accepted by all those concerned, given their
divergent cultural, political and social histories. Postmodernist thinkers

are inclined to reject the possibility of such a common foundation. They suggest that norms and values are historically determined and can therefore not claim universal validity. German moral philosopher Apel disagrees: if our morality is relative only to time and place and no universal standards can exist, we cannot condemn Nazi practices (Griffioen, 1990: 13). Following the relativist position the Holocaust could be justified with the argument that opinions about genocide in Nazi Germany were determined by the specific historical conditions of the time. If we accept global responsibility for the worldwide effects of our technological and economic activities, we absolutely need (according to Apel) interculturally and universally binding norms (Griffioen, 1990: 13).

The metaphysical arguments through which theologians attempt to justify norms and values will usually convince the believers only. If the moral foundation is revealed through the 'Word of God' this has authority only for those who accept the validity of this revelation.

If moral principles are founded upon the nature of the human being, this foundation will fail because it moves in unexplainable ways from a descriptive statement about human nature to a normative statement about human conduct. Moreover, the irresolvable question is upon which dimensions of human nature moral principles should be based. Human dignity? But this is a very vague notion with many different and conflicting interpretations. Upon qualities such as human skills? Those are, however, very unequally distributed among human beings and this would imply that rights and duties are assigned to different people in different ways. Can human needs provide a foundation? But someone's need for alcohol does not provide a right to liquor or the moral duty for others to get those in alcoholic need their booze. It is difficult to argue that people would be always entitled to the satisfaction of their needs.

In recent thinking about the development of morality the Canadian philosopher of science Michael Ruse has put emphasis upon an evolutionary model that perceives of moral acting as a genetically programmed altruism. However, it remains unclear why some species (human beings in this case) could stake – on the basis of biological facts – specific moral claims. Those who defend the rights of animals argue that acknowledging or rejecting moral claims based upon biological definitions constitutes forms of discrimination. We could also base the foundation for the distinction between good and evil upon personal intuition. This however renders arguments for or against certain moral choices extremely subjective and arbitrary to the extent that a serious dialogue with others becomes impossible.

Most problematic in the search for moral foundation is that most efforts are undergirded by the ambition to identify an absolute truth as the basis for moral behaviour. This is inspired by the notion that without the belief in some absolute value (which could be metaphysical or secular) there is no sufficiently strong motivation to act morally. One does not need to acclaim the postmodern position, however, to be very suspicious of absolute foundations. They are accessible only to those who believe the grand narrative these absolute truths stem from and tend to forms of religious or secular fundamentalism. Moreover, they offer no guarantee that their believers will know how to make distinctions between good and evil in concrete situations.

If we give up the expectation that there could be on a global level a shared foundation for morality, where does this leave us? How do we find a rationale to act in certain ways towards others? The contestability of moral foundations does not exclude the possibility that around the world people – inspired by different motivations – could agree to bind themselves voluntarily to a common set of moral principles. This would obviously require that their choice be sufficiently guarded against individual arbitrariness and partisanship. In the history of moral philosophy a common feature of different schools of moral thought is that they consider normative judgements based upon self-interest generally not morally justified: 'From ancient times, philosophers and moralists have expressed the idea that ethical conduct is acceptable from a point of view that is somehow universal' (Singer, 1979: 10). Thinkers as different as Kant, Hume, Bentham, Rawls, Sartre and Habermas 'agree that ethics is in some sense universal . . . that the justification of an ethical principle cannot be in terms of any partial or sectional group' (Singer, 1979: 11).

The demand for universalization has been articulated by Habermas in the following way: 'A norm is justified only if it is "equally good" for each of the persons concerned' (Habermas, 1993: 68). In Habermas' approach to moral justification the essence is the dialogue among the community of moral subjects. He argues for a communicative, inter-subjectivist approach. This is basic to the discourse ethics which was referred to in Chapter 1: 'Whether a norm is justifiable cannot be determined monologically, but only through discursively testing its claim to fairness' (McCarthy in Habermas, 1993: viii). Discourse ethics 'bases the justification of norms on the uncoerced, rational agreement of those subject to them' (Habermas, 1993: x). As Habermas concludes: 'Only those norms can claim to be valid that meet (or could meet) with the approval of all affected in their capacity as participants in a practical discourse' (1993: 66).

The consensus on the need of a universality of moral principles as basis for justification has run into trouble with the rise of postmodernist thought on moral philosophy: 'Postmodernism tends to claim an abandonment of all metanarratives which could legitimate foundations for truth' (Waugh, 1992: 5). In addition to its cultural-aesthetic manifestations, postmodern thought is mainly a critique of the modernity of the Enlightenment. It is 'a development in thought which represents a thorough-going critique of the assumptions of Enlightenment or the discourses of modernity and their foundation in notions of universal reason' (Waugh: 1992: 3). In a considerable volume of writings postmodernists have denounced the 'grand narratives' of the Enlightenment (Lyotard, 1979). Herewith they reject unitary thought systems, comprehensive moral theories, and the ambition to answer all questions of how to live with one all-encompassing philosophy.

Against this position one can object that it is possible to agree with the denouncing of the absolutism of past political doctrines and yet recognize that liberal pluralist societies require basic moral standards if they want to remain democratic. With the denial of Enlightenment principles like justice, and equality, one cannot differentiate between principles that are essential to the creation of democratic arrangements and principles that are not. As a result the body of postmodern reading on world politics provides no helpful insights for the future political practices of the world community. Postmodern thought leaves the world pretty much as it is.

The relativist defends the position that all morality is relative to culture. The variety of moral beliefs inevitably implies that they cannot be assessed by some universal standard. Relativists deny that there can be answers to moral questions that apply interculturally or intersubjectively. There are several fallacies in the relativist argument that undermine the validity of this position. If we accept that the conflicting moral beliefs of different cultures are equally true, then it is difficult to defend that someone from culture A would criticize a normative act by someone in culture B. One cannot apply the moral norms valid in culture A to culture B. However, this position is incompatible with the real-life observation that nobody would probably defend the thesis that you can never criticize any normative act by people in other cultures. This would imply that people would always condone whatever others did, including rape, murder, torture and child abuse. Moreover, even if we accept cultural diversity, there are remarkably few people who support racism, slavery or genocide! The problem is that relativism tends to insist on cultural differences while discarding cultural similarities.

If one accepts that moral standards are culturally relative, this does neither logically imply that there cannot be universal moral standards, nor that we could not make moral choices for solutions we can argue to be preferential to other choices. Moreover, the observation that people come to different moral judgements does not necessarily prove that the moral principles that undergird these judgements are fundamentally different. When people differ about the value of certain customs and practices, they may very well share the same basic moral premises. The ways in which cultural communities approach the treatment of the deceased, male–female relations, or the education of children may be totally different. Yet they may be based on the same moral principles. Burying, cremating, embalming or eating the dead may all be inspired by the same respect for those who passed away.

Postmodernists object to universal moral principles or truths, and favour the tolerance of pluralism. However, how can one hope to achieve tolerance without shared normative principles? Why should we be tolerant? Does tolerance of plural truths not imply the respect for the universal moral principle of the tolerance of diversity? The postmodern relativists claim that there can be no universal claims. It remains unclear though how they substantiate this claim. It would seem reasonable to expect that they demonstrate empirically that no universal norms exist. The issue is not whether all or most moral norms are universally accepted, but whether there are any shared principles at all. And, indeed, it is difficult to ignore that there is a limited set of basic norms that most people across time and space share!

One of the problems with a relativist position is that there is little hope for justification outside the boundaries of a specific situation. Thus moral relativism may ultimately lead to moral indifference for events beyond the confines of a local scheme of values. Against this, the universalist position accepts that there are values that transcend local boundaries and that these are applicable to all. The universalist refuses to abandon the world and people's common future to moral indifference.

Human rights

The principle that meets the requirement of universal validity is the defence of human rights. As Lukes rightly observes the principle is accepted virtually everywhere: 'It is also violated virtually everywhere. . . . But the virtually universal acceptance, even when hypocritical, is very important' (Lukes, 1993: 20). Human rights provide currently the only universally available set of standards for the dignity and integrity of all human beings. It is in the interest of all people that they be respected. The world political community has concluded a global social contract about the defence of human rights. It has recognized the existence of human rights, their universality and indivisibility, and has accepted a machinery for their enforcement. The United Nations World Conference on Human Rights in 1993 reaffirmed the universality of human rights. The final declaration states 'The universal nature of human rights is beyond question.' This tells us that international human rights law represents – however ineffectual – a set of moral claims that is accepted universally and that is worth defending.

The human species does not distinguish itself by a historical record that radiates benignity. For most of its history, the human being occupies himself (and to a more limited extent: herself) with an impressive variety of humiliating acts against fellow human beings. Against this gross indecency of human history, the more enlightened individuals have throughout the ages committed themselves to the articulation and codification of basic moral standards that were intended to restrain human aggression, arbitrariness and negligence. Most of such moral prescriptions had a limited scope in terms of the agents they addressed and/or the geographies they covered. This changed dramatically in 1945.

In response to the assaults against human dignity during the Second World War, the United Nations (UN) began to develop a universal frame-work of moral standards. This was to become the international human rights regime. Before 1945 there were human rights declarations, such as the Magna Carta of 1215, the British Bill of Rights, the American Declaration of Independence and the French Déclaration des droits de l'homme et du citoyen. In 1945 this long history of the protection of human dignity acquired a fundamentally new significance. The novelty of the international human rights regime – as it was established after 1945 – was the articulation of the age-old struggle for the recognition of human dignity into a catalogue of legal rights. Moreover, the political discourse shifted from 'rights of man' to the more comprehensive 'human rights'.

The protection of human dignity (previously mainly a national affair) was put on the agenda of the world community. Herewith, the defence of fundamental rights was no longer the exclusive preoccupation of national politics and became an essential part of world politics. The judgement whether human rights had been violated was no longer the exclusive monopoly of national governments. More importantly yet, the enjoyment of human rights was no longer restricted to privileged individuals and social élites. The revolutionary core of the process that began at San Francisco – with the adoption of the UN Charter in 1945 – was that 'all people matter'. Basic rights were to apply to everyone and to exclude no one.

The new regime that transcended all earlier moral codes since it incorporated 'everyone', claimed universal validity. This claim has time and again been challenged. In spite of this, however it was confirmed by the 1993 United Nations World Conference on Human Rights in Vienna that the international human rights regime embodies the only global moral framework the world has at present.

> The World Conference on Human Rights reaffirms the solemn commitment of all States to fulfil their obligations to promote universal respect for, and observance and protection of, all human rights and fundamental freedoms for all in accordance with the Charter of the United Nations, other instruments relating to human rights, and international law. The universal nature of these rights and freedoms is beyond question. (United Nations, 1993: 3–4)

Although this was an important step, the recognition of universal validity did not resolve the question of the admissible variety of cultural interpretations. Universal validity does not mean that all local forms of implementation will be similar. A variety of cultural interpretations remains possible. This has provoked the question of the degree to which local cultural interpretations can be accepted. There is increasing support for the view that culturally determined interpretations reach a borderline when they violate the core principles of human rights law. Moreover, this view holds that the admissibility of the interpretation should be judged by the international community and not by the implementing party.

An important characteristic of these rights is that they are formulated in very similar ways in a variety of international, regional and national constitutional instruments. Therefore, it seems sensible to accept the political reality and adopt the moral standards of the human rights regime as guidance for human conduct in all domains of social activity.

The new regime did evolve around a set of basic texts (some codified as legally binding instruments and others adopted as customary law) and mechanisms for their enforcement. The foundation for the regime was laid down in United Nations Universal Declaration of Human Rights (adopted on 10 December 1948 by the UN General Assembly) and the two key human rights treaties, the International Covenant on Economic, Social and Cultural Rights (in force since 3 January 1976) and the International Covenant on Civil and Political Rights (in force since 23 March 1976). In these three documents (commonly referred to as the International Bill of Rights) one finds 76 different human rights. If one were to take the totality of some 50 major international and regional human rights instruments the number of rights would obviously increase even further. There is also presently a tendency among human rights lobbies to put more and more social problems in a human rights framework and thus to add to the number of human rights.

Since this proliferation of rights does not necessarily strengthen the cause of the actual implementation of human rights, various attempts have been made to establish a set of core human rights that are representative for the totality. One effort concluded to the existence of twelve core rights (Jongman and Schmidt, 1994: 8). These are:

1. The right to life.
2. The right not to be tortured.
3. The right not to be arbitrarily arrested.
4. The right to food.
5. The right to health care.
6. The right not to be discriminated against.
7. The right to due process of law.
8. The right to education.
9. The right to political participation.
10. The right to fair working conditions.
11. The right to freedom of association.
12. The right to freedom of expression.

These rights are the legal articulation of fundamental moral principles and their implied standards of human conduct. These principles and standards are:

- Equality and the implied standard that discrimination is inadmissible.
- Security and the implied standard that intentional harm against human integrity is inadmissible.
- Freedom and the implied standard that interference with human self-determination is inadmissible.

The principle of equality

The principle of equality implies that there is equal entitlement to the conditions of self-empowerment. Among the essential conditions of people's self-empowerment are access to and use of the resources that enable people to express themselves, to communicate these expressions to others, to exchange ideas with others, to inform themselves about events in the world, to create and control the production of knowledge and to share the world's sources of knowledge. These resources include technical infrastructures, knowledge and skills, financial means and natural systems. Their unequal distribution among the world's people obstructs the equal entitlement to the conditions of self-empowerment and should be considered a violation of human rights. For the analysis of governance in CyberSpace the equality principle will be used in the sense of 'equal entitlement'.

The principle of security

The human rights regime proposes standards of conduct against attacks upon people's physical, mental and moral integrity. The right to the protection of privacy as provided in Article 12 of the Universal Declaration of Human Rights and in Article 17 of the International Covenant on Civil and Political Rights, protects people against arbitrary interference with their private sphere and against unlawful attacks on their honour and reputation. For the analysis of governance in CyberSpace the security principle will be used in the sense of protection against harm to both physical and psychological integrity.

The principle of freedom

The freedom principle is found in human rights instruments in a range of applications. There is recognition of among others the freedom of movement, the freedom of religion and the freedom of peaceful assembly. For the analysis of governance in CyberSpace the equality principle will be used in the sense of freedom from interference with expression and access to information. Various international and regional instruments provide for the right to freedom of expression, the limitations on this right, the legitimacy of these limitations, and legal recourse against violations of these provisions.

Technology and human rights

In various declarations the international community has proposed moral standards for the evaluation of technological developments.[1] These standards point to the right of protection against harmful effects of technical applications, the right of access and enjoyment of technological progress, and the right of participation in decision-making about technological development. With regard to the protection against harmful effects there are provisions such as:

- The right to human dignity (e.g. in the Universal Declaration of Human Rights, 1948, Articles 1, 5, 6, and 29). This is pertinent when technologies in general, and ICTs in particular, are deployed for surveillance, decision-making by electronic systems and automation in business and government.

- The right to freedom of expression and the right to collect information (e.g. Universal Declaration of Human Rights, Article 19). This is pertinent when technologies in general, and ICTs in particular, are deployed to censor the provision of information, to hinder the access to information, or to divulge 'disinformation'.
- The right of access to technology is provided in Article 27.1. of the Universal Declaration of Human Rights where it is stated that 'Everyone has the right to . . . share in scientific advancement and its benefits'. This right is inspired by the basic moral principle of equality and the notion that technology belongs to the common heritage of humankind.

Problems with human rights

The choice for a human rights-based social ethics and its implementation is not without difficulties. At different levels pertinent questions can be raised.

The claim to universalism

International human rights standards represent a system of morality that has universal ambitions. Against the realization of this ambition there are major roadblocks. These are established by the emotivists (who claim that moral beliefs are a matter of emotion), the decisionalists (who claim that moral beliefs are a matter of choice), the dogmatists (who confuse their feelings with objective certainty), and the relativists (who claim that moral systems are a matter of social/cultural perspective). The latter, who were discussed above, hold the best cards. The relativists do not deny that forms of rational moral reasoning may be possible, but they do deny that there can be answers to moral questions that apply interculturally or intersubjectively.

There are several fallacies in the relativist position and among them is the argument that the idea of human rights is exclusively Western. The fact that many nations (cultures) were not present in San Francisco at the founding of the United Nations and did not take part in the UN General Assembly on 10 December 1948 which discussed the Universal Declaration of Human Rights does not undermine its universal character. In the years after 1948 when all the absent nations were formulating their national constitutions, they borrowed concepts and phrases from the Universal Declaration. The universality of human rights is reflected in the basic legal documents of such diverse countries as Cambodia, Nepal and South Africa. Also, in the major religions one finds components that plead for the cross-temporal and cross-cultural validity of human rights.

Individualism

It is often objected that the human rights tradition is exclusively focused upon individual rights. It is certainly true that human rights are to an important extent articulated in the language of a Western individualistic liberal tradition. This, however, does not hinder the provision of collective rights, such as the rights of minorities. In the evolution of human rights the link between individual and collective rights has become stronger. Moreover, individual rights are always tied to the rights of other members of the community and to the community at large. As Article 29 of the Universal Declaration of Human Rights provides, 'Everyone has duties to the community in which alone the free and full development of his personality is possible'.

Enlightenment

The proposal to make human rights the focus of social ethics can be criticized from the position that human rights are products of a modern, Western, rational Enlightenment mode of thought. In this vision human rights represent a colonial, racist, sexist culture that through its conflicts of body versus soul, matter versus spirit, man versus nature, subject versus object, produces a materialist and individualist type of thinking that ultimately destroys society. In this Enlightenment critique the philosophies of Kant and Descartes form the prelude to the twentieth-century Holocaust.

Against this analysis it can be argued that the Enlightenment philosophers were primarily supporters of decent forms of public governance (Gay, 1973: 397). Thinkers such as Montesquieu, Diderot, Beccaria, Voltaire and Lessing strongly emphasized the need for social morality. Important moral principles for them were tolerance, pluralism, international peace, abolition of slavery (Montesquieu) and capital punishment, and the humanization of criminal law (Beccaria). If even a minimal portion of these ideas had been implemented, there would have been much less suffering during the nineteenth and twentieth centuries. For enormous numbers of victims this would have made a significant difference.

There are conflicting positions held on the issue of the Enlightenment. One option is to completely reject its rationalism. The opposite option is to embrace it as foundation for contemporary morality. A third position is represented by among others the German philosopher Jürgen Habermas and the British sociologist Anthony Giddens. In a general sense they propose that one should treat the ambitions and pretences of the Enlightenment philosophers with scepsis, but one should also recognize that the project of human emancipation is not yet completed.[2]

The Enlightenment suggests that scientific knowledge which is rationally discovered will eventually end human insecurity. The pretence is that a universal science can be developed which can explain the world in an authoritative and comprehensive narration. This universalist claim already contains the core of relativist thinking. Precisely since Enlightenment puts so much emphasis upon the independence of human thinking which liberates itself from religious dogma, the Enlightenment begins to instil doubts about the general truth of human knowledge. For this reason, Habermas and Giddens consider contemporary scepsis regarding the claims of an objective social science not as a clean break with the modernism of the Enlightenment. Habermas sees a realistic possibility to continue the process of emancipation through a communicative ethics. This perspective has been severely criticized by Michel Foucault. For Foucault, Habermas is a naïve utopianist who mistakenly thinks that the proposed public dialogue can take its cue from universal principles. This is impossible because such principles do not exist, Foucault argues.

This discussion actually represents the core of the modernist/postmodernist controversy: can a critical theory of society be founded upon a normative premise? Postmodernist thought offers promising and inspiring criticism of the hierarchical structures of patriarchal societies and the cultural imperialism of modern science. It remains doubtful, however, whether this criticism can lead towards alternative forms of social organization and lifestyles without normative standards. This is a pertinent question since both modernist and postmodernist analyses of current social realities point to the fundamentally threatening nature of our situation and thus share the need to design alternatives.

The inadequate enforcement

The most important issue for the significance and validity of the human rights regime is the enforcement of the standards it proposes. There is abundant evidence that these standards are around the world almost incessantly violated and by actors with very different political and ideological viewpoints. Usually, in wars of liberation, for example, one finds gross violations both by the oppressors as well as by the liberators.

And if one studies the depressing annual reports from Amnesty International, there appear to be no countries where human rights are not violated. For moral philosophers this is actually not a terribly surprising problem. It concerns the classical gap between the moral knowledge human beings possess and their intention to act morally. The mechanisms the international community have developed to deal with the 'moral gap' are largely inadequate.

Present procedures are mainly based upon the Optional Protocol (OP) to the International Covenant on Civil and Political Rights (ICCPR) (1966) and Resolution 1503 adopted by the Economic and Social Council (ECOSOC) of the UN in 1970. The Protocol authorizes the UN Human Rights Committee to receive and consider communications from individuals subject to its jurisdiction who claim to be victims of a violation by that State Party of any of the rights set forth in the Covenant. Individual complaints can only come from nationals of states that are party to the OP (presently 75 states). The OP provides for communications, analysis and reporting, but not for sanctions. Resolution 1503 recognizes the possibility of individual complaints about human rights violations. It authorizes the UN Human Rights Commission to examine 'communications, together with replies of governments, if any, which appear to reveal a consistent patterns of gross violations of human rights'. The 1503 procedure is slow, confidential, and provides individuals with no redress.

The institutional mechanisms for implementation are in addition to the UN Commission on Human Rights, and the Human Rights Committee to monitor the ICCPR, the Committee on the Elimination of Racial Discrimination, the Committee on Economic, Social and Cultural Rights, the Committee on the Elimination of Discrimination against Women, the Committee against Torture, and the Committee on the Rights of the Child.

However important the work of all these bodies is, their powers to enforce human rights standards are very limited. The UN Commission on Human Rights is a permanent body of the ECOSOC. Its members are state representatives. Findings of the Commission have a certain significance but are not binding. The ICCPR Human Rights Committee consists of 18 experts supervising the implementation of the Covenant. The work of the Committee covers only parties that ratified the covenant (presently 129 states) and provides international monitoring on the basis of reports provided by states. The Committee's monitoring does not imply any sanctions, but it can generate some negative publicity on a country's human rights performance. For the implementation of the Race Convention the Committee on the Elimination of Racial Discrimination has been established. The Committee can receive complaints among states, but only

14 states authorize the Committee to receive communications from individuals.

The implementation body for the 1979 Convention on the Elimination of Discrimination Against Women is the Committee on the Elimination of Discrimination Against Women. The Committee is not authorized to receive individual communications.

The Committee on Economic, Social and Cultural Rights (ICESCR) has no right to receive complaints from individuals or groups. In its submission to the 1993 UN World Conference on Human Rights the Committee argued for a formal complaints procedure in stating,

> As long as the majority of the provisions of the Covenant (and most notably those relating to education, health care, food and nutrition, and housing) are not subject of any detailed jurisprudential scrutiny at the international level, it is most unlikely that they will be subject to such examination at the national level either. (United Nations, 1993: para 24)

In 1997 the fifty-third session of the UN Commission on Human Rights discussed a draft protocol for a complaints procedure and affirmed in a resolution the interest of its members for the draft. This was the first step in the long process towards an optional protocol.

A special problem with the enforcement of economic, social and cultural rights is the standard by which implementation is measured. Article 2.1 of the ICESCR requires state parties 'to take steps, individually and through international assistance and cooperation, especially economic and technical, to the maximum of its available resources, with a view to achieving progressively the full realization of the rights recognized in the present Covenant'. This standard of 'progressive realization' is much more complicated to monitor and less compelling than the requirements the International Covenant on Civil and Political Rights imposes on state parties in Article 2.1: 'Each State Party to the present Covenant undertakes to respect and ensure to all individuals within its territory and subject to its jurisdiction the rights recognized in the present Covenant'. The measurement of 'progressive realization' demands the collection of comparative, statistical data over time and is complicated by the notion of 'to the maximum of available resources'. In recent discussions on this issue, a shift from this approach to a 'violations' approach has been argued:

> While requiring further specification, violations are more readily defined and identified, particularly for non-governmental organizations and perhaps for governments and international bodies as well. The work of the Committee on Economic, Social and Cultural Rights attests to the fact that

it is possible to identify violations of enumerated rights without first conceptualizing the full scope of a right and the obligations of State parties in relationship to it. (Chapman, 1995: 31)

Horizontal effect

Conventional human rights thinking mainly focuses on the vertical state–citizen relation. This ignores the possibility that concentration of power in the hands of individuals can be as threatening as state power. Whenever citizens pursue different economic interests, individual human rights will be under serious threat. Citizens also need to be protected against each other. Here the idea of human rights entails an ambivalent position on the state–civil society interaction. The realization of civil rights requires limitations on the power of the state, yet the realization of social and economic rights needs the authority of the state. A solid protection of human rights needs both a civil defence against the powers of the state as well as the support of the state in cases of 'horizontal' abuses of fundamental rights and freedoms. An adequate enforcement of human rights has to be clear on the need for a horizontal effect of basic constitutional rights. Increasingly such rights are threatened by private parties and the defence of human rights needs to be extended to the relations between citizens themselves.

This is particularly important since the world political arena is no longer the exclusive forum of states. In recent years a growing number of non-state actors has begun to play a decisive role in such domains as security, environment, human rights and communications. There should be more adequate remedies (complaints procedures and legal processes) than prevail today in the defence of basic rights against the actions of fellow-citizens, be they individuals or corporations. This increases even further in importance as more and more social domains are being privatized in many societies.

Political interests

International human rights law remains a weak and largely non-enforceable arrangement. It should not be ignored that this is a conscious political choice. Most nation-states have shown little interest in interference with their human rights record. As a result today's world system remains largely a case of criminals policing themselves. The state-centric arrangement of world politics in which states are unwilling to yield power over their citizens is still dominant and stands squarely in the way of universal respect for human rights. In current world politics states still retain a considerable measure of sovereignty in the treatment of their citizens. Yet, the United Nations World Conference on Human Rights of 1993 reaffirmed that 'the promotion and protection of all human rights is a legitimate concern of the international community' (United Nations, 1993: 4).

It is particularly harmful to the implementation of human rights that the more powerful Western nations in particular have repeatedly been very hypocritical in their enforcement of human rights standards. Usually, human rights violations in so-called client states have been generously overlooked whereas the readiness to intervene in countries of progressive leaning if they violated human rights has been much greater. Often a double standard has been applied that served geopolitical and economic interests. Cases can be found in the different ways the international community has treated its 'enemies' in Iraq or in former Yugoslavia. An illustrative recent case is also the way in which the US government at the same time helps the Palestinian Authority to violate human rights (for example through the order to President Arafat in 1995 – by the US Vice President Al Gore – to establish a military tribunal for terrorism) and accuses the Palestinians of human rights violations.

Moreover, there is an abundance of cases to demonstrate that many states are very willing to trade their business interests for the defence of human rights. The motivation to defend human rights only rarely survives the attractions of commercial contracts. Western attitudes towards the Chinese People's Republic are a case in point. A particularly serious problem in this context is caused by the stakes the five permanent members of the United Nations Security Council have in the world's arms trade. Almost 90 per cent of the world's weaponry is sold by these five countries. And as Garcia-Sayan rightly observes: 'Weapons on the world market are one of the major sources of corruption of both political and, especially, military institutions. If this issue is not clearly and directly tackled, it is impossible to speak seriously about economic, social and cultural rights in the Third World' (1995: 76).

Finances

There are important financial obstacles to the implementation of human rights. If one would like to combat the exploitation of children in sweatshops in poor countries, one would have to find means to keep the victims of this exploitation alive when they lose their jobs and also to find ways to support the exploiters who now need to employ adults at higher wages which increases the prices of their products and makes them less competitive on the international market.

It is not so difficult to think of myriad creative programmes to implement human rights in poor countries, but then the question is how will the necessary resources for these programmes be mobilized: by the international community, by the rich nations?

The 'new world order'

The protection of human rights is in serious danger around the world with the rapid deterioration of socioeconomic conditions. Poverty is no longer a Third World phenomenon, it proliferates in the East and Central European countries and in the big cities of the rich countries where increasing numbers of people live below poverty lines and in cardboard boxes. This globalization of poverty is a structural condition and not the incidental fringe effect of an otherwise benign system. It is the result of the economic policies of the rich countries and the international financial institutions, notably the IMF and the World Bank, and the worldwide withdrawal of public support for the vulnerable members of society.

In the 1980s and 1990s most sub-Saharan African countries have adopted – more or less voluntarily – programmes of economic reform designed by the international financial institutions. They include, in general, the decrease of government expenditure on public services, the abolition of price controls, the devaluation of the local currency, the reduction of trade and foreign exchange controls, and the privatization of public enterprises. These policies sustain poverty, destroy the environment, encourage civil and ethnic conflict and erode women's rights. Loan conditionalities almost everywhere lead to massive poverty.

The World Bank concedes in its 1995 Report *Workers in an Integrating World* that the poor have in particular suffered from structural adjustment. It has meant the reduction of public services, recession and unemployment. For many countries it has been well documented that Structural Adjustment Policies adversely affected health and education. Attempts to remove food subsidies have directly threatened the right to food. The liberalization of labour markets has led to a reduction in wage levels, unemployment and restrictions upon free trade unions:

'The experience of developing countries, in particular in South Asia, abundantly documents that structural adjustment programmes and development strategies hurriedly introduced, without social policies and mechanisms to protect the vulnerable and the weak, have had negative impacts on human rights and impeded sustainable development. (Hossain, 1997: 11)

The emerging new world order within which human rights standards are to be implemented is characterized by the following realities:

- Some 25 per cent of the world population does not benefit from any economic growth, and lives in conditions worse than 15 years ago.
- In 89 out of the present 174 UN member states the economic situation is worse than a decade ago.
- The top 358 billionaires in the world are worth the total income of 45 per cent of the world population.
- The 20 per cent poorest people receive only 1.4 per cent of the total world income and the 20 per cent richest receive 83 per cent.
- In the past few years the South has transferred more money to the North (in terms of debt-servicing and corporate profits) (some $50 billion per annum) than the total international spending on development assistance.
- Some 1.3 billion people live on less than one dollar a day.
- More than 2 billion people do not get enough food and 800 million are chronically undernourished.
- Over 1 billion people lack access to safe drinking water.
- Almost 1.5 billion people lack access to health services.
- For more than 100 million children there are no schools.
- Almost 1 billion adults are illiterate.
- The 1.4 billion working people in the Third World earn on average $695 per year. (UNDP, Human Development Report, 1997 and World Bank Report, 1998, 1999).

This actual state of affairs adds up to a gross violation of human rights and there are no indications that this situation might change in the near future.

Human rights and the market

At the core of the 'new order' stands the belief in the constructive role market forces play in the realization of a decent society. The common reasoning goes something like this. The society that respects the defence of human rights is a democratic society. Democracy is a political arrangement in which people's needs and aspirations are freely expressed. The market is an economic arrangement by which people's needs and aspirations are satisfied. A marriage made in heaven! The market is the perfect tool for a democratic social order. The trouble is, however, that the market only caters to the needs and aspirations of those people who can pay for their satisfaction. The market is selective and exclusive in its treatment of people whereas a human-rights inspired democratic order should be inclusive and egalitarian. Moreover, the market does not meet all needs and aspirations equally well. It prioritizes some needs and aspirations over others. Priorities are not determined by substantial moral standards such as human security but by monetary value. Those needs and aspirations that can be defined in hard monetary terms are the definite winners.

Characteristic for 'free market' societies is the 'money culture' that judges all human activity in terms of its monetary value.[3] Everything is provided with a price tag: even basic resources, such as water, air, maternal care, security, time. Everything can be acquired through money and be traded in against more money. In this culture people engage in contractual and calculating relations with each other. Its greatest problem is the totalitarian nature of the money culture. It is worldwide the most prominent model for the organization of societies. As a result the relations that people have in the marketplace spill over into domains such as education, health care, care for the elderly, science and culture. The contractual and calculating relations are to mutual advantage. In the marketplace people do not entertain affective relations with each other. Buyers and sellers do not necessarily have to take the interests of their counterparts into account. It can even be an unnecessary additional complication if business exchanges are burdened with an affective dimension. In the market people survive best if they are good at calculating. This attitude is, however, disastrous for the quality of human relations when affection and trust are required, such as in health care. In caring institutions the key principle is solidarity between the various parties. As in more and more countries the principles of the market are introduced solidarity disappears. In the market the primary motive is self interest. Choices people make are tested against the yardstick of 'What is in it for me?' As health care institutions introduce the rules and standards of commercial operations all decisions are tested against their stockholder value. Whether patients leave hospitals horizontally or vertically is less important than their contribution to the annual balance. The money culture has winners and losers. The money culture is unsuitable for the caring professions and institutions. Most people find it unacceptable that some people would be excluded from health care, even if this is due to their own faults. When however the notion of profit begins to dominate health care, the aim to provide care to as many people as possible is rapidly eroded. The market approach causes in the USA a situation whereby some 40 million out of the 266 million American citizens have no health insurance. They only get medical assistance in extremely critical conditions.

The 'money culture' has also begun its devastating journey into the domain of science. Science acquires the features of top sports. It is increasingly a ruthless game in which competition is more important than cooperation. Quantity is more important (numbers of quotes, numbers of students) than intellectual quality.

The essential assessment criteria are fundraising, top ten lists, production output and money flows.

By applying market principles in more and more social domains people are not merely calculating consumers, but become calculating citizens. This poses a serious obstacle to the implementation of human rights. In the market people entertain contractual relations because they expect to gain from these exchanges. Within this mental map human rights only fit insofar as respecting them yields a profit.

The social contract and self-interest

The adoption of human rights as normative guidance for social ethics is founded upon a global social contract that the international community has concluded. The notion that common moral standards can be based upon a social contract already occurs in biblical thinking, in Aristotle's *Politics*, in Roman law and in the eighteenth-century philosophies of Locke, Hume and Rousseau.

The social contract is essential to the thinking of a contemporary philosopher of law and politics, John Rawls. The common question is how can people who do not know each other live together? This is an extremely urgent question in societies that are increasingly anonymous, complex and multicultural. An essential objection against the conclusion of social contracts is that they are mainly inspired by self-interest. As American philosopher Gauthier writes, 'the contractarian insists that a society could not command the willing allegiance of a rational person if, without appealing to her feelings for others, it afforded her no expectation of net benefit' (1986: 11).

People agree to impose certain moral restrictions upon themselves if they expect to benefit from this. The critical question is whether the expectation of self-interest is a sufficiently strong motivation to respect the defence of human rights. It can be argued that defending human rights may not always be in one's best self-interest. Violations of someone else's human rights often presents a situation in which one's self-interest is best served by looking the other way. The protection of human rights, however, implies that people take the interests of others seriously and are prepared to – if necessary – restrain their own interests. People may take the interests of others into account usually when this is ultimately also to their own benefit. And indeed it cannot be denied that enlightened self-interest may serve good causes. It may have a positive effect upon the implementation of human rights. People may fear to become victims themselves of human rights violations. Or they may have learnt that respect for human rights is part of a society's good manners. Or they may be afraid they will be punished for committing human rights crimes.

However, within the morality of the 'money culture' all of this is not sufficient to bring people to sustained forms of restraint vis-à-vis others. Ultimately it is decisive that people feel solidarity with victims, feel that injustice is unacceptable and that caring for others is more important than self-interest. The choice whether to respect human rights is largely based upon a form of empathy with the conditions that others – even people one does not know – experience. This is to a large extent a non-rational choice inspired by a strong sense of disgust against avoidable suffering. This revolt is not motivated by social contracts or well understood self-interest and cannot be legally enforced. The most powerful affective motive for the protection of human rights is 'compassion'. Respecting human rights requires an altruism that does not thrive within the money culture. In a culture where the accumulation and expansion of private property has the highest priority, human rights do not stand much of a chance. They need a very different biotope: a culture of compassion.

Samuel and Pearl Oliner investigated the motives of people who rescued Jews during the Holocaust. The rescuers – often of people they did not know and at great peril for their own lives – are characterized by feelings of compassion, care and solidarity. They tend to come from families where affective relations were important, where it was explained that negligent conduct to others is unacceptable and where parents provided caring role models:

> The differences between the basic values and world views of rescuers and nonrescuers can be traced in part to their parents' significantly different views about appropriate standards and the importance of self and others. Excessive self-interest – self-preoccupation – generally precludes attention to others, reducing not only one's ability to recognize others' needs, but also one's motivation to do so. (Oliner and Oliner, 1988: 160)

The rescuers are more focused upon others than the non-rescuers. The rescuers also are less interested in materialist and pragmatic considerations: 'Altruistic rescue obviously required the abjuring of practical and instrumental goals' (Oliner and Oliner, 1988: 161). It is important to realize that compassion is not a fixed part of the human genetic constitution. It is not a hereditary personality trait. It can be learnt and therefore it should be taught!

Good global governance

The implementation of human rights, as Hossain rightly observes requires 'good governance': 'Governments as well as powerful corporations must adhere to respect human rights and be accountable for their conduct measured by human rights standards' (Hossain, 1997: 20). The Universal Declaration of Human Rights offers important guidance in Article 28 that was quoted at the beginning of this chapter. It provides that 'Everyone is entitled to a social and international order in which the rights and freedoms set forth in this Declaration can be fully realized.' This claim is equally valid for the organization of physical as well as of virtual societies. The relevant question thus is which standards should guide the social and international order that guarantees the protection of human rights and freedoms in CyberSpace?

In recent years the notion 'good governance' has become very fashionable in international development cooperation. In this context it has often amounted to a rather paternalistic assessment of the performance of governments in poor countries by standards such as respect for human rights, rule of law, multi-party democracy, and accountable administration. To judge one's partners by standards of social morality seems in itself a useful idea lest one ends up with parties that demonstrate more talent for corruption and gross human rights violations than for sustainable social development. However, within the framework of international human rights law such standards would apply equally to all the parties involved. They would thus be the moral measure for governments in both poor and rich countries, for intergovernmental development agencies, but also for non-state actors such as transnational corporations and the development assistance non-governmental organizations (NGOs). This is not the case today. International institutions such as the IMF and the World Bank have in the past few years not contributed to the development of democratic institutions in poor countries. Most of their programmes have rather undermined such institutions (Korten, 1995: 171). They have also themselves not been paragons of democratic governance (Korten, 1995: 165). One also finds in the world of the NGOs a lack of public accountability and democratic structure that competes with authoritarian government institutions. Equally, most global business corporations do not live up to the standards of good governance. Moreover, development assistance agencies tend to be most cavalier in applying good governance standards when they hurt good business prospects in recipient countries.

Key requirements for good governance of CyberSpace

The international human rights instruments point to a democratic organization of societies as prerequisite for the realization of human rights. Human rights cannot be realized without involving citizens in the decision-making processes about the spheres in which freedom and equality are to be achieved. This moves the democratic process beyond the political sphere and extends the requirement of participatory institutional arrangements to other social domains. It claims also that culture and technology should be subject to democratic control. This is particularly important in the light of the fact that current democratization processes (the 'new world order' processes) tend to delegate important areas of social life to private rather than to public control and accountability. Increasingly large volumes of social activity are withdrawn from public accountability, from democratic control, and from the participation of citizens in decision-making.

The requirement of broad participation in social decision-making processes needs to be complemented with the requirement of public accountability. The Universal Declaration of Human Rights (United Nations, 1948) states in Article 1: 'All human beings are born free and equal in dignity and rights. They are endowed with reason and conscience and should act towards one another in a spirit of brotherhood.' This conception of the human being as gifted with reason and consciousness leads to the obligation of accountability. The gift of reason and conscience means that people can know what they are doing, can reflect on their acting in terms of normative categories, and they can thus be held responsible for what they are doing! They should act in a certain way ('in a spirit of brotherhood' which could be translated as 'with compassion') and can be held accountable for their conduct. Since in social ethics government institutions and business corporations are 'moral agents' they can and should be held accountable by those who are affected by their moral choices.

In line with the proposal to base social morality upon the normative standards of internationally adopted human rights and freedoms, the social and international order within which this can be realized should be guided by global governance 'with a human face'. At a minimum this implies that global governance of CyberSpace should have a democratic and inclusive architecture and should recognize the public responsibility of all actors. The leading questions for the following chapters have now been stated. Chapters 4–6 will address the question whether current CyberSpace governance rules and practices are guided by the defence of human rights standards. The concluding Chapter 7 will address the question whether the institutions of global CyberSpace governance meet the requirements of 'good governance'.

Notes

1. By way of illustration: Resolution 3384 (XXX) of 10 November 1975 by the General Assembly of the United Nations: *The Declaration on the Use of Scientific and Technological Progress in the Interests of Peace and for the Benefit of Mankind* proclaims that:

    1. All States shall promote international co-operation to ensure that the results of scientific and technological developments are used in the interests . . . and for the purpose of the realization of human rights and freedoms in accordance with the Charter of the United Nations.
    2. All States shall take appropriate measures to prevent the use of scientific and technological developments . . . to limit or interfere with the enjoyment of human rights and fundamental freedoms. . . .
    7. All States shall take the necessary measures, including legislative measures, to ensure that the utilization of scientific and technological achievements promotes the fullest realization of human rights and fundamental freedoms without any discrimination whatsoever on grounds of race, sex, language or religious beliefs.
    8. All States shall take effective measures, including legislative measures, to prevent and preclude the utilization of scientific and technological achievements to the detriment of human rights and fundamental freedoms and the dignity of the human person.'

    Resolution 1986/9 by the Commission for Human Rights, *Use of Scientific and Technological Developments for the Promotion and Protection of Human Rights and Fundamental Freedoms*: 'Calls upon all States to make every effort to utilize the benefits of scientific and technological developments for the promotion and protection of human rights and fundamental freedoms.'

2. Also Foucault tends towards this third position. He warns that we should not be trapped in the either/or choice in connection with the Enlightenment (Waugh, 1992: 103). We are to a large extent determined by Enlightenment thinking and will have to try to now proceed independently with our critical self-examination. We have not yet achieved the maturity to which the Enlightenment invites us and as Foucault states 'I do not know whether we will ever reach mature adulthood' (in Waugh, 1992: 107).

3. James Buchan (1998) wrote an enlightening book about the significance of money.

Equal Entitlement in CyberSpace 4

Everyone is entitled to all the rights and freedoms set forth in this Declaration, without distinction of any kind, such as race, colour, sex, language, religion, political or other opinion, national or social origin, property, birth or other status.

Universal Declaration of Human Rights, Article 2

The key task for any system of governance is the distribution of essential social resources. For the governance of CyberSpace this implies the distribution of society's information and communication resources. The basic human rights standard of 'equality' has a direct bearing upon the way in which a society should deal with the distribution of resources. The standard claims that no one should be excluded from access to and benefit from those resources that are essential to the participation in the community's life. Therefore, the international community has provided through Article 27 of the Universal Declaration of Human Rights that 'Everybody has the right freely to participate in the cultural life of the community, to enjoy the arts and to share in scientific advancement and its benefits.' Equally, the International Covenant on Economic, Social and Cultural Rights provides that the States Parties to the Covenant recognize the right of everyone 'to enjoy the benefits of scientific progress and its applications' (Article 15). The 1966 UNESCO Declaration of the Principles of International Cultural Co-operation states: 'to enable everyone to have access to knowledge, to enjoy the arts and literature of all peoples, to share in advances made in science in all parts of the world and in the resulting benefits, and to contribute to the enrichment of cultural life' (Article IV.4). A non-discrimination provision is also incorporated into the Outer Space Treaty (1967): 'The exploration and use of outer space . . . shall be carried out for the benefit and in the interest of all countries, irrespective of their degree of economic or scientific development, and shall be the province of all mankind' (Article I). Already in 1991 this standard was applied to the use of telecommunications satellites through a resolution by the General Assembly of the UN: 'Communication by means of satellite should be available on a global and non-discriminatory basis' (Res. 1721D [XVI] in

1961). In the Principles Governing the Use by States of Artificial Earth Satellites for International Direct Television Broadcasting (1982) it is emphatically claimed that 'Access to the technology in this field should be available to all States without discrimination' (Article 5).

When using the standard of 'equality' one should note that in the conventional human rights theories there is a bias towards an interpretation which assumes that all human beings are equally capable in asserting their rights and in which the legal system is formally based upon the assumption of the initiative of free citizens to defend their rights. These liberal foundations of human rights law tend to neglect the reality of the widely differential capacity to such initiative. In reality, the powerful are always better in asserting their rights through litigation than the less powerful.

Whenever the concept of equality is used this usually pertains to the Lockean interpretation of 'one rule for rich and poor' or to the Kantian interpretation of non-discrimination: the law should treat all citizens as equals. In these interpretations the law recognizes a formal concept of equality that is related to the perception of inequality as a form of social differentiation which can and should be corrected. Law is anti-discriminatory in the sense of repairing social disadvantage by the equal treatment of unequals. This, however, does not change the structurally unequal relations of power. The equal treatment can even reinforce the inequality.

Providing equal liberties to unequal partners functions in the interest of the most powerful. In a more adequate interpretation 'equality' means equal entitlement to the social conditions that are essential to emancipation and self-development. Increasingly access to digital ICTs is seen by many as a social condition that is equally essential for the members of a community as water, energy or road systems. One could raise the question whether at present the access to CyberSpace does constitute a service that is essential for people's participation in social life. It would seem that most people can live reasonably well even without a mobile phone and Internet connection. There are for those outside the Internet world still many other information sources available. Actually, in most societies it is possible to function quite well even without access to TV. There are enough other sources ranging from libraries to daily newspapers. For many it is still easier and cheaper to communicate by writing letters or by just talking to other people. If, however, as might well happen, the functions of the Internet keep expanding and more and more people are connected, it may be expected that lack of access will cause serious social exclusion.

The global digital divide

> The network society is creating parallel communication systems: one for those with income, education and – literally – connections, giving plentiful information at low cost and high speed; the other for those without connections, blocked by high barriers of time, cost and uncertainty and dependent on outdated information. (UNDP, 1999: 63)

The principle of equality meets in the literature and debates about ICTs with a great deal of consensus. As the Independent Commission for World Wide Telecommunications Development (1984) states, it is in the interest of humanity that the majority of the world population is not excluded from the use of new technologies. The Commission, chaired by Sir Donald Maitland, writes in his report *The Missing Link*, 'that by the early part of the next century virtually the whole of mankind should be brought within the reach of a telephone' (1986: 4). Yet, there seems general agreement in the scientific literature and in public policy statements that the ICT gap between the developed and developing countries is widening and that this hinders the integration of all countries into the so-called Global Information Society. Nowhere in the world have the aspirations of the Maitland report been achieved. Universal access has not been realized anywhere in the world! For some 5.7 billion people there are one billion telephone lines. In some 500 million households (34 per cent of the total in the world) there is a telephone. Early 1997 62 per cent of all telephone lines installed were in 23 rich countries with less than 15 per cent of the world's population.[1] Although over half the population of poor countries lives in rural areas, some 80 per cent of all telephones are connected in the urban areas.

Unequal access holds for all new networks and services. In rich countries one finds 84 per cent of cellular phone users, 91 per cent of fax machines and 97 per cent of all Internet host computers.[2] In 1999 there are an estimated 170 million people with access to the Internet. This represents some 4 per cent of the world population. Over 80 per cent are in North America and Europe.

Another indicator of present disparities are revenues from telecommunications services. In 1996 they reached a world total of US$620 billion. Europe, the USA and Japan combined 77 per cent of these revenues and the African countries a mere 1.5 per cent. Investments in the telecommunications sector show a similar distribution. In 1996 the world total is worth US$166 billion. Europe, the USA and Japan are responsible for 67 per cent of these investments and Africa for 1.7 per cent (ITU, 1998a).

The expenditures for electronic data processing per capita of the population show great variety across the world. In 1995 the world average was US$46. In the USA these expenditures were US$315, in Japan US$400, in Singapore US$1,500, in Brazil US$39, in Thailand US$29, and in India US$0.87 (Mansell and Wehn, 1998: 35). Large disparities can also be seen in the world trading of ICT. In 1996 the share in worldwide computer equipment imports for the USA, Japan, Germany and the UK alone was 60 per cent. The share in worldwide computer equipment exports for the USA, Singapore, Japan and the UK was 57 per cent. The share in tele-communications equipment exports for the USA, Japan, Germany, the UK, Sweden and Singapore was 60 per cent. The share in telecommunications equipment imports for the USA, Hong Kong, the UK, Japan, Germany, China and Singapore was 58 per cent. The share in world imports of sound and TV recorders for the USA, Hong Kong, Germany, the UK and Japan was 67 per cent. The shares on the world market for computer software in 1996 of the USA (46.2 per cent), Japan (11.4 per cent), Germany (8.6 per cent) and the UK (5.7 per cent) combined to 72 per cent.

Whatever the economic benefits of ICT deployment may be, at the present time the worldwide distribution of ICT resources is enormously unequal. In terms of availability, accessibility and affordability of equip-ment and services as well as the mastery of technical and managerial skills there are great disparities between affluent and developing countries, but also between different social groups within all countries. In the United States, for example, the 'digital divide' follows a clear geographic pattern: 'The West Coast and Eastern Seaboard from New Hampshire to Virginia are at the forefront of the 21st Century Economy. The Deep South and the upper Midwest lag far behind' (*Business Week*, 2 August 1999: 39).

The present disparity is no new phenomenon. When new technologies are introduced in societies the chances to benefit from them are always unequally distributed. Some people will benefit, others will mainly experi-ence the negative impact. This is a recurrent pattern. When a technology that promises financial benefits is introduced in social situations where unequal power relations prevail, a small group will enjoy advantages and the majority will often experience regressive development. Access to the global network society is mainly available to those with good education and those living in the OECD countries with sufficient disposable income. In most countries men dominate access to the Internet and young people are more likely to have access than the elderly. Ethnicity is an important factor and in many countries the differences in use by ethnic groups has widened: 'English is used in almost 80 per cent of Websites and in the common user interfaces – the graphics and instructions. Yet less than 1 in 10 people worldwide speaks the language' (UNDP, 1999: 62).

Gender

A particularly skewed distribution of ICT resources and uses concerns the position of women across the world. An immediate problem is the fact that ICT skills are largely based on literacy. Actually, 'it seems likely that the vast majority of the illiterate population will be excluded from the emerging knowledge societies' (Mansell and Wehn, 1998: 35). This affects women especially, since around the world illiteracy rates for women are higher than for men. According to the latest data from UNICEF, there are among the one billion illiterates in the world some 130 million children. Among these kids for whom there are no schools, two of every three in the developing world is a girl (UNICEF, 1999). In terms of sharing ICT knowledge women are also disadvantaged since their numbers in enrolment for science and technology education lag far behind the figures for male enrolment. If one takes access to tertiary education in science and technology, there is a clear gender inequity. In 1990 the percentages of female enrolment are for Africa some 10 per cent, Latin America 40 per cent, Western Europe 32 per cent, Eastern Europe less than 30 per cent and Asia/Pacific 34 per cent (UNESCO, 1996).

ICTs offer potentially new forms of communication that enable women to break through their often isolated social situation. They also create new opportunities of employment for women in jobs that require new skills. However, the technologies themselves will not achieve this. Unless robust policies are in place and are enforced, the possible benefits of ICTs will have no impact on women's lives. The realization of opportunities that are in principle created by the deployment of ICTs will depend upon such social variables as cultural capital, class and age: 'Although faced with these changing skill requirements and the need for continuous upgrading of skills, few women have access to the relevant education and training' (Mansell and Wehn, 1998: 249).

As Mansell and When (1998) report:

> Some women at grassroots level, even in extremely poor countries, have managed to use ICTs to improve their businesses, reproductive health, and basic human rights. (p. 250)

> The sustainability of women's initiatives in 'knowledge societies' depends on an enabling environment which can be created through the efforts of national policy-makers, donor agencies, and United Nations bodies. (p. 250)

> In the emerging 'knowledge societies' access to communication is becoming the key tool for social inclusion. (p. 250)

There is still considerable gender inequality in the access to and use of ICTs and a great deal of creative policy-making is needed in order to ensure that women may also share the benefits of ICT deployment in their societies. Across most developing countries women are disadvantaged in terms of scientific and technological literacy, in opportunities for education and training for the acquisition of technical skills, and in real access to information and knowledge.

Universal access: historical development

From the first design for telecommunications networks, universal access was considered a fundamental factor. The availability of telecommunications services to the general public has been a basic standard in international regulation since the ITU Convention of 1865. This conference convened by Napoleon III to promote the international standardization of telegraphy led to the establishment of the International Telegraphy Union (the predecessor of the International Telecommunication Union) and to the conclusion of the world's first international treaty on telecommunications. The 20 European countries signing the treaty decided that the norm of universal availability of telecommunications services should be the fundamental standard for international regulation. This first multilateral accord codified the right of everyone to use international telegraphy as standard. Many countries followed this decision and recognized that minimal telecommunications services should be provided on a universal basis.

The US Communications Act of 1934, for example, proposed 'to make available, so far as possible, to all people of the United States, a rapid, efficient, nationwide and worldwide wire and radio communications service with adequate facilities at reasonable charges'. And American telephone company AT&T used in its annual report of 1909 the slogan 'One System, One Policy, Universal Service' (Pool, 1983: 22).

The world community has expressed its political choice on the availability of telecommunications services in the 1961 landmark resolution on space communications that was quoted above (UNGA Res. 1721D (XVI). The agreement for the operation of the satellite consortium INTELSAT (signed by parties at Washington, 20 August 1971 and entered into force 12 February 1973) made reference to this resolution in its preamble: 'Considering the principle set forth in Resolution 1721D (XVI) that communication by means of satellite should be available to the nations of the world as soon as practicable on a global and non-discriminatory basis.'

The standard of availability obviously demands international coordination. It requires that telecommunications networks are technically compatible and that common rules are adopted about access to and use of these networks. From the mid-nineteenth century through the 1970s this coordination was governed by a stable and robust multilateral accord. The world community had adopted common standards on the technical compatibility of networks and the price setting for access to and use of these networks. This public-service type agreement was based upon the principles of natural monopoly and cross-subsidization. Monopolies of equipment and services were seen to provide efficient and equitable public service. Cross-subsidization meant that tariffs for small users were not based upon real costs, but were kept affordable by subsidies from such revenue generating operations as international telephony.

The political developments and the technological innovations of the 1980s eroded this arrangement and caused important reforms in telecommunications regulation. It had become clear meanwhile that the monopolistic position of companies like AT&T in the USA had not delivered universal telecommunications services. Also the European monopoly public telephone operators had not succeeded in connecting everyone to their national networks. The first century of international telecommunications agreements had served monopolies well against competition, but had not contributed to the implementation of the fundamental standard of universal availability. In the regime that emerged in the 1980s the issue of universal access was again on the policy agenda.

US President Clinton has repeatedly stated that universal access to the means of communication is critically important. Also the poor in the USA should have access to the electronic highway. During the ITU conference in Buenos Aires (1994) Vice President Al Gore launched a proposal for a Global Information Infrastructure (GII). This project received ample political and industrial support. According to Vice President Gore everyone should have access to the GII: 'The GII . . . will circle the globe with information superhighways on which all people can travel. These highways – or, more accurately, networks of distributed intelligence – will allow us to share information, to connect, and to communicate as a global community.'[3] At the G-7 meeting on the Information Society (held in February 1995 in Brussels) the implementation of this global infrastructure was a priority item on the agenda. At this meeting most government representatives were very concerned about the backward position of the developing countries. They committed themselves to the promotion of 'universal service to ensure opportunities for all to participate'.

Definition of universal access

For inventor Alexander Graham Bell (in 1878) universal access implied that 'the poorest man cannot afford to be without his telephone' (Pool,

1983: 21). Over a century later the Director-General of British telecom company watchdog OFTEL defined universal access as 'affordable access to basic voice telephony or its equivalent for all those reasonably requesting it, regardless of where they live' (Garnham, 1997: 207). This definition reflects the now generally adopted notion that telephony should be available and affordable for all.

As a result of technological developments the access to electronic networks and information services has become increasingly important. Therefore, the universal access debate no longer exclusively focuses on access to the infrastructure of telephony. In November 1993 the European Commission communicated to the Council of Ministers and the European Parliament that the principle of universal access should be extended from 'access to telephony' to 'access to new information services'. In 1996 the Commission proposed to define universal access as 'the provision of voice telephony service via a fixed connection which will also allow a fax and a modem to operate as well as the provision of operator assistance, emergency and directory enquiry services and the provision of public pay phones' (European Commission, 1996b). Herewith the Commission confirmed that users should have access to all services provided by the existing telecommunications networks. The European Parliament has defined this extension from access to service in the sense of a 'minimum package of services that should be available to all users irrespective of their geographical location against an affordable price'.[4]

The European Parliament has put 'universal service' in a broader social context and linked telecommunications to other domains such as energy and water supply, postal services and public transportation. In the perspective of the European Parliament governments should intervene whenever the market fails to guarantee this universal service.

In several countries the notion of universal access has been expanded in recent years. In the USA, for example, the new Telecommunications Act (1996) provides that 'Access to advanced telecommunication and information services should be provided in all regions of the Nation'.

When the development of telecommunications moves beyond the plain old telephone service (POTS) the universal access concept becomes fairly complex. With the growth of the Internet, for example, the issue has been raised about the inclusion of such new telecommunications services.

It may be well to note that universal access in its various conceptions has never meant 'free access'. In all European Union countries universal access implies that the user pays for both the connection with the infrastructure and its usage. However, most EU member states have not adopted in their national telecommunications policies the provision that access to networks should be affordable for users. Belgium, the Netherlands,

Luxembourg, England, Finland, Greece, Ireland, Italy, Portugal, Spain and Sweden have no specific rules on affordability. The telecommunications laws of France and Germany have, since 1996, a rule on access with affordable tariffs. Denmark has proposed in its telecom policy that it wants to offer the world's best and cheapest telecom services.

The critical question evidently is what universal access means when a price tag is attached to it. This becomes even more complicated if the scope of access is broadened. Should users also have access to ISDN facilities and broadband optical fibre networks? How should this be financed? By the users themselves? From public means? By way of cross-subsidization schemes? Taxes on digital traffic? Or through the forces of the market-place?

Conventionally in developed countries, universal access means 'a telephone in every household'. In the developing countries the meaning has shifted to a telephone within reasonable distance. This reflects a change in emphasis from individual service to forms of community service. According to telecommunications expert Heather Hudson it is essential that universal access not only applies to individuals but also to institutions:

> Therefore, the unit of analysis used to measure universality needs to be rethought. In the past, universal service was defined in terms of individual access, typically using the household as the unit of analysis. However, this definition needs to be broadened to encompass access to services that telecom can deliver to individual residents through community or institutional access. (Hudson, 1997: 399)

Income inequalities

> Buying a computer would cost the average Bangladeshi more than eight years' income, compared with just one month's wage for the average American. (UNDP, 1999: 62)

There is substantial research evidence of a strong correlation between access to telecommunications and income. In the UK, for example, 30 per cent of the households with less than £100 per week has no telephone (Mitchell, 1997: 444). Consumer organizations in the USA complain about the fact that the national information infrastructure is primarily constructed in the richer neighbourhoods. As Mitchell concludes: 'it seems to be a fact that all the trials and initial plans for the Information Super-highway in the US involve prosperous residential and business areas, leaving middle and lower income areas unconnected' (1997: 445). And as research by the National Association for the Advancement of Colored

People shows: 'low-income and minority communities are under-represented in United States telephone companies' initial plans for installing advanced communications networks' (Lohr, 1994).

There is ample empirical evidence to conclude that today income disparities grow rapidly everywhere in the world. In 1960 the 20 per cent richest people were thirty times richer than the 20 per cent poorest people. In 1991 this ratio was 61:1 and in 1994 78:1. The part of the poorest 20 per cent in the total world income was 1.1 per cent in 1997 (this was 2.3 per cent in 1960). In 1997 out of 5.7 billion people some 1.3 billion lived on less than one dollar per day. At the same time the 358 top billionaires had 45 per cent of the world's total income (UNDP, 1997).

Poverty is one of the features of economic globalization as it no longer affects only the poor countries of the Southern hemisphere. In Eastern Europe, for example in the former Soviet Union, the number of poor people (who live on less than four dollars a day) has risen from 14 million in 1988 to 119 million in 1994. In Western Europe more than 70 million poor people are threatened with social exclusion. Against these depressing observations it can be argued that there is economic growth in many countries. And it is certainly true that the elimination of poverty is unlikely without any economic growth. However, for poverty to be reduced economic growth is effective only if there are well-defined political programmes for poverty alleviation and public policies for the redistribution of wealth.

Experience teaches us, moreover, that where economic growth reduces poverty, this does not necessarily mean that social inequalities are reduced. In most countries the rich benefit more from increases in the gross domestic product than the poor. For example, in most Latin American countries over the past years the income of the 20 per cent poorest people decreased. The unequal distribution of economic benefits would seem to be further reinforced by the so-called globalization process. For the least developed countries (with some 10 per cent of the world population) the share in world trade diminished from 0.6 per cent in the 1970s to 0.3 per cent twenty years later.

Do people want universal access?

What would happen if people were asked whether they really want universal telecom access? There are many examples of situations in poor areas of big cities or rural areas where access to communication means is not itself a real problem, but where people prefer TV to the telephone. If people are capable of paying they may prefer the entertainment TV provides more than the use of interactive telephony. It may well be that many people prefer to be passively entertained rather than actively communicate with others. Should public money be spent for consumers who if given the choice would not see telephones and PCs as priorities but would rather have the latest in digital TV technology in their homes? What should public policy be vis-à-vis people who do not want to be interconnected? Not only because of the costs, but also since they find the equipment much too complicated and have no interest in all the information that is on offer.

As societies become more 'digital' the self-imposed exclusion will become more of a burden and will be seen as socially undesirable. Becoming digital (or becoming digitally literate) entails an ambivalence similar to conventional forms of literacy. People need to be literate in order to participate in social life. Social institutions, such as public services and banks, can only function effectively if sufficient numbers of people are literate. Learning to read and write has always been proposed as an effort that primarily benefits the student. It enriches people's minds, increases their knowledge and thus liberates them. Thanks to international programmes of technical assistance (run by organizations such as UNESCO) many people have become literate in order to achieve higher economic, social and cultural standards. Literacy, however, also has the dimension of political and social control. As more people can read and write, it becomes easier for social élites (in governments, industry, banks) to exercise influence. If large numbers of people refused to become literate this would pose serious problems for those who manage today's societies. A modern society can no longer function without the basic skills of literacy.

The same applies to digital (il)literacy. It would be naïve to assume that governments and corporations promote universal access to CyberSpace for charitable reasons only and out of great concern for otherwise socially excluded people. Universal access is also motivated by the wish to incorporate as many people as possible within the discipline of the market. Government and industry have a vested interest in getting more people interconnected. With more people on the Net forms of 'Orwellian' control for political and commercial purposes become more effective.

What information should be accessible?

If all the necessary financial means can be generated to provide universal access to CyberSpace and everybody also wanted this, then we face the question about the kind of information that should be made accessible.

The Internet appears to be developing into the world's largest vehicle for commercial information and the competition for future advertising income on the Internet has begun. This is only logical since the investments for the construction of a global information highway have to be recouped through advertising. In this sense, the Net may just develop like television. One wonders though whether the universal access to commercial messages equates to the realization of a crucial common good?

Universal access could mean that everybody has access to games, entertainment and pornography. Can this justify the social efforts to provide universal access? This is complex because who is to decide what information is socially more acceptable: free access to the *Encyclopaedia Britannica* or to erotic entertainment? CyberSpace technology offers great chances to give citizens information about public policies and to involve them in the decision-making process. However, is this what citizens want? Is this what governments want? Although governments often claim that general access to public information is essential, they will usually make sure that they themselves draw the lines of what is accessible. An additional problem is that not only should state institutions make information physically accessible, but the information should also be presented in formats that are intelligible for the average citizen.

It also needs to be noted that the democratic nature of a society not only depends upon the equality in distribution of information but also upon the ways in which citizens use the available information. Citizens themselves will also have to be ready to actively participate in public decision-making processes. This participation is wanting in many societies and it is too simple to just blame the failing provision of information. A much more basic problem is the low level of interest citizens have for politics and the lack of credibility politics has. If people were to choose between the political discourse of the Athenian Agora and the Roman Colosseum (where Christians were devoured by lions) many may indeed prefer the entertainment over the political debate. Even where there are possibilities to access alternative information sources, there usually is a small minority only that actively engages in the search for information. People have very different information needs and different information interests. This is related to the differential distribution of 'information capital' in societies.

Distribution of information capital

The French sociologist Pierre Bourdieu (1985) has proposed that the position of social actors is not only determined by economic capital, but also by their cultural, social and symbolic capital. Cultural capital is made up of such features and skills as knowledge about wines, fine arts, music and literature, good manners and mastery of foreign languages. Social capital is based upon the social networks that people develop. Symbolic capital represents social prestige and reputation.

To these forms of capital, the category of 'information capital' should be added. This concept embraces the financial capacity to pay for network usage and information services, the technical ability to handle network infrastructures, the intellectual capacity to filter and evaluate information, but also the motivation to actively search for information and the ability to translate information into social practice. Just like other forms of capital, information capital is unequally distributed across societies. Its more egalitarian distribution would require an extensive programme of education, training and conscientization. To just have more 'surfers' on the Web does not equate to the equal possession of information capital.

The issue of sustainability

An important concern that has arisen in connection with the possible proliferation of digital technologies across the world is the question whether ICTs can be applied in environmentally sustainable ways. If, as a result of the deployment of ICTs economic productivity increases, does this also imply that levels of consumption increase? And, is this an acceptable course from the perspective of sustainable development?

It would seem naïve to assume that the mere deployment of ICTs implies the sustainable development of societies. There are both environmentally positive and negative scenarios thinkable. When information replaces tangible goods production processes could emerge with lower levels of environmental pollution. However, the rise in economic productivity (even assuming this could be done with lower pollution levels per produced unit), implies the strong likelihood that more industrial output leads to higher levels of consumption and therefore in the end to more pollution (Jokinen, 1996). If one, for example, assumes that digital technologies would improve the productivity of the automobile industry, then even if cars could be manufactured with lower levels of pollution, the overall increase in car purchase and use would probably lead to overall higher pollution levels. The core problem with a more equal global access to ICTs is that this would increase the level of energy use (per capita) in the developing countries to the average levels in the rich countries. As Makridakis (1995: 800) suggests, 'it is doubtful that the climatic equilibrium of the earth can be sustained' if this were to happen. The global use of ICTs would also drastically increase the emission of carbon dioxide (by printers, copiers and computers) to environmentally untenable levels. Providing more access to more ICTs implies producing more computers. The production of a single PC requires approximately as much energy as the average electricity consumption of a mid-European household per year.

In 1998 IBM presented a technology that makes it possible to diminish the energy use of chips. The production of low-energy chips is primarily intended for the cellular phone market. For some time to come most computers (with Pentium processors and Microsoft operating systems) will function without such chips. At the ever higher speeds they operate their energy use will increase.

PCs are obsolete after three to four years and the question is what to do with a rapidly growing mountain of electronic garbage that contains all kinds of poisonous materials like PVC, broom, antimoon, lead and cadmium (Malley, 1996). All this has to be seen in the light of a rapidly growing world population which could by the mid-twenty-first century amount to some 8–10 billion people. For policy-makers this may be one of the toughest questions: can a global digital grid – accessible for all – be combined with environmentally sustainable development?

The challenge of sustainability concerns not only the environmental dimension, but also has financial, institutional and technical aspects. If foreign investments have facilitated the growth of national networks, can they be maintained, upgraded and renovated in the future through an independent generation of funds? Can – particularly in the smaller and weaker economies – the development of local production capacity for ICTs and the effort to gain an export position on a longer term be sustained in view of international competition and fluctuations on the world market? Will sufficient financial resources and training be invested in developing adequate management skills and technological mastery to secure the longer-term local control?

Solutions

Eliminating the distinction between information rich and information poor countries is critical to eliminating economic and other inequalities between North and South, and to improving the quality of life of all humanity. (Nelson Mandela at Telecom 95, 3 October 1995, Geneva)

Serious concerns about the growing digital divide inspire many public and private donor institutions to propose plans for the elimination of the

ICT-rich versus ICT-poor disparity. The World Bank, for example, established in early 1995 the Information for Development Program with the brief to assist developing countries with their integration into the global information economy. In 1995 the ITU established WorldTel – an ambitious project to generate private investments to bridge the tele-communications gap in the world by developing basic infrastructures. WorldTel aims at making some 40 million telephone connections in developing countries in the next ten years. It aims at an investment fund of a minimum of $1 billion.

AT&T planned that its Africa One project would have a fully operational optical fibre cable around the whole continent of Africa by 1999 to provide connections for all the major coastal cities. Also Siemens and Alcatel have designs (Afrilink and Atlantis-2 respectively) to provide telecom connections, especially to West Africa. Both the International Satellite Organization (IntelSat) and the Regional African Satellite Organization are actively promoting the expansion of e-mail services for the continent.

It needs to be questioned, however, how realistic the expectation is that this disparity can indeed be narrowed, let alone be eliminated. It may well be an illusion to think that ICT-poor countries could catch up or keep pace with the advancements in the Northern countries. In the North the rate of technological development is very high and is supported by considerable resources. It would be wasting scarce resources if poor countries did attempt to follow a 'catching up' policy which would – in the end – only benefit the designers and operators of ICTs. This does not mean that poor countries should not try to upgrade their ICT systems but they should not do this in the unrealistic expectation that those who are ahead will wait for them. As a result, the situation may improve for the poorer countries, but the divide will not go away. As long as ICTs are embedded in the institutional arrangements of a corporate-capitalist market economy, the equal entitlement to information and communication resources will remain a normative standard only.

The present discussion on the ICT gap provides no convincing argument that the owners of technology will change their attitudes and policies towards the international transfer of technology. Throughout the past decades the prevailing international policies on transfer of technology have erected formidable obstacles to the reduction of North–South technology gaps. Today, there is no indication of a radical change in the current practices of technology transfer. This makes it very unlikely that the relations between ICT-rich and ICT-poor countries will change in the near future.

Development support

The equitable sharing of communication infrastructures (the electronic highway systems created by telecom carriers such as satellites, cables, fixed lines and mobile transmissions), computing capacity (computers, peripherals, networks), information resources (databases, libraries), and ICT literacy (intellectual and social capabilities to deploy ICT in beneficial ways) demands an enormous effort on behalf of the international community. Massive investments are required for the renovation, upgrading and expansion of networks in developing countries, for programmes to transfer knowledge, for training of ICT skills – in particular for women.

In 1985 the Maitland Commission estimated that an annual investment of some US$12 billion would be needed to achieve its aspiration that early in the twenty-first century all people in the world should have easy access to a telephone. In 1996, Gautam S. Kaji, managing director of the World Bank, said in a talk to the WTO Ministerial Conference (December 8 1996):

> We estimate that telecommunications infrastructure investments in developing countries, which averaged roughly US$30 billion over the 1990–1994 period, will need to double over the next five years, in order to implement the necessary upgrades. The magnitude of these investments is clearly beyond what can be financed from tax revenues and internal public sector funding sources. The private sector will need to come in. (I-Ways, 1996: 32–4)

It can be debated whether the expectation that private funding will create worldwide equity in the access to and use of ICT resources is fully justified. It would seem that in any case the international governmental community and national governments of affluent countries should be reminded that solutions are not hindered by a paucity of financial resource but rather by political will. Creating worldwide adequate access to ICT resources should be no problem in a world economy of some US$22 trillion income. The core issue is that the expenditures for development assistance represent only US$55 billion and thus a mere 0.25 per cent of this income. As the UNDP reports in 1998: 'Official development aid is now at its lowest since statistics started' (UNDP, 1998: 37).

If one makes an educated guess of the funds needed to provide universal access to basic ICT equipment and services, the calculation would have to include basic infrastructural investment costs and recurrent service charges. Adding one billion telephone lines, subsidizing over 600 million households that cannot afford basic telephone charges, providing PCs and access to the Internet for schools, the annual costs for all developing countries – over a period of ten years – could amount to an annual US$80–100 billion. This should not be an insurmountable level of funding. It represents some 11 per cent of the world's annual spending on military projects, some 22 per cent of total annual spending on narcotic drugs, and compares to the annual spending on alcoholic drinks in Europe alone (UNDP, 1998).

For a variety of political and economic reasons many donor governments are presently cutting down on their financing of ICT development. Between 1990 and 1995 multilateral lending for telecommunications decreased from US$1,253 million to US$967 million. Bilateral aid for telecommunications decreased from US$1,259 million in 1990 to US$800 million in 1995 (ITU, 1997).

The account rate settlement system

An important component of global ICT governance is the so-called account rate system. Traditionally, the telecommunications system was based in bilateral relations between telecom carriers. The general regulatory framework for the settlement of charges between carriers (often the monopoly telecom operators) was provided by the International Telecommunication Regulations, a treaty administered by the ITU and last revised at the World Administrative Telegraph and Telephone Conference (WATT-C) in 1988. Over the past years with the innovations in technology, the drive towards liberalization and privatization, this regime came under severe pressure. Today, not only will more and more private commercial companies be the operators in both countries of origin and destination, they will also offer new services (such as phonecards or Internet telephony) that bypass the settlement system.

One of the essential motives of telecommunications regulation as it was enacted in the first International Telegraph Convention (1865) was to find an adequate system for the division of revenues from international calls among countries of origin, transit and destination. Basically, the public telecommunications operator (PTO) in the country of origin would charge the customer a certain price, then the PTO in the country of destination and the PTO in the country of origin would agree a price for the services by the destination PTO (providing international lines and switching and delivering calls to local customers). This is called the account rate. This amount forms the basis for the charges of operators in destination countries to operators in originating countries. These charges are called account settlement rates. The general recommendation by the ITU has been to divide the charges on a 50/50 basis between carriers. This worked well in situations where monopolies dealt with other monopolies and where international telecommunications was seen as a jointly provided service. However, this is all changing with the availability of more private operators and more competition, and more technical options to bypass the existing system.

For some time now a reform of the existing account rate settlement system has been discussed by the OECD (since 1991), the ITU (since 1992) and the WTO. In the past the existing system has served the interests of the developing countries well. Since developing countries have usually applied relatively high charges for the completion of international calls at their end, the account rate settlement was an important source of foreign exchange. According to the ITU each year up to US$10 billion may go to developing countries in net payments. This income can – at least in principle – be used to support access to the telecom infrastructure for people in rural areas who would otherwise remain disconnected.

When negotiations about reform did not progress quickly enough, the US administration decided to announce its preferred solution. The Federal Communications Commission in the USA has argued that the US loses billions of dollars each year in payments to other countries. It has therefore introduced (in November 1996) the Notice of Proposed Rulemaking which came into force in January 1998). Herewith a revised system was proposed that determines how much US operators can pay to operators in foreign countries. This would on average be half of what was paid in the past.[5] The critics of the conventional system have argued that payments above real costs are no longer adequate in an increasingly commercial tele-communications marketplace. They suggest that it is unacceptable for countries of origin to pay so much above-costs for the completion of their calls that countries of destination can subsidize their universal access policies. For example, in 1997 the United States paid US$154.7 million to Brazil on the basis of 495 million minutes of telephone calls from the US to Brazil and only 159 million minutes of calls from Brazil to the US.

Those who defend the system will refer to the critical significance of these payments for the provision of universal access in poor countries and will argue that lowering the account rate payments will lead to an increase in costs to local customers in those countries. Over the past 15 years, the USA transferred some US$1.2 billion to China, US$1.3 billion to India, and US$7.6 billion to Mexico in settlement fees (*Business Week*, 11 October 1999: 84).

In March 1998 the issue of the reform of the international account rate system was an important topic on the agenda of the ITU World Telecommunications Policy Forum. The shape of the eventual governance system on account rates will have a critical impact on issues such as accessibility of ICTs in poorer countries but also on the overall economic situation of these countries. The unilateral decision by the US Federal Communications Commission to cut the settlement rates means for a country such as Senegal a decline in settlement income from US$19.4 million in 1996 to US$10 million in 1998 (*Business Week*, 11 October 1999: 87). If other countries follow the US example, the country faces a loss of some 80 per cent of its hard foreign currency income. The government of Senegal gambles that by lowering tariffs for international calls it may boost traffic and can thus deal with the prospective losses. In Sri Lanka, however, the government has decided to double the prices of telephone calls to compensate the losses in settlement fees.

Free access to the Internet

In the course of 1998 and 1999 more and more providers began to offer free services; for example, Freeserve in the UK bypassed giant AOL in 1999 with 1.3 million accounts against AOL with 600,000 and CompuServe with 400,000 accounts. This is a definite trend by now. All providers charging subscription fees are getting into trouble and find the only solution may be to join the free providers.

One wonders though how free can 'free access' be in a capitalist economy? Is there such a thing as a 'free lunch'? There is always the need to recoup investments and to make profits. Therefore, the user will inevitably pay. The market is not a charitable institution. The delivery of free access is compensated through telephone call charges, advertising, paid information services and entertainment offerings hidden behind the decoder. Since offering free services will not change much unless a more attractive rate system is in place, several activist campaigns are underway to attack the present system. Groups like the UK Campaign for Unmetered Telecommunications (CUT) want to change the current common European local call charge regime which makes using the Internet expensive. CUT wants the pay-as-you-go regime changed to a US-style flat phone rate regime. In June 1999 CUT and other advocacy groups (like the Association of Angry Belgian Surfers and the Portuguese Internet Strike) joined forces for Europe-wide action.

The most problematic aspect of the free services may be that providers of such services recoup their investments from the sales to marketeers of the personal data they collect about the usage their clients make of the Internet. Such customer profiles are very valuable commercial commodities.

The bit tax

The 1999 UNDP *Human Development Report* has proposed a bit tax as a way to finance a more equitable distribution of Internet usage. The report recommends 'a very small tax on the amount of data sent through the Internet. For example sending 100 email messages would cost one dollar cent. . . . Globally in 1996, it would have yielded $70 billion – more than total official development assistance that year' (UNDP, 1999: 66). Levying a tax on data flows could, however, have a negative impact on those who can hardly afford the present charges of Internet access and usage. The tax may have a positive impact if it were used as a new form of cross-subsidization through which big corporate users are charged so that these revenues could subsidize small business and residential users in digitally deprived locations. Given the current resentment against public interference with the 'free market' (in institutions such as the World Trade Organization) the prospects for the bit tax are not very promising. Moreover, the enforcement of this new tax could imply very doubtful consequences for the privacy of Internet users and the confidentiality of their communications.

Access and equality

A difficult problem is that if indeed greater global equality in access to information could be achieved, this would not guarantee an improvement in the quality of people's lives:

> Even when these disparities are recognised and new organisational models such as telecentres are proposed, the policy emphasis is frequently biased towards improving access to networks rather than towards content creation and the social processes whereby digital content can be converted into socially or economically useful knowledge. (Mansell, 1999: 8)

Including people in the provision of basic public services does not create egalitarian societies. The existing social inequality means that people benefit from these services in highly inegalitarian ways. Actually, the growing literacy in many societies did not bring about more egalitarian social relationships. It certainly did have some empowering effect, but did not significantly alter power relations. Catching up with those who have the distinct social advantage is not a realistic option. They too use the new developments, such as ICTs, and at a minimum the gap remains and might even increase. It is a common experience with most technologies that the powerful players know best how to appropriate and control new technological developments and use them to their advantage. In the process they tend to further increase their advantage.

Global governance

The prevailing pattern of thought that guides global governance in relation to ICT-infrastructures is:

- telecommunications infrastructures are essential to development;
- their installation and upgrading is expensive;
- private funding is needed;
- to attract private funding, countries will have to liberalize their ICT markets and adopt pro-competition regulatory measures.

The governance of ICTs is in fact left to freely operating private entrepreneurs. The basic thought is that a country's telecommunications infrastructure can be managed by private companies and that whenever parts of the network are unprofitable the state can provide the public means to ensure that no citizen is disenfranchised.

In the course of the 1980s deregulation became the leading principle for public policy. Its main aim of 'less state and more market' has begun to affect more and more social domains and now reaches out in many countries also to primary facilities such as the provision of water and energy, thus rendering their access and usage problematic for those with little income. For national and global ICT markets the new policy implied privatization and liberalization. According to the deregulators, the creation of competitive markets and the shift from public to private ownership would facilitate the universal accessibility of telecommunications and information services. In this spirit the G-7 summit held in Brussels in 1995 adopted as guiding policy principles for the global information highway 'liberalization of the market' and 'universal service'.

By combining these principles it is suggested that they are complementary and mutually reinforcing. This is grossly misleading. The liberalized world market is the expression of an economic arrangement that promotes social inequality worldwide.

This is very visible in the policies of the most important forum for the free world market, the World Trade Organization. This organization supports the freedom of the most powerful players on the world market and protects them against the competitive prices of the less powerful players. Within the neo-liberal policies of the WTO, low prices for Third World products are seen as unfair competition, whereas the monopolization of market sectors by transnational corporations is considered free trade. Free market policies cannot guarantee the level of tariffs that is needed to secure universal accessibility to CyberSpace services.

The World Bank

In the spirit of deregulation, the World Bank Group has recommended the creation of investor-friendly business environments, the protection of investments and the security of repatriation of revenues. Since there may be losses in revenues as a result of the change in service charges or severance payments when public companies are privatized, the World Bank offers to finance the adjustment costs of the adoption of liberalization schemes in individual countries.

The World Bank policies are characterized by a strong emphasis on economic growth and a key role for the private sector. The expectation is that in a sufficiently free market, economic growth will also benefit the poorer sector of society. Within this perspective the contribution of the ICTs is to provide the essential infrastructure for economic development. This position bypasses the question whether indeed the deployment of ICTs leads to more economic productivity and – if so – whether the growth in economic productivity will be equitably distributed.

The ITU

The International Telecommunication Union (ITU) largely follows a similar governance pattern. During the Second World Telecommunication Policy Forum on Trade in Telecommunication Services (Geneva, 16–18 March 1998) the ITU Secretary General Pekka Tarjanne underlined the major points that were prominent in the contributions from member states. The telecommunications world has changed fundamentally as a result of the World Trade Organization (WTO) Agreement on Basic Telecommunication Services and the General Agreement on Trade in Services (GATS) which preceded it. According to the ITU member states, the telecommunications industry now operates, for all intents and purposes, under a trade regime. In this transition to a market-orientated environment, it is important that all countries are able to benefit fully from the new opportunities that a liberalized and dynamic world telecommunications market will create.

On 18 March 1998 the 593 Forum participants from 119 countries endorsed three non-binding opinions on the trade in telecommunications services. Opinion A addressed the implications of the GATS with respect to basic telecommunications services for ITU member states. Participants acknowledged that ITU member states that are also members of the WTO are obliged to apply the general principle of most-favoured nation (MFN) treatment to services and service suppliers from other WTO members.

The World Trade Organization

The Marrakech Agreement Establishing the World Trade Organization completed in 1994 (15 April) the Eighth Multilateral Round of Trade Negotiations held under the GATT (Uruguay Round). Part of the final treaty was a General Agreement on Trade in Services (GATS). The most elaborate annex concerned the trade in telecommunications. The Annex defined basic telecommunications services and networks as:

- Public telecommunications transport service: any telecommunications transport service required, explicitly or in effect, by a member to be offered to the public generally.
- Public telecommunications transport network: the public telecommunications infrastructure which permits telecommunications between and among defined network termination points.

Among the 125 signatory countries of the Marrakech Agreement some 60 made commitments to open their markets for telecommunications services although most did not commit themselves on the issue of basic telecommunications. The commitments range from full competition for all telecommunications services to exceptions for basic telecommunications services or cellular services or for local services.

The Marrakech meeting established the Negotiating Group on Basic Telecommunications (NGBT) which was to deal with telecommunications services and to conclude its work by April 1996. The NGBT failed to reach agreement by this date. Several issues remained inconclusive, such as the liberalization of satellite services and the settlement arrangements for international telecommunications rates. The negotiations did lead though to an agreement on some basic rules that were provided in a so-called 'Reference Paper' which deals with competitive safeguards, interconnection, universal service obligations, transparency of licensing criteria, independence of the regulator and the allocation and use of scarce resources.

A new group, called the Group on Basic Telecommunications, continued the work after July 1996. Open to all WTO member states and with monthly meetings, its main mandate was to stimulate more countries to make commitments, to deal with the issue of liberalizing satellite services and to solve a number of issues related to the provision of telecommunications services. The new series of negotiations focused among others on the matter of restrictions on foreign ownership. In particular, the US government pushed hard for allowing maximum foreign ownership in domestic telecommunications. In making their commitments, restrictions on foreign ownership were fully waived by many countries; others however retained 25–80 per cent domestic control. Whereas some countries consider foreign ownership an opportunity to attract necessary foreign investment (ITU, 1997: 102), others perceive it as a threat to national sovereignty. Although national governments have full control over the scope, the phasing and the timing of their commitments, once they have made those commitments they cannot in the future change their concessions. A complex matter for the negotiations became the issue of mobile services provided through satellites. Although the allocation of satellite frequencies is the responsibility of the ITU, there is a trading angle when national governments use national procedures for spectrum allocation as barriers to trade. Following the provisions of the GATS, such procedures should not be discriminatory.

On 15 February 1997, 72 member states of the WTO (representing some 93 per cent of the world trade in telecommunications services) signed the Fourth Protocol of the General Agreement on Trade in Services. On 5 February 1998 the Protocol came into force. This World Telecommunications Agreement demands that participating states liberalize their markets. They are allowed some leeway to implement universal access in ways they deem desirable but there are significant qualifications in the agreement which seriously limit the national political space. The Agreement has far-reaching implications for the governance of the basic infrastructures of telecommunications. It states on the issue of universal service:

> Any member has the right to define the kind of universal service obligation it wishes to maintain. Such obligations will not be regarded as anti-competitive per se, provided they are administered in a transparent, non-discriminatory and competitively neutral manner and are not more burdensome than necessary for the kind of universal service defined by the member.

This seriously limits the space for independent national policy-making on the access issue. Since foreign industries cannot be placed at a disadvantage, the national standards for universal service standards have to be administered in a competitively neutral manner. They cannot be set at levels 'more burdensome than necessary'. If a national public policy would consider to provide access to telecommunications services on the basis of a cross-subsidization scheme rather than on the basis of cost-based tariffs, this might serve the interests of the small users better than those of telecommunications operators. Foreign market entrants could see this obligation as 'more burdensome than necessary'. As a consequence the policy would be perceived as a violation of international trade law. It would be up to the (largely obscure) arbitration mechanisms of the WTO to judge the (il)legitimacy of the national policy proposal.

The focus of the Agreement is rather on the access that foreign suppliers should have to national markets for telecommunications services, than on the access that national citizens should have to the use of telecommunications services. The simplistic assumption is that these different forms of access equate. As a result, social policy is restricted to limits defined by the commercial players. Trade interests rather than sociocultural aspirations determine national telecommunications policy. Following the Agreement, the WTO has suggested that by the year 2004 there will be an almost worldwide open market (probably up to 93 per cent) for basic telecommunications services as most trading partners have agreed to liberalize their domestic markets. The establishment of worldwide free markets for any type of services does not, however, necessarily imply the availability of such services or the equitable use of these services for all who could benefit from them.

Judging from the growing participation in the telecommunications negotiations and the increase in market opening commitments, the conclusion is that more and more countries believe that liberalizing their telecommunications markets is beneficial to them. The real political issue is no longer whether countries will liberalize or not, but rather when they will do so. Yet, opinions continue to differ, as the *World Telecommunication Development Report* observes: 'Market access, for example, will be viewed by some as an opportunity, while others that are attempting to develop their own domestic telecommunication service industry might see it as a challenge and a threat to nascent local operators' (ITU, 1997: 102). In some countries there will be an increase in revenues for domestic operators as a result of liberalization, in other countries most revenues may accrue to foreign entities. As the ITU report rightly notes 'there will be winners and losers' (1997: 106).

As part of the opening up of their markets many countries have also begun to privatize their public telecommunications operators (PTOs). Whereas liberalization can be defined as the opening of markets to competition, privatization refers to the transfer of state-owned institutions or assets to various degrees of private ownership. These two processes can be in conflict with each other. Liberalization may clash with the desire of governments to get the highest price for its monopoly PTO and privatization may conflict with market liberalization when the incoming operator wants monopoly control for an initial period.

Governments pursue privatization and/or liberalization policies for quite different reasons. These policies may – especially in poorer countries – be more related to troublesome economies than with the desire to improve and upgrade telecommunications services. They may be related to the political wisdom of the day (for example neo-liberalism) or with the hope to get technology transferred in the process. The new policies are neither an unequivocal recipe for disaster nor do they guarantee successful economic and technological performance. Results will be different in different countries and much more study is needed to establish what social conditions determine benefits and costs.

Privatization has been implemented in a fairly large number of countries. Since 1984, 44 PTOs were privatized (ITU, 1997: 2). These privatizations have raised some US$159 billion. The 12 major privatizations in 1996 raised over US$20 billion. These investments were roughly 50 per cent domestic and 50 per cent foreign. The overall trend has been that over 30 per cent of the invested capital comes from foreign sources. As the ITU reports the PTOs themselves are usually the most active investors.

However, in 1997 majority shares in 29 out of the top 40 international carriers were still owned by states: 'Rather than full privatization, it is corporatization of state-owned telecommunication companies that has instead proceeded across all regions' (ITU, 1998b: 9). Also liberalization has not proceeded such as to create competitive markets across sectors in all countries. In many countries basic telecommunications services are not open to competition. Most liberalized are markets for mobile telephony but also in this sector several countries do not (yet) allow competition.

The arguments that are used to support privatization point to the expansion and upgrading of networks, the improvement of services and the lowering of tariffs for access and usage of networks. Experiences are however varied. Frequently, one of the results of privatization is the expansion of the telecom network. In several countries (for example Peru, 1997 and Panama, 1997) privatization considerably improved teledensity. According to the ITU: 'One reason is that network expansion targets have increasingly been made a requirement of privatization concessions' (1998b: 71). The added telephone lines benefit of course those users who can afford the service. The privatization scheme does not enlarge the group of citizens who have the purchasing power that is required for the use of telecommunications networks.

In several countries tariffs have gone down but mainly for big corporate users whereas the telephone bills for ordinary consumers have hardly benefited. Experiences with the provision of services are also differentiated. This is partly due to the fact that the expectation of more competition and more choice as a result of privatization was not always fulfilled. As a matter of fact, in smaller and less advanced states national telecommunications operators have lost out against big global coalitions, the new monopolists. It is highly questionable whether markets controlled by a few global operators will actually benefit the consumer. It remains dubious how much competition in the end will remain. The reduction of prices and the increase in investments for technological innovations tend to shake competitors out of the market and as a result market liberalization almost everywhere tends to reinforce market concentration. This follows the historical experience that free markets inevitably lead to the formation of monopolies since competitors will shake contenders out of the market or will merge with each other.

Conclusion

The moral standard of equal entitlement represents the ideal of an egalitarian society in which all people can claim access to those basic services that are essential to participate in social life. This standard does require that access to and usage of CyberSpace are available and affordable to all without discrimination. In the current world situation this requirement is not met by far. The current practices of global ICT governance pose crucial obstacles to its realization.

The prevailing commercial environment for the development of CyberSpace resources collides with the standard of equal entitlement. Market imperatives allocate resources according to what people can buy and not according to what they need. They defeat around the globe the aspirations of egalitarianism and equitable social development. Increasingly, social inequalities are no longer seen as structural problems, but as marginal phenomena to an otherwise benign system.

All the public concerns about the global digital divide and all the lip-service paid to the aspirations towards universal access and universal service do not change this. This is largely so because most expressions of concern ignore the real underlying issues. There is little or no space for critical social analysis to understand why technology does not normally change unequal power relationships but tends to reinforce them. Even if the efforts to reduce the global digital divide were successful this would not necessarily mean the ideal of a more egalitarian society was achieved. Actually, greater equality in access to and usage of ICTs – within the constraints of the current political-economic order – is likely to even strengthen current inequalities.

Notes

1. The 23 rich countries are Australia, Canada, European Union members, Japan, Iceland, New Zealand, Norway, Switzerland and the USA (ITU, 1998a).
2. In some more detailed figures:

   Of the total number of 47,972,000 fax machines in the world in 1996, Europe had 10,942,500, the USA: 17,000,000, and Japan: 14,300,000. This combined 88 per cent contrasts with the 0.5 per cent for Africa. Of the total number of TV sets in the world in 1996, Europe, the USA and Japan had 47 per cent and Africa had 3 per cent (ITU, 1998a). Internet host computers were distributed across the world such that the USA (51.5 per cent), the EU countries (23 per cent), Canada (6.1 per cent) and Japan (5.2 per cent) combined 85.8 per cent of the world's total in 1997 (OECD, 1998b).

3. Address at the Conference of the International Telecommunication Union in Buenos Aires, 21 March 1994.
4. European Parliament: Directive 97/33 by the European Parliament and the Council of Ministers (30 June 1997) on interconnectivity in telecommunications, universal service and interoperability by application of the principles of Open Network Provision. Resolution by the European Council of Ministers (7 February 1994) about the principles of universal service in the sector of telecommunications.
5. As part of its liberalization and pro-competition policies, the European Union has decided that the account rate system will be discontinued for telecommunications traffic between members of the Union. The Union prefers a system of cost-based charges for interconnection services.

Digital Risks and Security in CyberSpace 5

The human rights standard of security poses relevant questions for social ethics since the pervasive application of digital technologies creates new forms of social vulnerability. This chapter addresses the security risks caused by the unreliability and fallibility of digital technologies, and the mental attitudes of decision-makers towards digital risks. It also deals with the threats to information security caused by the current proliferation of surveillance technologies.

Risks to physical security

On its first voyage from Southampton to New York on 14 April 1912, the *Titanic* collided with icebergs. Out of 2,200 people on board over 1,500 died. The new technologies applied to the construction of the ship had suggested it could not sink. However, against the power of the iceberg the new steel plates of the ship had little chance. Although this was technically the cause of the disaster, another factor was the complete confidence the crew had in the perfection of the vessel. Since nothing could happen anyway, the ship sailed much too rapidly through an area with icebergs. Moreover, since the *Titanic* was thought to be absolutely safe, insufficient lifeboats had been stocked. Actually, this assumed technical perfection caused people on boats in the vicinity to conclude that the emergency flares were fireworks to celebrate the great ship.

The *Titanic* catastrophe symbolizes all those situations in which avoidable harm is inflicted as a result of an overdose of confidence in the safety of technological products. This misplaced confidence can be extremely hazardous. It would seem a rational attitude to acknowledge that technology does not come without risks and see to it that sufficient lifeboats are stocked!

The security risks implied in the use of digital systems are especially urgent in the light of the extremely high global risks the late-twentieth-century presented. As sociologist Ulrich Beck writes, 'we live on the volcano of civilization' (1992). The philosopher John Leslie even points to the real danger of the extinction of the human species (1996). According to the British social theoretician Giddens it is impossible – in the late-modern society – to live on 'automatic pilot' since no single lifestyle can be adequately protected against the globalization of life-threatening risks (1991b: 126).

Our security is threatened by warfare (nuclear, biological and chemical), terrorism, organized crime, changes in the environment (increasing ultraviolet radiation, rising temperatures, disappearance of rain forests, shortage of drinking water, desertification, depletion of fossil fuels, decreasing biodiversity), carcinogenic ingredients in food supplies, pollution by poisonous materials (acid rain, chemical products from insecticides to deodorants), series of natural disasters (asteroids, comets, volcanoes, floods, tornadoes), and genetic experiments. To this discouraging list we have to add the observation that also the deployment of digital systems implies enormous risks.

Software failures

We find today that digital systems are applied in a wide variety of applications – from microwave ovens to cockpits of aeroplanes. Such systems are guided by software. This implies that the instructions for the actions that systems must perform are written in thousands of rules in a computer program. The obvious intention is that the systems do precisely what they are instructed to do. Often this works well. But all computer users are familiar with the nuisance of computer programs that malfunction or with programs that – upon their installation – delete existing software. Since even the simple PC is never fully reliable, users are constantly advised to make so-called 'back-ups'.

In general, it has to be said that digital systems are unreliable. In many big projects, the software demonstrates serious flaws. In 1992 the manager of British Nuclear Fuels announced that in an essential part of the system's software several thousands of errors had been detected, hundreds of which caused serious danger for the secure operation of the company (Leslie, 1996: 95). Such problems have been known about since the 1960s but have still not been satisfactorily resolved. Yet, in more and more fields systems are deployed that are dependent upon software. Aviation provides a good illustration.

The A320 Airbus is considered the first complete digital 'fly-by-wire' aeroplane. This means that the pilots no longer direct the plane directly but through instructions to the computer system. The role of software in the flight-control system is essential. Specially programmed software determines the routing and the flight altitude, distributes fuel from the various tanks, boosts the engines, shuts them off or withdraws the landing gear. The pilot, who used to have a more direct link to the plane, now activates the software that steers the plane. A series of accidents has demonstrated that this impressive technological progress is not without risks. Between 1988 and 1993 four A320 planes crashed with the probable cause being the digital 'fly-by-wire' system. In the various accidents the system failed to warn for high speed during landing, or to warn that the plane had landed. In some cases the system reported after landing that the plane was still in the air. On 20 January 1992, an Airbus 320 of Air Inter crashed just before landing at Strasbourg airport: the system had to process too much data and had 'parked' the information automatically away for later retrieval. The overload of data caused the electronic guidance to fail. Eighty-seven people died.

Failures of software can also cause problems in other applications:

- On 20 November 1985 the Bank of New York lost over $5 million as a result of an error in the software of the digital system that registered all the bank's financial transactions.
- In January 1990 a software error stopped all computers that ran national telephone traffic for AT&T. For nine hours all US telephone traffic was in complete disarray.
- On 25 February 1991 28 American soldiers were killed and 90 were wounded in an attack with an Iraqi Scud missile. The air defence system failed to intercept the missile as a result of a software error.
- In 1992 a software problem created total chaos in the communication system of ambulance services in London. The delay in communications caused the death of 30 people.
- On 4 June 1996 the launching of the European Ariane-502 rocket failed due to software errors in the flight control and guidance system. During the repeated and extensive tests this specific system had not been adequately tested.
- On 7 August 1996 the computer system of Internet-provider America Online (AOL) failed for 19 hours when new software had been installed. Over 16 million subscribers were affected. Before this took place, the AOL experts had strongly suggested that the system was immune to this kind of disaster.

Much work is at present being carried out to improve the reliability of essential software. All kinds of control mechanisms are being explored that would detect failures much earlier. The production of software has certainly improved in the past few years and will be further refined by the application of more strict methodologies in software design. However, it is not possible to completely avoid errors. Error free software remains – possibly for ever – a dream. One important problem in this context is that measures to make software more secure always cost time and money. There is always the need to balance these costs against the consequences of possible failure.

Why is software unreliable?

Errors in computer programs can be caused because the software producers make mistakes, they may be negligent or work too fast in order to beat the competitor. Software designers sometimes assume that systems will be regularly checked and small errors will easily be detected. This can be a fatal mistake, when in reality such systems have to function permanently. A general rule is that every 4,000 lines of code contain at least one error. Large digital telephone systems need programs with millions of rules of code. This increases the number of errors accordingly.

For software to be completely reliable, it would be necessary to consider all the possible conditions under which the digital system will have to function. A system that takes care of the landing of an aeroplane would have to be tested under all the weather conditions that may impact the plane: extreme heat or cold, sudden winds, unexpected hail or icing, the weather obviously being only one of the many variables. The system designer develops a model of the reality within which the system will operate. In spite of the efforts, it will never be possible to incorporate all possible situations and conditions in the model. Some variable is likely to be left out.

It is impossible to detect all the errors in programs that contain millions of lines of code before their actual use. Even with repeated testing, errors remain and will incidentally cause problems. If errors are detected, they can obviously be repaired. However, the repairs can lead to new errors. Moreover, sometimes errors are not caused by the software designers, but evolve later because a part of the code in the programs reproduces itself and transmits faulty instructions to the system. With the growing complexity and capacity of digital networks, the risks of self-mutating viruses that can evade anti-virus software only increases. Testing is difficult since even very minute errors may have dramatic consequences and one should therefore not miss even the smallest detail. Human beings do the testing, so they are prone to forget something. If testing is left to computers, the problem is again the reliability of the testing software. The software that is used to chase the so-called 'bugs' (for example, viruses) may itself contain errors. An almost classical scenario is the extended test of a system that has many millions of lines of code. After three months of trials, everything looks perfect. Then a small detail (for example, three lines of code) is changed. The designers know precisely what they may expect from the change. There is no reasonable argument to go though another three months of testing. The system is installed – and crashes!

Even when tests are satisfactory, there is still no certainty since some problems only occur after a period of actual use of the system. If the system then fails, it is often a complicated and time-consuming affair to find the cause. In fact, one only knows that a system fails when it fails and thus when it is too late! A simulation test gives important indications about the reliability of systems under different conditions. However, the ultimate real test is in prolonged daily usage of a system. Even if digital systems function perfectly in prolonged testing, there is no guarantee that the same behaviour will occur in real applications.

Digital systems are usually very complex. This complexity causes unexpected effects because the systems may do things they were not instructed to do. An illustration is where the anti-theft detectors in shops reprogrammed customers' pacemakers, with sometimes fatal consequences.

Can software be less complex? Simpler software is of course possible, but this will diminish the number of functions the systems may perform. If users demand more of their ovens, washing machines, PCs, cockpit systems, control panels for nuclear reactors, and so on, this increases the complexity of operating systems and thus the chances of failure. Even when users do not need all the functions their dishwashers may have, the manufacturers just build them into their systems in order to suggest a superior quality.

The protection of complex systems make systems even more complex. If a system is to anticipate all possible errors, the complexity will inevitably increase. The more complex a system is, the more difficult it becomes to foresee all possible errors. As complexity increases the margin for surprises also grows. An additional problem is that software usually steers systems which consist of parts that are interrelated and that influence each other. If one part malfunctions, the whole system may be affected. One of the many components of an electronic system may be a weak element in the chain that impacts the quality of the total system. It is also impossible to predict how components that by themselves may be safe will function when they form a system. Even the application of proven software offers no guarantee for reliability since software that operates in a new system may behave in unexpected ways.

Software and its users

A minor error made by a systems operator (July 1997, at Internic in Virginia, US) made the Internet inaccessible for several hours. The network is very vulnerable to simple human errors like the inputting of a wrong command in organizations such as Internic, which manages databases with addresses.

On 3 July 1988 the US aircraft carrier *Vincennes* shot down an Iranian civil plane (Iran Air flight 655) carrying 290 passengers who all died. The crew on the *Vincennes* mistook the plane for a hostile, military F-14 fighter. The Aegis air defence system, that had cost billions of dollars and that used the most advanced digital electronics, provided its users with more data than they could handle in the critical few seconds they had for their decision. The system designers did not reckon with this. The system could handle high-speed data processing, but the human operators could not. In nuclear reactors a similar problem arises. The digital warning systems have enormous electronic panels that provide the operators with vast amounts of data that they need to interpret in too little time.

Particularly troublesome with the users of software is the tendency to be more cavalier about security as the technologies become safer. If a car is equipped with safety belts, ABS and excellent tyres, people are inclined to drive faster than they should. It is a general finding in research on automobile traffic, that the more protection is provided, the more risks people will take. With regard to computers this may imply that the more users trust the technology, the less inclined they are to take all kinds of control measures.

One also has to contend with the almost inexhaustible creativity of the human being to use technology for utterly destructive purposes. Although electricity and axes were designed for different purposes, people use them for torture and murder. Until societies leave the running of electronic systems to cyborgs, computers will be managed by the human species which has a highly developed proclivity to create ruin and chaos. Many people are also overconfident with regard to their own technical abilities. Most people that own cars believe they are good drivers. Experienced airforce pilots fly their planes without parachute because they believe they are too good to crash.

Systems may also be so complicated and so user-unfriendly that this causes errors in their use. If, however, systems are made more user-friendly, their security will normally diminish. The system would then, for example, not require that the user upon seeing an error message checks all the data put into it before retrial. This was one of the problems with the radiation system Therac-25. When the system refused to perform, it did not ask to provide all the specific data about the patient concerned before retrying.

Human failure is, however, only one of the many variables that cause accidents. If one replaces the fallible human operator with technology, there will be other problems since perfect software does not exist. The security risks of fully automated systems have been amply discussed in connection with the plans of the Reagan administration (during the 1980s) for a Star War scenario in the Cold War. This scenario, called the Strategic Defense Initiative (SDI), proposed a defence system that could intercept Soviet land-based intercontinental ballistic missiles in the so-called 'boost phase'. This is when the engines of the rockets are firing. A critical element of the SDI was that the decision-making capacity would have to be left to the technical system. Given the need to make enormous volumes of calculations in high sequence and process vast quantities of data, human choices would be too slow and the use of automatic control systems would be required. The implied launch-upon-warning strategy would then be based on decisions made by digital electronics. The organization Computer Professionals for Social Responsibility (which was established in 1982) warned at the time that military warning systems would become increasingly dependent upon unreliable computers.

Security risks may occur when the effort to resolve problems with digital systems focuses too much on finding and repairing one specific cause. If this has been detected the search for other possible variables stops. Security problems are, however, often caused by several factors. A good illustration is provided by the accidents caused by the digitally-run Therac-25 radiation system. A number of cancer patients who received treatment with Therac-25 in the USA and Canada between 1985 and 1987 received such an overdose that three of them died and several others were seriously injured. These accidents were partly caused by software errors. Leveson and Turner (1993) demonstrated after extensive study that in accidents like these there is a series of causes:

> Most accidents involving complex technology are caused by a combination of organizational, managerial, technical and, sometimes, sociological or political factors; preventing accidents requires paying attention to all the root causes, not just the precipitating event in a particular circumstance. (1993: 69)

There is a strong human tendency to identify one specific cause and when it is believed this factor (for example, a software bug) is found, the search ends. Another characteristic for the majority of approaches to risks is that all involved solve their own problem. In an interdependent system this makes no sense. In complex network situations there are often numerous causal connections and access to a complete overview of all the connections and the possible effects of even minor events is impossible.

Digital sabotage and cyberwar

Some risks to security are caused by deliberate efforts to wreak damage in computer systems. Acts of digital vandalism may include denial of service attacks whereby outsiders instruct computer systems to crash. Special programs (among them WinNuke) have been designed to send so much information to other computers that they stop functioning. The popular Microsoft operating system Windows is particularly vulnerable to such attacks as it makes it fairly easy for outsiders to infiltrate hard disks as soon as users log on to the Internet.

Although the intentions of the so-called 'hackers' may not always be devious, there can be no doubt that their activities can cause great damage to essential digital systems. It is difficult to give a precise estimate of the damage that can be caused by hacking. The American FBI thinks it may be as much as $700 million annually (1997) (Hoboken, 1998: 9). Some examples illustrate the vulnerability of digital systems to sabotage:

- In 1996 there were 250,000 attempts to break into the computers of the Pentagon. Some 75 per cent were successful. The 150 hackers that were eventually prosecuted had managed to get into the central computers of the airforce.
- In December 1997 the World Wide Web homepage of search engine Yahoo! was hacked and the hackers warned users that they would install a virus infecting all Yahoo! user computers. Yahoo! is one of the search programs through which Internet users seek information. In October 1997 the WWW site of Yahoo! was used more than 17 million times. Experts reacted by saying that the likelihood of the hackers planting the virus was very small, but it was certainly possible.
- In February 1998 the US Ministry of Defense was confronted with a forceful digital attack against 12 nodes in the networks for the airforce and the navy. Two 16-year-old hackers turned out to be the culprits.

- In early March 1998 a computer hacker crashed thousands of computers with Microsoft operating systems in the USA, among them the digital systems of the NASA.
- Also in March 1998 the Israeli police arrested an 18-year-old hacker who had been snooping in Pentagon computers.
- In April 1998 the computer systems of the Pentagon and the NASA were hacked. The hackers (calling themselves 'Masters of Downloading') reported their burglary in the cyber magazine *AntiOnline*.
- In 1999 the e-mail service of Microsoft (Hotmail) was hit by a security failure. The Swedish hackers Hack Unite discovered that from different websites it was possible to read personal messages from Hotmail subscribers. It is a recurrent feature of Microsoft that security failures in its operating system and its browser are exposed.
- In August 1999 common protective encryption codes of 512 bits, among others used for electronic payments, were decoded by scientists at the University of Amsterdam. This implies that the protection of electronic transactions needs a more expanded encryption which obviously after some time will again be outdated. There is probably no end to this game between encryption codes and the efforts to crack them.

According to security expert John Vramesevich (*NRC Handelsblad* 30 April 1998) the protection of vulnerable systems is generally very inadequate: 'Since we know of the break ins by MOD – "Masters of Downloading" – we received proof that six other hackers had managed to break through the security of army systems'. The Pentagon hackers are considered dangerous criminals by the US government. During a trial in May 1998 against one of them, Janet Reno, the US Minister of Justice, remarked that cybercrime could change the Internet into the Wild West of the twenty-first century. According to Reno we face a new type of criminal that uses computers for mass destruction. The hackers themselves state that they want to contribute to public awareness about the vital security risks in case essential systems are not sufficiently protected. Security is obviously of prime importance for military computer systems. The Pentagon spends over $2 billion on security. Yet, the systems remain vulnerable to attacks. After extensive research in 1996, the US General Accounting Office reported that terrorists or other opponents could take over the control of military information systems and seriously diminish the defence capacity of the country (*NRC Handelsblad*, 7 March 1997).

Security is the essential topic in current debates on new forms of warfare. The development of digitally-run weapons systems makes 'cyberwar' an attractive and 'clean' alternative to conventional armed conflicts. However, a deceptive aspect is that in a digital war there may be fewer victims in the short term than with old fashioned bombing, but the numbers of victims will rapidly increase as the effects of cyberwar set in. A successful digital attack would, among others, lead to disruption of the provision of electricity and water.

The possibility of 'cyberwar' implies that states have to design defensive policies to diminish their vulnerability. At the same time, several states, like the USA, actively develop the capacity for digital offensives. The USA has developed an extended digital system for espionage that costs some $30 billion annually. This is justified by the argument that the USA is the target for much industrial espionage and theft of intellectual property. The capacity of this espionage system can also be deployed to secure American economic interests abroad.

Digital weapons systems consist of: (a) software that renders the information networks of opponents inoperational through viruses; (b) advanced bugging devices, and (c) equipment that through electromagnetic pulses can disrupt electronic systems. The Pentagon has this recipe for digital warfare: 'Deny, destroy, or intercept adversary computer, network, or communications, while protecting one's own' (Schwartau, 1996: 464). A cyber attack could close all international communications of a country, render all air traffic impossible, sabotage the provision of electricity and water, paralyse the country's financial system. A scary prospect is the possibility that organized crime or terrorist groups could equip themselves with cyberspaceweapons.

Societies that apply many digital systems are extremely vulnerable to 'cyberterror'. With relatively simple tools the key functions of such societies can be disrupted.

Electromagnetic interference

Security risks in digital systems can be caused by totally unpredictable factors, such as earthquakes, floods, tornadoes, fire, lightning or extreme temperatures. Security can also be threatened by electromagnetic signals that suddenly open or close electronic gates or doors or set electronic toys in motion. Electromagnetic signals give instructions to the software that runs digital systems. Such signals are transmitted by computer screens, microwave ovens, mobile phones, alarm systems of transmitters for broadcasting.

During test flights of US Air Force Black Hawk helicopters 22 people died in crashes caused by radio waves that generated incorrect instructions for the software in the helicopters. Even with the installation of measures to protect the flight system against interference, Black Hawk pilots are not allowed to fly near certain broadcasting transmitters (Neumann, 1995: 158).

Several examples are known of cars that suddenly speed up while they are on cruise control, because the (digitally-run) motor management system is affected by the electromagnetic interference from an amateur shortwave transmitter (Association for Computing Machinery, 1991). In mechanical systems the driver decides which instructions will be given to the engine and will increase the speed by stepping on the accelerator. In a digitally run 'motor management system' the instruction can be effected by external factors such as the signals from a cellular telephone or a satellite transmitter. Digital 'motor management systems' are not only vulnerable to external electromagnetic disturbances but also to internal pulses that are generated by the system itself. It may also be the case that several internal and external factors operate simultaneously. However improbable this may sound, experience teaches that accidents are often caused by the completely unexpected simultaneous occurrence of different factors.

Ignoring alarm signals: the real problem!

It can be argued that more dangerous than the risks inherent in new technologies, is the limited human capacity to deal with these risks in rational and responsible ways.

The *Challenger*

The explosion of the Space Shuttle *Challenger* (flight STS 51-L) in January 1986 could have been avoided. Signals of serious risk were not taken seriously in the compulsion to be competitive in space and the refusal to deal responsibly with the possibility of the loss of human lives. Engineers of the rocket manufacturer Morton Thiokol Inc. tried to stop the launch, pointing to the risk that cold temperatures could compromise the primary seals on the shuttle's booster. As one engineer said, they all knew that if the seals failed, the Shuttle would blow up. They were overruled. In August 1985 there had already been a study by Thiokol that concluded there was a high probability that the back-up sealings would fail as well. Even already in 1983 NASA itself had concluded this. On the day of the launch, the engineers said no, but the general manager of the company conceded to NASA pressure and gave approval. In one of the meetings a senior manager of Thiokol said that they had to take a managerial decision and not a technical decision (Punch, 1996: 28). The lift-off was very important for

NASA because there had already been several delays and a $30 million investment was at stake in a fierce international competition in space. NASA management chose to ignore the warning signals and risked the gamble. Seventy seconds after launching the Shuttle blew up. The six astronauts and the school teacher on board all died.[1]

The DC-10

A similar gamble was made by aeroplane manufacturer McDonnell Douglas with the choice for a hazardous cargo door of the DC-10. The door was economically attractive but had structural weaknesses. In spite of the warnings about potential lethal risks, the company gambled on winning. As a Convair engineer who had worked on the DC-10 design pointed out in a memorandum of June 1972, 'It seems to me inevitable that, in the twenty years ahead of us DC-10 cargo doors will come open and I would expect this to usually result in the loss of the airplane'.

The choice was made under pressure of the competitive race against Lockheed and Boeing. The management of Convair recognized there was a moral problem but decided that Convair 'should not risk an approach to Douglas' (Punch, 1996: 109). The memo of the engineer was not transmitted to McDonnell Douglas. However, even without this information the McDonnell Douglas management knew there were problems with the cargo door. There had already been a number of near-crashes caused by the door.

On 3 March 1974 a DC-10 of Turkish Airlines lost the cargo door after take off from Paris and crashed: 346 people were killed. Also the management of Turkish Airlines was to blame. McDonnell Douglas had instructed all its clients to make a modification that would improve security. Turkish Airlines did not comply, again under pressures of time and competition and the related financial considerations.

Such fatal management choices are characteristic of situations in which decision-makers take the 'calculated risk' to ignore warning signals. This means that decision-makers refuse to listen to dissident voices, discourage critical thinking and silence people who ask awkward questions. Studies on managerial decision-making suggest a number of factors that reinforce the neglect of warning signals (Wissema, 1997). Among these factors are the complexity of situations, the feeling that one lives through an extraordinary historical period, the exultation of a winning mood, and the pressures of time and competition.

If we analyse key documents on the 'information society' a mental climate emerges which is very conducive to the neglect of warning signals.

The documents point to a time of important changes, a feeling of triumph, time pressures and competitive forces. By way of illustration, the Final Report of the Information Highway Advisory Council in Canada (September 1997) can be used:

- Time of transition: 'As the 21st century dawns, Canada and the world are making a profound transition that reaches into every aspect of life'; 'A new knowledge society is replacing the industrial society'; and 'A social, economic and cultural revolution is now transforming the world.'
- Winning mood: 'Canada has a leadership position in developing the Information Highway and progressing toward a knowledge society and economy.'
- Time pressure: 'It is urgent that Canada moves quickly'; and 'Canada must move quickly to lay a solid legal and technical foundation for electronic commerce.'
- Competitive climate: The task of 'building the high-quality, affordable information infrastructure needed to strengthen Canada's position in the global information economy. This task takes on growing urgency with the evidence that Canada trails some countries in per capita spending on information and communication technology.'
  The Bangemann Report (1994) demonstrates a similar ambience:
- Time of transition: 'Throughout the world, information and communications technologies are generating a new industrial revolution. It is a revolution based on information.'
- Winning mood: 'Europe can have a leadership position.'
- Time pressure: 'whether the opportunities will be realised depends upon how quickly we can enter the European information society. Quick action is needed.'
- Competitive climate: 'There is urgency since non-European competitors are increasingly active on the European markets.'

Such statements as can be found in important policy documents, represent an opinion climate in which it is unlikely that possible risks will be taken seriously. Policy-makers will rather tend to believe that the *Titanic* is unsinkable!

The Millennium Bug

The Millennium Bug problem provides a good illustration of the common approach to warning signals.[2] By now we know that no major social disruption occurred. This makes it easy to state that the whole Y2K story was a misguided and unfounded commotion. As a matter of fact immediately after 1 January 2000, many computer experts claimed they had all along known that nothing would happen and that all those who warned about possible failures were irresponsible troublemakers.

Several observations can be made in connection with the Millennium Bug. Although experts first wrote about the problem in the 1980s most computer users (including government institutions and commercial companies) chose the Titanic approach and refused to take lifeboats on board. In one way or another it was believed the problem was going to pass. In the early 1990s more and more publications appeared in which computer experts warned of the potential implications and very slowly a beginning was made in a relatively small number of countries to repair the problem. By 1997 in the USA only 35% of the commercial firms had given serious attention to the problem. Slowly people began to realize that problems could also occur with the embedded software in a large range of crucial applications, such as in transportation, health care, and social services. As at November 1999, there were however still numerous commercial companies and public institutions in many countries that neglected the issue. By late 1999 in the USA neither the Pentagon nor many smaller sized companies were prepared. In many countries around the world little had been done. In Russia the government hoped that it was all just a false alarm.

At the same time, important sectors in international business began to take the threat seriously and US companies alone spent over US$500 billion on solutions. In Singapore the government spent over US$40 million on the 'Operation Catch-the-Bug'.

We will probably never fully know what would have happened if nothing had been done. If all worked out well, this does not mean that the problem was handled with sufficient care, but could mean we escaped by sheer luck.

In an almost perverse way it seems a pity that – although more problems occurred than were reported in the mainstream media – no real accidents happened, which creates the impression that there is no need to consider human security in relation to cyberspace technology. The fact that so little happened seems to reinforce the Titanic feeling and will make it even more difficult in the future to anticipate seriously how societies can responsibly deal with the unpredictability of chain-effects in complex systems.

We might learn from the Y2K problem that it is important to design scenarios that are based on close cooperation since even if the Y2K problem was not a disaster there will be other critical technical failures.

We need to be better prepared for disaster. The importance of this was clearly demonstrated at the time of the Oklahoma City bombing in 1995. Although the bomb blast could obviously not have been foreseen, some weeks prior to it various organizations in the city had tested the community's capacity to deal with an emergency situation. The drill turned out to be an extremely important training in forms of civil cooperation: 'Many lives were saved and systems were restored at an unprecedented rate because people from all over the community worked together so well' (*The Futurist*, October 1998: 26).

One of the productive outcomes of the whole Y2K exercise has been that in several institutions (both industrial and public utilities) it was discovered that they were inadequately prepared for worst cases. And even if only on a modest scale in sensitive social institutions (such as energy provision) the need for back-up systems is now taken more seriously, it was worth all the commotion. It might serve our societies well if we had a Millennium Bug warning as a recurrent event!

An important aspect of the Millennium problem is the realization that we have become increasingly dependent upon digital electronics in our daily lives and that most of us seem to conveniently believe that technology will not fail us. In an ironic sense one should hope that the turn of the century has shown the world some problems with its digital dependency so we may begin to deal with this situation in a responsible manner. We would have to learn that in connection with this dependency we need to be prepared for 'worst case' scenarios. Not in any depressed or morbid state of mind, but realistically and responsibly as a sign of our awareness that digital technology has proliferated into almost all social realms in spite of its unreliability and fallibility. This observation constitutes no argument against the technology. It just tells us that the *Titanic* could sink. If we cannot be certain whether we may hit an iceberg, we may as well take enough lifeboats along. This means that we are ready to listen to experts such as Peter de Jager in his testimony on the Y2K issue:

> Computer Practitioners are the most optimistic people in the world. Despite all evidence to the contrary we believe the next application we write will be bug free. We believe the bug we just found is the last one. We believe the next release of a software product will solve all the errors in the prior release and introduce no new ones. Sadly, these beliefs are totally without foundation. (Testimony before the Commission of the US House of Representatives, May 1996)

If we are ready for 'worst case' scenarios we should also take the resource implications seriously. If we stock lifeboats, they need to be regularly tested otherwise the whole exercise is futile. Precautions demand permanent monitoring. As societies deploy more electronic systems, more people should be active in controlling, maintaining and servicing these systems. From the perspective of security, automation does not imply – as is often suggested – that we need less people. If a society wants technologies to perform tasks as desired, this implies that much time, attention, energy and money should be vested in their supervision. Socially responsible digitization requires the employment of large numbers of digitally trained people. The serious preparedness of a community to deal with high-tech risks demands considerable investments for protection against events that may never occur.

An extra complication that we should be aware of is that all the regular maintenance and repair includes the risk of new errors. Solving a problem may introduce new errors in software-run systems since new functions are added that may conflict with existing functions of the system at some point in the future.

Coping with uncertainty

One of the twentieth-century discoveries is that knowledge and certainty cannot be equated. More knowledge often implies more uncertainty. Much of today's knowledge may have to be revised tomorrow: 'In science, nothing is certain, and nothing can be proved, even if scientific endeavour provides us with the most dependable information about the world to which we can aspire' (Giddens, 1991a: 39). The knowledge we acquire in the process of reflection does not equate to certainty: 'We are abroad in a world which is thoroughly constituted through reflexively applied knowledge, but where at the same time we can never be sure that any given element of that knowledge will not be revised' (Giddens, 1991a: 39).

In the social sciences the insight that knowing is not the same as having certainty is even more valid than in the physical sciences. This is related to the observation that knowledge about social actions itself changes these actions. Moreover, however much knowledge we may collect, we will never know all the unintended consequences of social acts. It is possible that the number and scope of such consequences can be limited, but as Giddens suggests it is precisely the reflexivity of the modern world that destabilizes our knowledge of the social reality. Our reflection on social reality changes this reality in unpredictable ways. Moreover, the validity of our projections into the future is obviously dependent upon the robustness of the tools of inference. The social sciences have designed a range of such tools. Unfortunately, most of them are seriously flawed.

A very common type of prospective evaluation of technological impact is known as 'technology assessment'. The leading idea is that instead of finding harmful effects after the introduction of technology, such effects would be forecast in extensive studies and consequently avoided. Specific techniques employed in technology assessment are the Delphi technique, scenario writing, cross-impact analysis, or trend extrapolation. Prospective evaluation can be criticized from several angles. It tends to show a technological bias, in that it takes technology as a given and tends to focus on the control of its negative impact.

A further problem is that this kind of evaluation tends to rely on expert opinions. The trouble though is that predictions by experts have the peculiar tendency to be wrong. Practically all forecasts about technological developments over the past century have turned out to be wrong. In 1878 British mathematician Lord Kelvin, president of the British Royal Society, announced that radio had absolutely no future. In 1880 Thomas Edison thought that the phonograph had no commercial significance and in 1899 he predicted that it was even useless and dangerous. The *New York Times* wrote in January 1880 that we were not likely to hear again about the lamp of Edison. In 1932 Albert Einstein predicted that nuclear energy would be impossible. In 1977 Ken Olson, president of Digital Equipment Corporation thought there was no reason why people would want to have a computer in their homes. In the 1970s futurologists told us that by 2000 all food would be in powder form, there would no longer be any books and newspapers, and most of us would work on platforms in outer space.

A fundamental criticism of prospective evaluation addresses the assumptions that lie at the root of technology forecasting. Technology forecasting departs from an inductivist base. It is guided by the assumption that one can make statements about the future on the basis of a limited number of observations in the past. Against inductivism, David Hume proposed in the eighteenth century that there is no logical argument for reaching the conclusion that phenomena we have no knowledge about would resemble those we do know about. Inductivism has to assume an inherent continuity of the historical process. It needs to accept the existence of unalterable laws of historical destiny. Such laws may be formulated by the physical sciences for the regularities in the physical environment, but no empirical indication supports the belief that similar regularities are valid in the social environment. There are certainly trends to be observed in human social history, but these are distinct from natural laws that determine the movement of a society and thus provide a valid prediction about society's future.

Trends depend upon the specific configuration of historical conditions which themselves are not unequivocally determined. It is possible to establish correlations between trends and historical conditions, but these cannot in any way guarantee that a prediction based upon them is valid. This is caused by another flaw in technology forecasting: the poverty of social scientific theory. A characteristic of social scientific theories is that they are 'underdetermined', that is, there are always several theoretical perspectives that concur with the empirical observation of social reality. This implies that empirical observation does not provide an arbitration among divergent theories. The explanatory poverty of social scientific theory invalidates technology forecasting since this is based upon the assumption of the possibility of a valid explanation of the modes of interaction between technology and society. There is no theoretical perspective on technology and society available that could provide the basis for a solid prediction about their future interaction. Given the essential contestability of theory in the social sciences, there is no prospect of such a prediction emerging shortly either. This may be disguised by the sophisticated nature of some forecasting techniques, but this basic flaw makes them no better than ancient astrology.

It is so difficult to predict the future effects of technology since all the time new technologies are developed that influence the earlier technologies. It is easy to laugh at IBM's 'father' Thomas Watson senior, who said in 1953 that there would be no more than five or six computers needed in the world. He made his forecast on the basis of the technology available in his time and it might well have been that for the enormous, slow, expensive and unreliable computers of the 1950s there would not have been much interest. Computers began their success story only after the development of new generations of computers with integrated circuits and transistors. A technology sometimes becomes only really useful in connection with other technologies. A good illustration is laser technology. Lasers existed already for a long time but became really important only when optical fibre technology was available. The combination made new forms of telecommunications technology possible.

Moreover there are no simple cause–effect models for the interaction between society and technology. Technologies often create certain social effects when users handle them in specific ways. And the ways in which people use technologies is difficult if not impossible to predict. Uses may be very irrational and not based on regularities. Technical innovations may be used very differently from the intentions of their designers.

Since the available tools of inference show serious flaws in their capacity to predict the future outcomes and consequences of ICTs, there is always imperfect information. Actually the notion of imperfect information may even be too generous, and it seems more appropriate to accept that choices about these new technologies have to be taken in uncertainty. Dealing with future consequences of technological developments represents something of a classical Catch-22 situation. You only know it is wrong when it goes wrong and then it is too late. Early on in the development of technological innovations it is almost impossible to mobilize solid arguments for or against them. As the technology develops there emerges a network of relations and applications within which the technology entrenches itself so that halting or fundamentally changing course becomes practically impossible.

In conclusion, the extensive application of ICTs is not without serious social risks. It is, therefore, imperative to seriously consider these threats to human security and to stock enough lifeboats. Technology choice is often characterized by a lack of sensitivity for warning signals, lack of readiness to change course and an almost compulsive inclination towards flying blind. There are at present no adequate rules and institutions to address this concern. The current practices in governmental and commercial institutions are largely characterized by irrationality and irresponsibility. The Y2K problem has demonstrated that there is not even the beginning of a globally coordinated response to the possibility of digital disaster. Given the nature of digital technologies it is futile to expect that all risks can eventually be banned. Imperfect and fallible technologies require that societies take 'worst case' scenarios seriously, accept fundamental uncertainty regarding future developments and their impact and show the moral courage to change direction as serious alarm bells ring. The international community should at a minimum start with preparations for a global civil defence practice that takes the protection of human security seriously.

Risks to information security

> No one shall be subjected to arbitrary interference with his privacy, family, home or correspondence.
> Universal Declaration of Human Rights, Article 12

Surveillance in CyberSpace

In many countries electronic surveillance is mushrooming. As Gumperts and Drucker formulate, 'The sanctity of privacy has been eroded by the increasing intrusion of the technology of surveillance' (1998: 409). This has occurred through the use of video cameras in public spaces, the bugging of telephone calls, credit card firms, scanners in supermarkets, 'cookies' on the World Wide Web and international spy satellites. As the scope of 'surveillance' in a society grows the confidentiality of communications diminishes. Digitization renders surveillance easy and attractive. It facilitates what governments have always wanted to do: to collect as much information as possible about those they govern. Because of technological limitations this was always a difficult job. However, recent technological innovations have made grand-scale spying rather simple. One consequence is that the trading of surveillance technology from rich to poor countries has become an attractive sideline for the world's arms traders. Digitization facilitates the monitoring of all communications through fax machines, telephones (particularly mobile phones) and computers. It has become technically relatively easy to register all traffic that uses GSM cellular telephones. Swiss telecom operator Swisscom admitted at the end 1997 that it registered the communications traffic of more than one million users of cellular phones in the GSM (Global System for Mobile Communication) network. Also in other European countries police forces use the technical possibility to establish the presence of mobile telephones. The computer systems of telecom service providers can register where mobile phones are even when they are not used for calls but switched on to receive voice mail.

According to the report *An Appraisal of the Technologies of Political Control* (Omega Foundation, 1998) the US National Security Agency (NSA) uses intelligent search agents to monitor the communications traffic of European politicians and citizens. The British research bureau Omega Foundation prepared this report for the European Commission. The report found that the US espionage computer network 'ECHELON' detects keywords in military and political information as well as in economic information used by commercial firms and stores relevant data for later analysis. For a long time there had been indications of eavesdropping on world communication networks by the NSA and the Omega report now provided the evidence. The British-American surveillance programme targets all the Intelsat satellites that carry the major portion of worldwide telephone calls, fax communications and Internet traffic. The main justification is the struggle against terrorism and crime. There is, however, little hard evidence that there are indeed positive law-enforcement effects. In the meantime European Parliament members were informed that the NSA routinely intercepts valuable private commercial data about investments, tenders and mergers.

Besides ECHELON there is also an EU-FBI surveillance system (for police, security and immigration services) that facilitates interception of worldwide communications by the US National Security Agency.[4] In September 1998 the European Parliament discussed the NSA surveillance and adopted a consensus resolution asking for more openness and accountability for electronic spying activities.

Interestingly enough, in early 1999 a working group of the European Parliament proposed the establishment of an extensive tapping network for police and intelligence organizations to intercept all telecommunications traffic among citizens and companies. According to the working group, the permanent surveillance of all data traffic in real time is a 'must' for law-enforcement purposes. In May 1999 the European Parliament resolved to approve the establishment of a comprehensive surveillance system for all European telecommunications traffic on mobile phones, faxes, pagers, and the Internet. The electronic system that is being designed for this massive interception programme will track data on phone numbers, e-mail addresses, credit card details, PIN codes and passwords. Also in 1999 the European Parliament was informed (in the report *Interception Capabilities 2000*) about the planning by the NSA, the FBI and the European Union through the International Law Enforcement Telecommunication Seminar of a vast surveillance network that would combine national security and law enforcement activities.

As such plans are made the very technology of surveillance is making considerable progress. In 1999 for example a satellite was launched (by a commercial US company Space Imaging) that can detect from space very small objects and that can be used for commercial purposes. A growing number of commercial companies have now acquired licences to launch surveillance satellites. The US government uses (in late 1999) satellites with the capacity to see objects of 20 cm across. Work is also in progress to make the recognition of faces from space possible. Tests have already been done in big cities with the scanning of faces in large crowds and the analysis of the images by databases in remote computers.

Digital bugging devices have become so small that Japanese scientists claim they can build them into cockroaches. Digital miniature cameras and microphones can be incorporated into smoke detectors, alarm clocks, hearing aids, ballpoint pens and spectacles. Most important, however, is the development of increasingly intelligent software for the registering and filtering of information. Using so-called self-learning neural networks, intelligent agents search in vast databases for the specific information that creates complete commercial and political profiles of the objects of their search.

Equipment for surveillance and spying becomes cheaper all the time. Among the big buyers are employers who want to control their employees. In many countries the permanent electronic surveillance of the workforce has become standard practice. This ranges from bugging telephone and e-mail traffic to video cameras in toilets to check for the use of drugs, tracking employees' movements through smart badges, sensors to monitor whether workers wash their hands after visiting the toilet, and monitoring the use of inappropriate websites. By 1999, some companies had installed the 'Ascentor' software (designed by the British Business Systems group) that reads all the electronic mail traffic in a firm and checks it against certain keywords to assess whether the messages are legitimate company business.

Companies that have intensive telephone traffic with clients (such as travel agencies, airlines, phone companies, call centres for direct marketing) increasingly use 'Big Brother' systems to check the performance quality of their staff. With the help of a computer system management can register how many clients in a given timeframe can be approached, how many transactions are successful and what operators cost per transaction. Firms may ask their employees to accept forms of surveillance. However, even if staff consent to managerial bugging of their phone traffic, the client will often remain ignorant of the surveillance. Very few firms do indeed announce to their clients that they use surveillance methods. It is therefore advisable, particularly in communications with companies that use 'call centres', for clients to always enquire whether the conversation is recorded, if so why this is the case, for what purposes, how long the recording will be kept and whether he/she can get a copy.

In many of the digitally advanced countries the state has a strong desire to monitor civil electronic communications. The crucial argument is that although this violates people's privacy it is inevitable to guarantee security. As state institutions can compose rather precise profiles of the communications traffic of their citizens, the inequality in power relations between states and citizens increases. The civil claim to the confidentiality of personal communications is violated and the principle of information security is seriously eroded.

Encryption

The use of cryptography offers a measure of protection against surveillance. Communicating in secret codes is an age-old method to secure the confidentiality of communications. It is told that the Roman emperor Julius Caesar encrypted his correspondence by substituting each letter with another letter from the alphabet. At present the most popular methods for coding and decoding information are distinguished as symmetrical versus asymmetrical methods. The first method uses one key for the coding and decoding of messages. The system called Data Encryption Standard is based on this approach. Senders and receivers use a similar code. In the asymmetrical method different keys are used for coding and decoding.

Encryption technology is an important tool for the protection of the confidentiality of communications. This has obvious advantages for the users' privacy but also facilitates secret communication among members of criminal organizations. Most states claim the right to access information flows if they might endanger national security or in case the judicial process requires this. As a result they tend to hold ambivalent positions towards encryption. The dominant trend in the OECD (Organization for Economic Cooperation and Development) countries is towards the liberalization of encryption and the general acceptance of coding techniques. An issue still to be resolved is the matter of whether the codes used for encryption should be deposited with third parties so that governments could access them in case they were needed for security or law enforcement purposes. In March 1997 the OECD recommended regulations that demonstrated this ambiguity very clearly. The OECD *Guidelines for Cryptography Policy* form a set of non-binding principles on the use of cryptographic technologies (OECD, 1997d). The essential regulatory principles are the trust in cryptographic methods, the choice of cryptographic methods, the market-driven development of cryptographic methods, the need for standards in cryptographic methods, the protection of privacy and personal data, lawful access, liability and international cooperation. The rules emphasize that national policies on cryptography should respect the fundamental rights of individuals to privacy, the confidentiality of communication and the protection of personal data. However, the principle of lawful access remains very vague and can be interpreted in ways that do not provide a robust protection of privacy.

The OECD and other fora such as the Chambers of Commerce are inclined to adopt a system in which the encryption keys are deposited with trusted third parties. One question this raises is what this means in case law abiding citizens oblige but criminals design their own cryptographic systems.

In the European Union most governments tend to allow the users of electronic traffic to use forms of cryptography but at the same time they want to have access when they deem this necessary. A Council of Europe Recommendation stresses the need to minimize the negative effects of restriction on cryptography for criminal prosecution while allowing the legitimate use of the technologies (Council of Europe, 1995). In October 1997, the European Commission emphasized the significance of a robust protection of the confidentiality of electronic communications as it is concerned that the restriction of encryption technologies negatively affects the protection of privacy. As a matter of fact the Commission considers that restrictions could make ordinary citizens more vulnerable for the activities of criminals whereas criminals would probably not be hindered in using these technologies.

The US administration has suggested the use of the so-called Escrowed Encryption Standard (EES) (often named Clipper or Skipjack). As the details of the rules used in the coding system are secret, many Internet users are critical because the reliability and confidentiality of the coding key cannot be checked. The EES method implies that unique coding keys are deposited with trusted parties ('escrow' agents), such as the Treasury Department and the National Institute of Standards and Technology. One of the many problems with such proposals is that users would be expected to have complete trust that the software designers of the encryption keys did not leave software instructions that facilitate surveillance without the user noticing this. Users would also have to trust that the places where keys are deposited are completely safe from actions by criminals and terrorists. In its fear for encryption the US administration prohibited the export of software for cryptography. As American software firms saw this as a threat to their competitive position they persuaded the government to loosen its export restrictions (July 1998). Software firms managed to get permission to export encryption programs, but only to those 45 countries with adequate legislation to prosecute the laundering of criminal money. The initial condition that the key for encryption had to be given to the FBI was dropped. It remained prohibited to sell the software to private parties. More recently, in September 1999 the *International Herald Tribune* reported that the White House decided to relax rules on the export of computer encryption. Against the objections of law enforcement and national security institutions the US government allows US companies to sell powerful encryption techniques to overseas markets. The rule against exports was always somewhat ambiguous as US citizens were allowed any type of encryption technique. Bans on exports remain valid for Iran, Iraq, Libya, Syria, Sudan, North Korea and Cuba, and in any case, special permission is required for sales to foreign governments.

In other countries that initially supported restrictive policies, such as France, there has recently been a change in position. In Austria (law of 1998) the use of key escrow is prohibited. Belgium (law of 1997), Finland (law of 1999), Germany and Japan have no restrictions on cryptography.

In 1998 the so-called Agreement of Vienna, which revises and reinforces the Wassenaar Arrangement which was initiated in 1995 (and signed in 1996 by 31 countries), was approved by the USA, Canada, Japan and the EU member states. These treaties concern the export controls for conventional arms and dual-use goods and technologies. These instruments – largely promoted by the US government – restrict the export of arms technologies and of robust cryptography. Only cryptographic codes not exceeding 56 bits (meaning they can be fairly easily decoded) are permitted. The most important argument for this position is that in order to protect state security and for law enforcement governments should be able to decode all electronic traffic. Opponents of 'Wassenaar' argue that the restriction of cryptography and the protection of privacy are in conflict with each other. Without robust encryption, one cannot protect privacy. The Wassenaar Arrangement is the successor of the earlier Cold War arrangement called CoCom (Coordinating Committee for Multilateral Export Controls) which ended in 1994.

Cryptography techniques are considered dual-use technologies, that is, they can be used both for civil and military purposes. The member countries agreed in November 1998 (Vienna) to export controls on encryption software that uses lengths of 64 bits or longer.[5] The level of 64 bits is important since at this level it is possible with relatively little effort to break the encryption open.

Under the Wassenaar Arrangement companies would have to provide much commercially sensitive information (about clients, for example) and the basic codes of the encryption to governments in order to obtain export licences. This creates a large space for misuse by intent or default. Actually, as Gerald Wakefield warns, people using encryption codes longer than 64 bits on their laptop computers could have these confiscated by customs officers in the Wassenaar countries (in Goldman and Winsbury, 1998: 31).

It should be noted that the Wassenaar Arrangement and its Vienna revision are not binding treaties and they leave it up to the signatories to deal with export controls much as they prefer. Even so, the Wassenaar export controls and their restrictions on the length of encryption codes, could pose a serious obstacle to the freedom of encryption. They threaten information security since they tend to lower international standards for the protection of privacy.

The irony around cryptography is that governments in their pursuit of criminals propose measures that are likely to affect ordinary citizens more than criminals. It stands to reason that societies pay a price for an effective law enforcement, but it is dubious whether law enforcement institutions can ask citizens to give up their constitutional rights. The ordinary digital citizen is likely to benefit most from a robust system of encryption. If this system implies that keys are deposited with so-called trusted parties, the citizen is asked to trust parties that on several occasions have demonstrated their untrustworthiness.

In discussing the issue of surveillance it needs to be noted that this phenomenon is an integral and constituent component of modern societies. As societies achieve higher degrees of organization, mechanisms of social control will inevitably expand. The methodically organized society exacts social costs: to run efficient systems one needs a considerable amount of information about their participants. Effective taxation and insurance systems, for example, require a permanent supply of detailed data about persons. The surveillance this implies is not caused by the technology of CyberSpace. This mainly provides an excellent instrument that managers of bureaucratic organizations will gladly use. The dilemma is that if a society wants to offer public services (such as social security) that cater efficiently and equitably to individual circumstances, the individual client will have to provide much information about him/herself. The cost of such social service is the loss of privacy.

Privacy and information security

The permanent surveillance of people hampers their free participation in communication and information traffic. When personal data about individuals are collected, processed, stored and retrieved without their consent, their information security is under threat. Information security also means that people are free to determine what information about themselves they want to share with others. The standard implies that others cannot gather information about people without their consent. In a decent society citizens know who collects what information, where, how and to what purpose about them. In this context, the notion of privacy-protection refers to the space that societies accord to individual autonomy. Even though there are important cultural variations in the appreciation of privacy, we can observe that in almost all societies people show the desire to have a small space where they can withdraw from the gaze of others. Also, most people will keep at least some of their personal secrets to themselves. It is also a sensible strategy that we keep some thoughts about others to ourselves and do not share all our thinking with them. If we did not do this, there would be even more civil wars in the world. This protection of the intimate sphere of human life has to be balanced with the participation in social networks.

The individual preference to be left alone conflicts with the wish of societal institutions to gather information about the individual. The development of digital ICTs has increased the tension of this conflict and made it more urgent. The protection of personal data has always been a difficult challenge, but with recent developments such as the Internet the effort has become very discouraging. Information about how people use the Net is collected on a grand scale through a variety of means (such as the so-called 'cookies') and each act in CyberSpace contains the real danger of privacy intrusion. Using electronic mail for example inevitably implies a considerable loss of control over one's privacy unless users are trained in the use of encryption techniques and as long as these are not prohibited by law. Engaging in CyberSpace transactions implies we leave a digital trace through credit cards, bonus cards and client cards. And as online transactions grow, the collecting of person-related data will increase.

Not only is it attractive for entrepreneurs to know the preferences of their clients, it is also lucrative to sell such data to third parties. Acquiring data about people's biogenetical profiles as well as consumer data can be of great value to among others insurance companies. The combined information about high blood pressure and the purchase of alcoholic beverages helps the insurer to define the level of risks and therefore the costs the client will pay for the insurance policy.

Person-related data are stored in what are known as data warehouses. With the assistance of increasingly more intelligent information systems all these data can be analysed and in combination with data from various sources, detailed profiles of the data subjects can be composed. This permits in-depth enquiries into the behaviour of certain categories of clients. This implies on the one hand that they can be better served through the marketing of the goods and services they need. It also implies that their privacy is progressively undermined. Collecting, analysing and interpreting of personal data has become a 'data-mining' industry.

Whatever public or commercial interests may be served, in the end the development of the data-mining industry poses grave dangers to people's privacy and thus their information security. It is remarkable to note how often people themselves assist in this process. Even when people are relatively sensitive to the privacy issue, it is often fairly easy to get them to provide detailed personal information if they expect some gain out of the deal.

The village pharmacist

Those who are concerned about the loss of privacy are often told that we deal in fact with an old problem. In the good old days, the village pharmacist knew many secret details about his clients. This may be true, but then also many of the clients had information about the exploits of the pharmacist. There was to a certain degree some information symmetry. This is where the present problem lies. Extended data-mining creates a situation in which public and private institutions know far more about their citizens and clients than these know about them. This creates asymmetrical information relations. We do not know what others know about us, who these others are and what they do with the information about us. The core issue in relation to privacy protection is the question how we can repair the asymmetry. One way to do this is that as citizens and clients we set out to gather as much information as possible about the institutions that collect our data. It is odd that we would accept that banks and insurers want to know much about us whereas we know little about them, about their creditworthiness and reliability, for example. This does not solve the privacy problem but it relieves some of the feeling of disempowerment.[6]

Conclusion

With the globalization of electronic surveillance, the human rights claim to security in CyberSpace is under threat. The claim clashes with forceful public and private interests in the comprehensive surveillance of people's behaviour and opinions. Against the erosion of confidential communications, national governments and the international community are engaged in providing forms of legal protection for security in the private sphere.

A central concern in relation to the security of electronic commerce are the matters of the validity of digital signatures and the confidentiality of transactions. On the certification of digital signatures important work is done by the UNICTRAL (United Nations International Commission on Trade Law) through the proposal of a Model Law for electronic commerce which provides the basis for uniform rules on electronic signatures.

The European Commission sees electronic commerce as an issue that needs global regulation and wants particularly on the issue of digital signatures that national regulatory rules should be harmonized. The US government prefers a deregulatory approach and has no interest in an authority for the certification of digital signatures. In most European Union member states regulatory authorities recognize the importance of digital signatures but they follow different approaches. The European Commission (1998b) has therefore developed a proposal for a Directive on 'A Common Framework for Electronic Signature': 'The key aim of the proposed directive is to establish a harmonised Community-wide legal framework for electronic signatures and for electronic certification services' (Baresch and Schlechter, 1998: 8). The Directive provides that member states would ensure the legal validity of digital signatures and adopt the issue of a certificate to indicate the signature meets the legal requirements of a hand-written signature. The certification process by the certification body (CSP) proves to the recipients of electronic messages the authenticity of the sender. The Commission wants harmonization but at a minimal level and leaves technical details to the standardardization organizations and/or the market.

In the proposal for a European Parliament and Council Directive on certain legal aspects of electronic commerce in the internal market (European Commission, 1998a) it is suggested that firms are only bound by the legislation of the country of their residence when they perform trade transactions on the Internet. So far the rule was that traders also follow the laws of the countries where they sell their products or services. An implication could be that traders decide to set up residence in countries with the most relaxed privacy laws in fields such as pharmaceutical products.

On 1995 November 23 the European Parliament and the Council of the European Union issued the 'Directive on the Protection of Individuals with Regard to the Processing of Personal Data and on the Free Movement of Data'. Article 25 of this Directive, which came into effect in October 1998, has caused some controversy as it provides that the transmission of person-related data to countries without adequate data protection laws (such as the USA, Japan, Canada or Australia) should be limited. The export of person-related data to countries without a strict privacy policy is restricted. The implication for electronic trade is: when countries lack privacy protection laws, there can be no trading. The Directive intends to promote international trading but not at the expense of the privacy of European citizens. Connor sees five possible outcomes when the Directive will be enforced: it could isolate the European market; the rest of the world may adopt more strict privacy legislation; there could be unpleasant trade wars; Europe could back away from its commitment; or all parties could begin to negotiate a solution (Connor, 1998).

The EU privacy directive is seen by the US administration as a great obstacle to the growth of electronic commerce. By late 1999 the USA and the European Union had not yet reached a consensus on what constitutes an adequate protection of privacy. The US Department of Trade has repeatedly claimed that digital economies cannot develop without the unhindered flow of person-related data. Representatives of US companies have claimed that the EU Directive hinders legitimate business operations. A case that is often cited is the 1997 obligation to US airlines company American Airlines by a Swedish court order to delete all personal data about Swedish passengers from its US databank or to ask passengers for their consent in keeping the data.

In terms of global governance the following issues should be addressed.

We face a rapid proliferation and globalization of uncontrollable forms of electronic control by law enforcement agencies and commercial companies. The current practices of both governments (the increasing use of surveillance technologies for law enforcement and national security purposes) and commercial companies (the use of surveillance technologies for management purposes and the use of data-mining technologies for marketing purposes) erode the principle of information security. In connection with the protection of privacy there are only very general legal principles as codified in human rights instruments and regional agreements (under such institutions as the OECD or the Council of Europe). There are no effective global rules and institutions and no globally co-ordinated effort to protect information security.

It is often argued that the protection of privacy is best served through measures that guard against the abuse of person-related data. These measures are then of a technical or legal nature. This approach, however, bypasses the real issue. This is the question of how much personal data collection is socially acceptable. Without addressing this question, privacy protection remains futile. As long as considerable volumes of personal data are collected and stored, no amount of technological inventiveness or legal force can ultimately stop abuse. All such measures presume that governments are relatively benign. If one day a less benign government comes to power all that information in numerous databanks becomes extremely dangerous.

It is also illusory to expect that a capitalist market economy will provide robust privacy protection. In a market-dominated society it is logical that information and person-related information are tradable objects. An extensive trading of data from client databases, shopping cards, mail orders, telephone directories is integral to the capitalist marketplace. Free markets and privacy protection are on a collision course. This is demonstrated any time there are local or international efforts at more strict data regulation. Such attempts will almost inevitably be met with strong protest from the industry.

The real question therefore is not whether data collections can be adequately protected, but whether they should be there at all.

If the existence of large-scale data collections is the real issue, we are forced to deal with the social-ethical question of what kind of society we want. If we collectively want a highly organized, bureaucratic, market-driven, modern society we will have to accept digital surveillance, data-mining and the trading of personal information. Within this kind of society the interests of political and economic élites will collide with constitutional rights. In this confrontation legal and technical means provide some relief, but ultimately they are only measures of damage control.

Despite the fact that opinion surveys indicate worldwide an increasing concern about the violation of privacy, in many societies ordinary people themselves have begun to erode the sanctity of privacy. Not only by carelessly signing up for all kinds of client cards but even more by the use of cellular phones. As one can observe almost daily people use these phones in public places and share their private conversations without restraint with complete strangers. Intimate feelings are loudly broadcast in airport lounges, train compartments or restaurants. The compulsive communication neurosis of the mobile caller poses a fundamental threat to the protection of privacy: why protect a right that people give away in such a cavalier fashion?

Data collections are increasingly the property of private corporations. As these players do not operate with forms of public accountability it would constitute good governance if societies were to define the data they collect as a common resource. This implies measures that go beyond the demand that data subjects should know who collects data about them, what the collectors do with these data, and so on. This would mean the establishment of an information equilibrium between data holders and data subjects and provide the latter with access to information about the former. In exchange for collecting, holding and processing (possibly selling) data about an individual, this person gets access to details about the corporation. It constitutes gross indecency if companies are free to collect whatever data they deem necessary and individuals would have no rights of access to company files.

Good governance certainly implies that criminals are prosecuted and terrorists are arrested. But criminal pursuit cannot be the primary motive for good governors. They should primarily be driven by their mandate to offer citizens safe and secure spaces for communication and information. At stake is a fundamental moral choice between the protection of the public order and national security or the constitutional rights of citizens. There are both benefits and costs to the digital registration of person-related data. The ultimate judgement about the balance between costs and benefits can only come about in the public dialogue between those concerned. This would seem a logical proposition but in the daily practice it seldom happens. In fact, the citizen plays a marginal role only and mainly as victim. The citizen's voice is not at all decisive in current global governance practices.

Notes

1. The report of the official commission to investigate the causes of the Challenger accident, the Rogers Commission, states that already in October 1971 there were objections against the design of the rocket engine. See: *Report to the President by the Presidential Commission on the Space Shuttle Challenger Accident.* Washington DC, June 6, 1986.
2. In most computer programs years were indicated with the last two digits of

any given year. The year 1978 appeared as 78. This was expected to cause serious problems in the transition to the year 2000.

3. See *Wall Street Journal* of 4 May 1998. Edward Yardeni writes about 'Y2K – An Alarmist View' and David Wessel about 'Year 2000 Is Costly, But Not Catastrophic'.

4. See: www.optel.org.uk/statewatch/

5. EU states, USA, Canada and Japan.

6. Examples of possible questions are: Why do you want to know this? How and where will you store the data? Who has access to my data? What will you do with these data? Can I check the data? Can I correct the data? Can you guarantee that the data are used only for the purpose for which I agreed to provide them? What happens if I refuse to provide the requested data? Can you confirm this in writing? One could also probe with questions into the background of the data collecting institution: What is the creditworthiness of your institution? What do members of the board earn? In what operations does the institution invest its funds? How well did the institution do over the past ten years? Are management and members of the board ready to be publicly accountable for their decisions? Does the institution have a policy on privacy?

Free Speech and Knowledge in CyberSpace 6

> Everyone has the right to freedom of opinion and expression; this right includes the freedom to hold opinions without interference and to seek, receive and impart information and ideas through any media and regardless of frontiers.
>
> Universal Declaration of Human Rights, Article 19

Free speech

The human rights claim to the protection of free speech is always under threat by efforts to curb the flows of information among people, organizations and societies. George Orwell once wrote that freedom of expression means that everyone has the right to say things others do not want to hear. This nicely illustrates the complexity of the moral principle. It is undoubtedly very natural to silence those who say things one does not want to hear. Certainly in unequal power relations – as obtain in all societies – it demands a good deal of moral maturity to allow dissident voices to speak out.

All forms of communication are under threat of censorship. Each day people become victims of censorship measures. Journalists are killed, writers detained, radio stations blown up and films prohibited. Less dramatically, but even more frequently children are silenced by their parents and employees regularly find their right to free speech restricted. Censorship is common to all types of regimes – authoritarian, totalitarian or liberal-democratic – and to all kinds of human relationships. Not only the creative élites fall prey to censorship but in fact all those who want to be informed about what happens in the world.

Censorship in CyberSpace

Initially it looked as if with the development of the Internet a new and completely free, almost anarchistic space was created where state censors had no power. The first cybernauts certainly expected that virtual communication spaces would be exempt from state interference. To some extent this expectation has come true. There is already a series of illustrative moments where Internet communications have escaped state censorship. Dissident movements across the world (in Cambodia, Indonesia, Mexico, Sri Lanka and Tibet) have begun to use the Internet in their cause for political freedom. This is possible because it is indeed difficult to silence electronic communication through global networks. Materials can be distributed through many different channels and networks. As an Internet newsgroup gets closed down, the materials can move to other virtual spaces somewhere else in CyberSpace. Users can substitute one Internet provider for another with relative ease. Messages can be distributed through secret codes. For a really effective control one needs the assistance of the so-called Internet Service Providers (ISPs). But if they are willing to cooperate, they will have to violate the privacies of their clients in the process.

Although it may be complicated for national governments to establish national control over a global network, it is not fully impossible. The computers that provide access to the network are placed not in virtual but in concrete physical space and they belong to persons who fall under national jurisdictions. National lawmakers could in principle restrict the operations of both providers and users to a considerable extent. Such laws could be ignored, obviously, but that is not necessarily an attractive proposition in all countries, and least in authoritarian countries. Moreover, there is always the, albeit remote, possibility that national governments join forces and cooperate in efforts to curb network communications. Eventually, the censorship measures in one country can only be evaded through other countries with which no extradition agreements exist.

Around the world governments have undertaken efforts at forms of regulation of Internet traffic. Regulatory measures range from laws requiring self-censorship by ISPs (Australia, 1996), obligations for Internet subscribers to register with the authorities (China, 1996), control over individual access (Cuba, 1996), the application of laws on pornography and racism to CyberSpace (Germany, 1997), legislation against Internet offences (Japan, 1996), censorship measures (Philippines, 1996; Republic of Korea, 1996) or the monitoring of Internet contents (Malaysia, 1996).

In the Republic of Singapore the number of ISPs is limited and they have to use a type of software that hinders access to undesirable 'sites'. The Singapore government prohibits the use of certain websites and intimidates users by the announcement that it has detected a large number of illegal activities on the Web. According to an official measure of 15 July 1996 (the so-called Singapore Broadcasting Authority Class Licence Scheme) online services are considered broadcasting and thus require a licence.

Internet Service Providers need a permit and this forces them to apply the Internet Content Guidelines of the Singapore Broadcasting Authority. These Guidelines prohibit among others the distribution of materials that show contempt for the government or that insult the government. They also forbid the distribution of information about sexual perversities (among these are counted homosexuality and paedophilia). The licence holder is obliged to cooperate with law enforcement in investigations against users who are accused of violating the Guidelines. The ISP has to do all it can to prevent its services being used in ways that damage the public interest, public order, national unity, and the codes of good taste and decency. This kind of censorship can be avoided if users subscribe to foreign ISPs – but this implies more expense for them.

In China the number of Internet users has grown very rapidly in recent years. The China Internet Network Information Centre expects that in 2000 there may be 10 million Internet connected computers. This puts China on the list of top Internet user countries in the world. The Chinese authorities are not overly delighted with these developments. On 1 February 1996 they announced the Computer Network and Internet Management Regulations. These rules provide that all Internet connections must use state institutions and all efforts to distribute materials that threaten public security are punishable by law. In September 1996 the Chinese government closed down almost one hundred websites, among which were sites of the Tibetan Information Netwerk, Playboy and all US newspapers. At the end of 1997 the administration made it known that the usage of the Internet would be subject to important restrictions. The proposed measures addressed, in particular, the prosecution of CyberSpace crimes, such as divulging state secrets, spreading information that could be considered politically subversive (as in the case of insults to state institutions). Dissemination of pornographic materials, hacking and the distribution of viruses were also sanctioned with heavy penalties. Implementing censorship is made relatively easy since all Chinese ISPs have to register with the police. Also the Internet users have to register and must sign a declaration that they will not visit forbidden sites. Access is made additionally difficult because of the high costs of Internet usage.

But even when the authorities can block certain contents by direct and indirect measures, what escapes their censorship is the electronic mail that Chinese users receive. Even police authorities regularly receive through their e-mail services the contents of the pro-democratic electronic journal *VIP Reference*. In January 1999 a Chinese software engineer who gave 30,000 Chinese e-mail addresses to the journal was sentenced to a two-year term in prison. The basis for the sentence was the subversive use of the Internet that posed a threat to state security.

In Saudi Arabia there is only one state-controlled provider of access to the Internet. In Burma the authorities are very hostile towards the Internet and suspect that it is mainly used by the dissidents for political actions. In principle even owning a computer with a network connection constitutes a criminal act. In Vietnam all ISPs have to register. They must notify the government of all illegal activities on the Net. They must also allow the authorities to control all network traffic.

Such measures as are taken in Singapore, China, Vietnam and Burma imply that governments exercise enormous pressures against national network providers.

In 1996 the US Congress made an attempt to control indecent content though the Communications Decency Act which was struck down in June 1997 by the Supreme Court as unconstitutional. The Act imposed standards of decency to the provision of information and made distribution of offensive texts and images punishable. The Supreme Court judges ruled that the importance of the freedom of information exceeded the public interests of the censors. Against the censorship proposed by the Communications Decency Act the Electronic Frontier Foundation (EFF) organized a 'Blue ribbon campaign' on the Internet. All users who protested against the law put in their home page a small blue ribbon. The Supreme Court decision did not, however, mark an end to efforts to use censorship against digital materials. In different states of the USA proposals for legislation are debated that could restrict the freedom of information. Recently the EFF has reintroduced the blue ribbon to campaign against new efforts at censorship.[1]

In 1998 the Child Online Protection Act was proposed which was then blocked by a federal judge in Philadelphia as a violation of free speech rights. This decision by the judge is representative of the trend that US courts grant free speech protection to the Internet. This signals a development in which CyberSpace communications is treated in the same way as conventional media such as newspapers, magazines and books. In various judgments, courts have indicated that the Internet is understood as a new medium but they have preferred to focus on the message rather than on the medium. In this spirit Judge Leonie Brinkema ruled (November 1998) that a library could not install filtering software to block access on its web-connected computers to sites deemed harmful. The judge opined that when the library gave access to the World Wide Web, it could not restrict access to information without compelling governmental interest (*International Herald Tribune*, 16 September 1999: 8).

In April 1997 CompuServe manager Felix Somm was indicted on counts including the distribution of pornography involving children and animals. His lawyers argued unsuccessfully that a sentence against Somm would amount to punishing the telephone company for the contents of phone calls. On May 28 1998, a court of law in Munich found Somm guilty and sentenced him to a suspended prison sentence of two years on the basis of misuse of the Internet. Meanwhile the new German multimedia law had relieved the liability of ISPs somewhat but maintained the providers' complicity if they have not done all that is technically possible to stop distribution. The Somm judgment means that Internet providers in Germany are considered responsible if they could have suspected that illegal acts are conducted. This makes them in principle censors of the contents on their networks.

All these restrictive regulatory measures have been contested across the globe by ISPs, Internet users (such as the members of the Electronic Frontier Foundation), computer professionals (as in the French Association Française des Professionels d'Internet) and human rights organizations (like the American Civil Liberties Union). The protests usually focus on the danger that restricting Internet access for valid reasons eventually slips into forms of censorship that erode the constitutional principle of freedom of expression. Moreover, they point to the ineffectiveness of efforts at controlling the Internet technology. Even if national attempts were successful, this does not imply that control over the global decentralized infrastructure is feasible. A crucial issue that has not yet been resolved is the matter of liability. Does this rest with the users directly or indirectly with the ISPs? The problem is that the ISPs only facilitate the relay of messages without monitoring the contents which are provided by users, often under the guise of anonymity.

There is a trend to consider the ISPs solely as 'carriers' but still to make them accountable in cases where they could have intervened and could have deleted harmful materials. In response to the threat of forms of state regulation, several attempts at self-regulation (netiquette) have emerged. Also – as was discussed in Chapter 2 – various self-regulatory, voluntary codes of conduct have been designed, for example in the form of acceptable use policies and professional codes of conduct.

It should be realized that state censorship is – despite the decentralized nature of the networks – certainly possible. It is not so much the technical nature of the Net – as is often claimed – that hampers censorship, but rather the lack of international legal cooperation. A real concern is that the justified anxiety about child pornography could be used by states to introduce forms of censorship. The trouble is that however justified this censorship would be, it would easily and uncontrollably spill over in less legitimate, but politically convenient forms of silencing dissident voices.

It is ironic that exactly the technical infrastructure of CyberSpace communications causes a considerable vulnerability to censorship measures. As long as access to telephone lines and electricity is required, there is ample possibility for interference. This infrastructure also makes control by industrial interests a real possibility. To partake of CyberSpace traffic the Internet user must connect with a local ISP. This ISP must connect with the chief transporters of Internet communications. At present over three quarters of this global traffic is carried by one company: MCI/WorldCom/Sprint.

There is, moreover, the realistic possibility that in the near future the system of Internet domain name allocation will be used as a control system for electronic information provision. The allocation of domain names could be used to control entrance to CyberSpace upon certain conditions. The core of the Internet structure is the Domain Name System (DNS). This system transforms the common e-mail and website addresses into the numbers with which Internet computer communications operate. Users use top level domain names for countries (such as .be for Belgium) or for general categories (generic top level domain names, such as .com, or .edu). They also use second level names such as un.org or add a third level domain name. Users need to apply to a domain name registry with the authority to register such names. Until recently, the allocation of generic top level domain names was managed on the basis of a contract that was awarded in 1992 by the US Department of Commerce to the private company Network Solutions Inc. in the USA (Hendon, Virginia). Top level domain names for countries were assigned by public or private national information centres. The overall coordination of the Domain Name System was handled by the Internet Assigned Numbers Authority (IANA). In 1998 the Clinton administration decided that control over the allocation of domain names should no longer be a governmental responsibility, but should be managed by a self-regulatory mechanism.

Following the instruction of the US President to the Secretary of Commerce to privatize the management of the Domain Name System, the Internet Corporation for Assigned Names and Numbers (ICANN) was established. The mandate of ICANN covers such matters as DNS management and IP address space allocation. The articles of incorporation (21 November 1998) state that ICANN 'shall operate for the benefit of the Internet community as a whole'. With the formation of ICANN the dominant role of the US government in the management of Internet names and numbers was effectively transferred to a non-profit corporation. In 1999 the new organization faced serious financial shortages and needed the support of funding from corporations such as MCI WorldCom Inc. This sheds some doubt upon its claim to an independent status.

Moreover, ICANN ran into trouble with Network Solutions Inc. The contract that the company has concluded with the government expires in September 2000 and ICANN wants to break the monopoly positions

Network Solutions Inc. has on a thriving market. Since Network Solutions Inc. receives US$70 for a first registration and US$35 for the annual renewal, domain name registration is big business indeed, if one realizes that in the course of 1999 there may be some 20 million generic top level domain names in operation. It is unclear whether ICANN will manage to win its battle against Network Solutions Inc. All of this matters because the Domain Name System offers in principle a powerful tool of control. If the self-regulatory system of ICANN fails, government may step in again and determine the rules. It is conceivable that registration of domain names follows only upon an agreement to certain rules for CyberSpace conduct. Breach of the agreement could lead to loss of the domain name. It might well be that the system of domain name registration offers a unique chance for the enforcement of CyberSpace content regulation.

Censorship by the users

The information freedom for Internet traffic can also be threatened by the users themselves. Those who oppose state censorship will often argue that the users need to exercise self-censorship. They suggest that Internet users have to define and apply their own rules. They also must sanction violations of these rules, for example by refusing a user access to certain newsgroups. In spite of all good intentions this amounts to censorship and implies that the principle of 'silencing' undesirable voices is acceptable also for the Internet community itself. Expressions that are unwanted by a majority are expelled. With good arguments, of course. But then censors have always defended their interventions with reference to the good cause they served. The censorship that is applied in self-regulatory fashion by users themselves is not necessarily more benign than that imposed by governments. Moreover, often user groups offer even fewer possibilities for appeal and remedy than governments do. A much used argument in this context still needs to be mentioned. The Internet is seen as an enormous conference centre and should someone's expressions be unwanted in Room 1 he/she can speak in myriad other rooms. This, however, undermines the real significance of the right to free speech. This right implies the freedom to say things that others do not want to hear. This is not the same as speaking freely when no one is listening.

Who owns the Internet?

Internet enthusiasts are usually happy to explain that the Net belongs to all and nobody. This is only true insofar as the Internet is used as a metaphor, a manner of speaking about a global virtual network. This equates with the notion that Outer Space belongs to no one in particular and is common property. However, as soon as Outer Space could be militarily and economically exploited, the most powerful players in world politics became the de facto proprietors. Even if no one can own the Internet, it remains possible that some industrial players own all the technical means that are required to access and use the Net.

Initially the 'backbone' of the Internet consisted of the network of the American National Science Foundation (NSFNet) funded by the US administration. In 1995 NSFNet was privatized and commercial companies took responsibility for the running of the infrastructure. These were MCI, UUNET Technologies (now owned by WorldCom), BBN (now owned by GTE) and PSINet. The transfer looked like the change from a public monopoly to a commercial marketplace with competing companies. However, it soon became clear that the new state of affairs was in fact 'oligopolistic': a small number of providers who would prefer to cooperate rather than compete with each other; they dominate the market and control access to the Net.

The global online marketplace

> After all, with the exception of Bertelsmann, the world's third-largest media company, no European player has the resources, the experience, or (let's face it) the talent to match the Americans in the online business. (*Fortune*, 9 September 1999: 62)

Although the efforts of governments to control the new forms of digital information traffic should be taken seriously, it might well be that free speech is more fundamentally threatened by those social institutions that are responsible for the network infrastructures and for the production and distribution of network contents.

Free access to a diversity of information sources and creative products is under pressure as a result of the strong trend towards consolidation on the global online market. In all the essential domains of this market one finds a strong degree of concentration among the key players. These – predominantly American – commercial players are the manufacturers of ICT tools and appliances, and the providers of telecommunications services, of access to the Internet, and of audiovisual contents.

Several of the key players have in recent years consolidated their market position through the conclusion of merger deals. In 1998, for example, WorldCom Inc. merged with MCI. This created MCI WorldCom, the second largest telephone company after AT&T and the largest international provider of access to the Internet. MCI and WorldCom control some 25 per cent of the US market for long-range telephone connections. In October 1999 MCI/WorldCom paid US$115 billion for the acquisition of Sprint. Control over the US market long-range telephone has now risen to over 33 per cent.

On 24 June 1998 the US$48 billion merger between AT&T and cable giant Tele-Communications Inc. was announced. In July 1998 it was made public that AT&T plans to cooperate with British Telecom for the provision of global telecommunications networks to transnational firms. The expected joint revenues will exceed an annual US$10 billion.

The merger movements in the ICT-sector are largely the consequence of liberalization and privatization policies. These have caused pressures on the prices for telecommunications services and as a result have forced companies to develop adequate financial positions through merging with other companies. Mergers are part of an endless process since the economic benefits that accrue from mergers cause new competitive relations with other market parties who – in order to survive – are forced to seek new business partners.

In the struggle for dominance on the ICT market, an important part of all commercial activity is geared towards the control over access to CyberSpace. The gates that provide access to the World Wide Web – the so-called webportals – have become crucial targets. 'There's a big shakeout on the horizon', says Chris Carron, financial specialist of Forrester Research Inc. In his commentary to the *International Herald Tribune* (12 October 1998: 21) he added 'Everyone is getting in the starting blocks for a high-stakes fight'.

In 1998 a real 'portal-fever' emerged as more and more companies wanted to secure a piece of the expected profits. In June 1998 media giant Walt Disney announced it would spend US$70 million for the purchase of 43 per cent of the stock in search engine Infoseek. Again in 1998, the US broadcasting network NBC invested US$165 million for the purchase of online service Snap! from Cnet Inc. Time-Warner and News Corp. began the development of their own webportals. Among the leading contenders are:

- the manufacturers of personal computers (see Table 6.1);
- the vendors of operating systems (see Table 6.2);
- the producers of browsers (the software that is needed to search the World Wide Web) (see Table 6.3);
- the telecom operators which provide access to the telecommunications infrastructure (see Table 6.4);

- Internet Service Providers (see Table 6.5);
- the search engines that guide users to the sites they want to visit (see Table 6.6);
- the producers of information and entertainment (see Table 6.7).

The global market for PCs in 1998 is estimated at some $400 billion. In March 1999 IBM and Dell announced close cooperation: IBM will sell PC parts and technology to Dell for approximately US$16 billion.

TABLE 6.1   *The most important PC manufacturers (1998)*

Manufacturer	Sales ($m)
IBM (US)	81.667
Hewlett Packard (US)	47.061
Fujitsu (Japan)	41.018
Compaq (US)	31.169
Dell Computer (US)	12.327

TABLE 6.2   *The vendors of operating systems (1998)*

Vendor	Sales ($m)
Microsoft (US)	14.848
Sun Microsystems (US)	9.791
Apple Computer (US)	5.941

In 1997 Microsoft bought for $150 million a 5 per cent participation in Apple Computer. As part of the deal Microsoft insisted that Apple Mac-computers should be delivered with Microsoft 'browser' Explorer.

TABLE 6.3   *Browser makers (1998)*

Browser maker	Sales ($m)
Netscape (US)*	not available
Microsoft (US)	11.358
America Online (US)	3.052

In 1999 AOL acquired Netscape.

TABLE 6.4   *Telecommunications companies (1998)*

Telecommunications company	Sales ($m)	Telecommunications company	Sales ($m)
AT&T (US)	53.588	L.M. Ericsson (Sweden)	23.190
Deutsche Telekom (Germany)	39.710	BellSouth (US)	23.123
Bell Atlantic (US)	31.566	MCI Communications (US)	17.678
SBC Communications (US)	28.777	Ameritech (US)	17.154
British Telecom (Britain)	28.324	Sprint (US)	17.134
France Telecom (France)	27.409		

In 1999 Sprint was bought by MCI/WorldCom. The worldwide revenues in the telecommunications industry were in 1998 close to US$800 billion. Almost 75 per cent of these revenues came from sales of equipment and the rest from services. Various analysts expect this to grow to some US$1,400 billion by the year 2000.

TABLE 6.5 *Internet Service Providers (1998)*

ISP	Sales ($m)
WorldCom (US) (1997)	7.351
America Online (US)	3.052

WorldCom controls some 60 per cent of worldwide Internet traffic and can be seen as a major gatekeeper of access to lines and networks. In September 1997 America Online acquired CompuServe through a complicated construction that made WorldCom owner of CompuServe's infrastructure (the access to Internet). WorldCom paid $1.2 billion to H&R Block (Columbus, Ohio) for the purchase of CompuServe. The subscribers of CompuServe were sold to America Online. Through this deal AOL became the largest ISP on the European market with 1.5 million subscribers. On the world market AOL has some 12 million subscribers. In the period June 1998–June 1999 AOL received US$1 billion in advertising revenues against Yahoo!'s revenues of only US$240 million. For a newcomer this compares very well to the US$1.7 billion advertising revenues of Time Inc.

The ISPs provide access to the services on the Internet and exercise considerable control over access to CyberSpace. Some of them conclude agreements with the search engines. Provider MCI for example concluded a deal with Yahoo! in order to guide its clients to the Web page of this search engine. The world market of ISPs is concentrated. In case the interest for the Web continues to grow, ISPs are likely to grant certain websites – against payment – a right of 'priority'. This implies that if too many clients browse the Web, the customers of the privileged sites get priority and they will have to wait less time than other clients.

TABLE 6.6 *The search engines (1998)*

Search engine	Sales ($m)
Yahoo! (US)	203
Excite (US)(1997)	89
Infoseek (US)(1997)	52

Also in this domain there is a concentrated market and there are many linkages among the players.

TABLE 6.7 *Producers of information and entertainment (1998)*

Information/entertainment producers	Sales ($m)
Disney (US)	22.976
Sony Music Entertainment (Japan) (1997)	16.900
Time Warner (US)	14.582
News Corp. (Australia)	12.995
Bertelsmann (Germany)	12.803
Viacom (US)	12.096
Seagram (Canada)	10.743

Bertelsmann is very active on the Internet. Since 1997 it has a 50/50 partnership with America Online Inc. for Internet services in Europe and on 7 October 1998 it invested US$300 million in a 50/50 joint venture with Barnes & Nobles Inc. for online sales of books. As a result of energetic merger movements in the past ten years, there are at present less than 10 firms that control this segment of the global market.[2]

This measure of concentration is largely due to the fact that the development of digital technology facilitated the convergence of formerly separate sectors. Technical convergence has made it very attractive for companies to combine hardware and software activities. Illustrative for this development are the activities of Bill Gates' Microsoft. In April 1997 Gates bought (for US$425 million) WebTV Networks – a company that produces set-top boxes for World Wide Web surfing with the TV set. In June 1997 Microsoft invested $1 billion in cable company Comcast Corp. (the fourth largest cable system in the US). In June 1998 Microsoft acquired together with Compaq Computer Corp. 20 per cent of the stock of cable company Road Runner. Meanwhile Microsoft had already begun to cooperate with TV network NBC in a new cable TV channel: MSNBC. The purpose of all these acquisitions is to find a bigger market for Microsoft software and for a range of online services such as sales of cars and travel. Even media mogul Rupert Murdoch has become worried and stated in the *Guardian* of 8 December 1997 (Media: 10): 'We have to stay on our toes to make sure Bill Gates doesn't erect a tollgate in every house'.

Competition, concentration and consumers

In defence of the market often its competitive effects are mentioned. However, in this argument there is – by design or default – a misleading confusion between the notions of 'free market' and 'open competition'. On the global market these notions are mutually exclusive. The freer the market is, the more concentration will develop and as a result less competition prevails. The idea of a non-regulated market proposes that there is competition among equal parties. However, in reality there are more and less powerful parties and their competition produces winners versus losers. Competition on the global market is 'cutthroat competition': a military, aggressive variant of competition in which the opponent is shaken out of the market. This type of competition leads to increasing concentration. Only powerful public intervention can guarantee free and fair competitive relations. However, this intervention restricts the freedom of the market. It is a classical Catch-22 situation. Even Adam Smith who saw self-interest as the prime motive of economic growth and believed that this would ultimately be in the collective interest, saw that totally uncontrolled self-interest would harm competition and lead to monopolies. Smith was, with regard to public intervention, certainly less dogmatic than many of his late-twentieth-century disciples.

Market concentration implies that companies buy their competitors or merge with them or that the control over the market is controlled by ever fewer parties. Ironically, it is exactly the need to develop a strong competitive position that forces companies to collaborate with others. To play on the global market, it is essential to control a sufficiently large share of that market. Only in this way will revenues exceed investments. An important issue here is obviously whether consolidation is to the benefit of the consumer. Will prices and tariffs go down? In the initial process this may indeed be the case, but once the market is controlled by one leading monopolist, this company will be able to determine price levels, for example for Internet access.

All the mega deals of recent years have been praised for their competitive effects and thus benefits to consumers. So far these suggested benefits are far from clear. For most consumers (in the USA) tariffs have gone up and services have deteriorated. Magazine *Business Week* has baptized the 1990s as the Age of Consolidation. Mergers, acquisitions and joint ventures are the essential facets in all sectors of the global market economy.

Conclusion

There is today no globally coordinated response to the threats posed by various forms of censorship. As a matter of fact, the commercial variant of censorship is even generally supported through the widespread belief in the blessings of the free marketplace. The common argument in favour of an unregulated marketplace in the provision of information is that it guarantees a creative and competitive marketplace with a diversity of contents. There is, however, abundant empirical evidence to suggest this did not happen in the mass media sector where increasingly markets – through concentration and consolidation – are oligopolized and tend to produce a limited package of commercially viable contents only. It is unclear why virtual marketplaces would behave in a different manner.

Against the reality of private censorship through the consolidation of the marketplace, current governance practices offer little remedy. The World Trade Organization's rules, for example, stress the need for competition. However, the major concern is that public policies should not be anti-competitive in the sense of hampering free access to domestic markets. Current competition rules mainly address the dismantling of public services and the liberalization of markets, not the oligopolization of markets or the conduct of the dominant market parties.

The WTO Basic Telecommunications Agreement of 15 February 1997 governs market access but has little to say about the conduct of parties on the market. It does not guarantee that there will be an effective, open competition between commercial actors. The non-discrimination principle that provides for most favoured nation treatment of foreign competitors is inadequate to secure competition on domestic markets.

The WTO provisions on anti-competitive practices do not exclude the possibility that local telecommunications markets would be controlled by only three or four foreign suppliers. The WTO reference paper on basic telecommunications (in paragraph 1 on Competitive safeguards) does provide that anti-competitive practices may include cross-subsidization policies. Such policies could, however, imply considerable benefits to local users. The lack of a serious competition policy supports unhindered market concentration and reinforces foreign ownership of essential market domains, particularly in developing countries.

One of the main policy issues is the question whether the infocom market is so substantially different from markets for other commodities (such as automobiles or detergents) that it should be treated in a different way. Is the question whether there should be public intervention different in the case of cultural products from the case of food products? Could it be that if the shopping mall functions best if the state does not intervene, this does not necessarily apply if the mall is the main provider of information and culture?

Moreover, there is the question whether a genuine international competition policy (Holmes et al., 1996: 755) that governs anti-competitive conduct of market parties is a realistic option. Such a policy would imply more regulation and would thus clash with the predominant concern of the major market players to reduce regulation. Serious global governance to curb the formation of cartels will in any case be very difficult. The approaches to cartels differ widely across national legal systems and traditions and most free trade supporters believe that free markets will eventually create open competition and that anti-cartel rules create trade barriers.

In an economic environment where mega mergers are almost natural and are loudly acclaimed by financiers and industrialists, the tendency towards public control is likely to be minimal. The European Commission does indeed stop and prohibit industrial mergers but in a limited and modest way. The Commission may propose demands that make companies decide not to merge. According to merger legal expert Jean Paul Marissing (law office of Caron and Stevens/Baker and McKenzie) out of several thousands of mergers that have been registered with the Commission only ten were really prohibited (*NRC Handelsblad*, 22 July 1998).

Among other factors this is caused by the fact that mergers are considered serious problems only when consolidated companies may control over 40 per cent of a market. European regulation can prohibit abuse of monopoly positions, but not the development of market monopolies. Equally, in US regulation there is only a threat to competition once two companies following their merger control more than 60 per cent of a market.

If the current trend continues, governance of and access to CyberSpace will be in the hands of a few gatekeepers and a global system of digital toll-roads emerges that is controlled by a small group of mega market leaders. At present, most public authorities (Clinton-Gore administration, European Commission, the G-7 countries) want the construction of the digital superhighways to be a private investment business. If, however, information freedom is indeed an essential public good, then 'good governance' would require more public control (nationally and globally) over the conclusion of corporate 'mega-deals'.

The right to knowledge

Ignorance is the curse of God. Knowledge
the wing wherewith we fly to heaven.
William Shakespeare

Knowledge is an essential human resource. For its development and application a proper balance should be established between the ownership interests of knowledge-producers and the public good interests of knowledge-users. It is very doubtful whether the emerging global governance of intellectual property rights could provide such a balanced approach.

There is a widely held belief that we should not be ignorant. Ignorance is perceived as something negative. It is a privation, an absence of knowledge. The dissemination of knowledge 'is essential to creative activity, the pursuit of truth and the development of the personality' (Art. VII, Declaration of the Principles of International Cultural Co-operation, UNESCO, 1966). When UNESCO was established in 1945, its Constitution stated as a fundamental norm the free exchange of ideas and knowledge. In order to realize the organization's purposes, the States Parties to the Constitution pledged, to 'maintain, increase and diffuse knowledge'. In 1966, the UNESCO Declaration of the Principles of International Cultural Co-operation defined as aims of cultural cooperation, 'To spread knowledge, to stimulate talent and to enrich cultures, . . . and to enable everyone to have access to knowledge, to enjoy the arts and literature of all peoples, to share in advances made in science in all parts of the world and in the resulting benefits, and to contribute to the enrichment of cultural life'.

These aspirations find a solid basis in the various freedoms that are articulated in the Universal Declaration of Human Rights. Such as the right to freely participate in the cultural life of the community, to enjoy the arts and to share in the scientific advancement and its benefits (Article 27). Or the right to education: education shall be free, at least in the elementary and fundamental stages, says Article 26. And, in particular, Article 19 that provides the right to the freedom to seek and receive information and ideas through any media and regardless of frontiers. Herewith an international human right to knowledge is constituted, the actual articulation of which could read as follows.

1. Everyone has the right to knowledge. This right includes that everyone is entitled to have access to knowledge.
2. No one shall be arbitrarily deprived of sources of knowledge.
3. The right to knowledge shall imply due recognition and respect for the rights and freedoms of others.
4. All peoples and all nations have the duty to share with one another their knowledge.

Measured against this normative standard, the real world proposes a rather different standard of achievement. Knowledge is not freely and equally available to everyone. Much of the world's knowledge is not shared. The production of knowledge is increasingly privatized and commercialized. The marketplace has become the leading actor in determining the direction and scope of knowledge production. When knowledge is created and controlled as private property, knowledge as common good is destroyed. The privatization of knowledge deprives communities of their common heritage and renders this the entitlement of individual owners.

The emerging global rules on intellectual property rights (IPRs) transform common heritage into exclusive, private (corporate) property. A case in point is the world's biological systems which are common heritage, but which through technological innovations (for example in biotechnology) are now becoming private property. In today's global rules on intellectual property rights, the biotechnology industry is allowed to commercialize and privatize the biodiversity of the Third World countries. This industry uses the genetic resources of the Third World as a free common resource and then transforms them in laboratories in patentable genetically engineered products. In the process the industry manipulates life-forms that are common heritage. This means that whereas formerly plants and animals were excluded from the domain of intellectual property rights, biotechnology has changed this. Life can now be the object of ownership. This has many perplexing implications, one of which is that thousands of years of local knowledge (about life organisms) are devalued and replaced by the alleged superior knowledge of Western scientists and engineers. This development upsets the delicate balance between private ownership and common heritage.

Global governance

Global governance in the field of intellectual property protection finds its origin in the nineteenth century. It emerges as an effort to create and maintain a balance between a set of rival claims to control of knowledge and dissemination of knowledge. From its inception, the protection of intellectual property rights has been inspired by three motives. The first motive was the notion that those who invested in the production of intellectual property should be guaranteed a financial remuneration. With the establishment of the first international treaties on intellectual property protection (the Paris Convention for the Protection of Industrial Property of 1883 and the Berne Convention for the Protection of Literary and Artistic Works, 1886) a monetary benefit for the creator was perceived as a necessary incentive to invest in innovation and creativity. During the 1928 revision of the Berne Convention the notion of moral rights was added to the entitlement to economic benefits. The introduction of the moral value of works recognized that they represent the intellectual personality of the author. Moral rights protect the creative work against modification without the creator's consent, protect the claim to authorship and the right of the author to decide whether a work will be published.

Early on in the development of intellectual property rights (IPR) law it was also recognized that there is a public interest in the protection of intellectual property. As a common principle it was acknowledged that IPRs promote the innovation and progress in artistic, technological and scientific domains, and therefore benefit public welfare. The US Constitution, for example, articulates this as follows: 'to promote the Progress of Science and the useful Arts, by securing for Limited Time to Authors and Inventors the exclusive Rights to their respective Writings and Discoveries'. The protection of intellectual property is thus in fact a delicate balancing act between private economic interests, individual ownership, moral values, and public interests.

With the increasing economic significance of intellectual property, this system of governance has moved away from the moral and the public interest dimensions and has emphasized in its actual practice mainly the economic interests of the owners of intellectual property. Today, such owners are by and large no longer individual authors and composers who create cultural products, but transnational corporate cultural producers. The individual authors, composers and performers are low on the list of trade figures and as a result there is a trend towards IPR arrangements that favour institutional investment interests over individual producers. The recent tendency to include intellectual property rights in global trade negotiations demonstrates the commercial thrust of the major actors. Copyright problems have become trade issues and the protection of the author has conceded place to the interests of traders and investors. This emphasis on corporate ownership interests implies a threat to the common good utilization of intellectual property and seriously upsets the balance between the private ownership claims of the producer and the claims to public benefits of the users. The balance between the interests of producers and users has always been under threat in the development of the IPR governance system, but it would seem that the currently emerging arrangements provide benefits neither to the individual creators, nor to the public at large.

The commercial tendency to focus resources on the generation of patentable knowledge also leads to a reduction of available variety for consumers. This development disturbs the balance between the claims of knowledge-producers and the claims of knowledge-consumers even further.

It would seem sensible that holders of copyrights would want to protect their interests against theft. Even the most active defenders of neo-liberalism (the protagonists for withdrawal of the state) will encourage states to act decisively against the piracy of their properties. Protecting intellectual property is however not without risks. The protection of intellectual property also restricts the access to knowledge since it defines knowledge as private property and tends to facilitate monopolistic practices. The granting of monopoly control over inventions may restrict their social utilization and reduce the potential public benefits. The principle of exclusive control over the exploitation of works someone has created can constitute an effective right to monopoly which restricts the free flow of ideas and knowledge.

The development of fair intellectual property rights requires delicate balancing of different interests. In recent developments this balance is seriously threatened and distorted to benefit primarily the commercial interests of large transnational cultural producers. These are in general more concerned about their battle against 'piracy' and the implied losses thereof than in the protection of the moral integrity of creative works or the quality of cultural life in the world.

Piracy

CyberSpace is one enormous photocopying machine.[3] The ease, speed and perfection of the digital copying of sound, text and image has contributed to the vast international growth of piracy. Particularly music is illegally copied in great quantities. In Russia, for example, in 1995 73 per cent of total sales of musical recordings was illegal (representing a value of US$222 million); in Romania it was 85 per cent (US$22 million); and in Italy the illegal trade reached 33 per cent (almost US$22 million).[4] Piracy caused USA-based software firms, entertainment companies and publishers in 1995 to lose a combined revenue of over US$14 billion.

The International Federation of Phonogram and Videogram Producers estimates that some 25 per cent of all musical recordings is pirated. The biggest pirates are in Asia (US$6 billion), in Western Europe (US$3.6 billion), in Latin America (US$1.8 billion), and in Eastern Europe (some US$1.8 billion).[5] The Business Software Alliance has discovered that in Indonesia and Russia over 90 per cent of all computer programs are illegal copies; in Japan this is 67 per cent and in the Netherlands 58 per cent.

Controversy

In 1994 US Vice President Al Gore launched the initiative for a National Information Infrastructure (NII). The NII project promised enormous opportunities for the entertainment industry – provided action could be taken against digital piracy. A powerful lobby of Hollywood producers pushed hard for effective measures. In 1995 the Clinton administration presented a White Paper that contained a strong plea for forceful protection of copyright on the digital highways. The argument was that if Internet surfers can read books, listen to music and watch films in CyberSpace, these acts constitute forms of illegal copying and are thus violations of copyright laws. The White Paper defined the temporary storage of a computer file in a computer memory (and thus browsing, downloading and scanning) as copying in the sense of copyright law.

Several interest groups began to resist this position. They formed a coalition (called the 'digital future coalition') to oppose Clinton's White Paper. The coalition consisted of libraries, educational institutions, consumer organizations, telecommunications firms and ISPs. In early 1996 the US Congress rejected the White Paper.

Next the Clinton administration tried to get support for its position internationally at the 1996 WIPO (World Intellectual Property Organization) conference.[6] This conference was convened to debate the adequacy of existing copyright regulation for the digital age. At the conference the US government was supported by the European Commission that also held the opinion that making temporary digital copies (like one does all the time when surfing on the Internet) was a violation of copyright. This position was backed up by a lobby from the music and entertainment industries in which the Motion Pictures Association, the International Federation of Phonographic Industries, the Federation of European Publishers, and the Business Software Alliance (with among others Microsoft, Apple, and IBM) joined forces.

Against this lobby stood a coalition of telecommunications firms including AT&T, Philips, British Telecom and France Telecom, browser company Netscape, libraries and private users of the Internet. The controversy focused on a draft Article 7 in the proposed new WIPO treaty which was to considerably expand the protection of reproduction rights. Under copyright protection would be 'direct and indirect reproduction . . . whether permanent or temporarily, in any manner or form'. The defenders of Article 7 saw this as the much-needed protection of a billion dollar market that would be lost if consumers could make perfect digital copies and distribute them through the Net without paying for this. Those opposing Article 7 argued that it would seriously limit the interest in the Net and would hamper the free flow of information. Network providers were afraid that they might be held liable for infringements of copyright. The implication would be that they would have to monitor the traffic of their clients to check whether copyrights were respected or not. In fact this would amount to the exercise of censorship!

On 20 December 1997 it was decided to delete the contested Article 7 from the new treaty. This is, however, not necessarily the end to the efforts to expand the current scope of copyright protection. The European Union Directive (11 March 1996) on the legal protection of databanks provides that electronic and written collections of data fall under the protection of copyright. The Directive subjects the free access to databanks to the provisions of copyright protection and moves towards a situation in which all digital formats of music, text and images will be protected so that consulting and copying them would yield more revenues.[7] If this were implemented it would add considerably to the control tasks of ISPs. The measures could lead to more technical provisions to be installed by providers and more costs for libraries and educational institutions.

The question about the proliferation of copyright claims and the implications for the right to knowledge is an urgent topic. If for example freely accessible information (which is in the so-called public domain, meaning there are no longer copyright claims against users, as in the case of the works by Shakespeare or Bach) is stored in digital format in electronic databanks that are entitled to copyright claims, public access to this kind of information may be seriously restricted. Current European regulation on intellectual property tends towards less rather than more access to information for the general public. A disturbing trend is also that the audiovisual industry tries to restrict the so-called 'fair use' of copied works. Copyright legislation has always made exceptions for forms of 'fair use' of images and sounds produced by others. The 'fair use' doctrine (as enacted in different countries) by and large excludes the use of materials in the home and for non-commercial purposes from copyright obligations. The classic case on this has been the *Sony Corporation of America* v. *Universal City Studios* 1984 where the US Supreme Court supported the legality of home videotaping. The Court found the copying in people's homes was an act that did not infringe copyright law. The freedom to copy at home has, however, since 1984 become more complicated, for example because more and more people work from home offices.

A further problem is also that courts of law have tended to accept 'fair use' on the basis that the control of individual usage would constitute a breach of privacy rights. This control would amount to issuing special licences to large numbers of individual users. Apart from the privacy implications, courts have also generally seen this procedure as technically too complicated. However, the technological obstacle is no longer a real problem. There are at present technologies available that make it perfectly possible to check on individual usage of copyrighted materials and automatically charge users.

Conclusion

At present the essential governance institutions in the field of intellectual property rights are the World Intellectual Property Organization and the World Trade Organization. The WTO plays an increasingly important role since it oversees the execution of the legal provisions of the agreement on Trade-Related Intellectual Property Rights (TRIPS). This global agreement emerged under the GATT negotiations (as Annex 1C to the General Agreement on Tariffs and Trade in the Uruguay Round of Multi-lateral Trade Negotiations, 1993). TRIPS contains the most important current rules on the protection of intellectual property rights. It is implemented within the WTO regulatory framework. In this agreement the economic dimension of IPR protection is reinforced. As Venturelli correctly summarizes, 'The balance has tipped entirely toward favouring the economic incentive interests of third-party exploiters and away from both the public access interests of citizens and the constitutional and human rights of creative labor' (1998a: 63). As IPRs have achieved a prominent place among the world's most important tradable commodities, the current trade-oriented IPR regime favours the corporate producers (publishers, broadcast companies, music recording companies, advertising firms) against individual creators. The provisions of the TRIPS agreement protect the economic rights of investors better than the moral rights of creative individuals or the cultural interests of the public at large.

The type of global governance that currently emerges is neither in the interest of the consumer, nor to the benefit of producers of artistic and literary works. For the dissemination of their products the performing artists, writers and composers transfer increasingly their rights to big conglomerates with which they sign contracts. Ultimately, these companies will determine how creative products will be processed, packaged and sold.

One of the serious problems with the current trend in IPR protection is that the emerging regulatory framework stifles the independence and diversity of creative production around the world. The regime is particu-larly unhelpful to the protection of the 'small' independent originators of creative products. It establishes formidable obstacles to the use of creative products since it restricts the notion of 'fair use' under which – traditionally – these products could be freely used for a variety of, among others, educational purposes. Its narrow economic angle focuses more on the misappropriation of corporate property than on the innovation of artistic and literary creativity.

A particularly worrying phenomenon is that the current rules provide that once knowledge in the 'public domain' is put into electronic databases it will come under IPR protection. This will imply a considerable limit to freely accessible sources. Moreover, the present system of governance threatens to render the new global forum that CyberSpace potentially offers (through the new ICTs) a marketplace where a controlled volume of ideas will be traded.

The one-dimensional emphasis upon the commercial facets of copyright protection is reinforced by the progressive shifting of negotiating fora from the WIPO to the WTO. In this process the protection of intellectual property becomes part of the global free trade agenda. This implies that the public interest is secondary to the economic interest of the largest producers of intellectual property. The social value and common benefit of cultural products is not on the transnational corporate agenda. Good governance would imply that societies respect the non-commercial dimensions of copyright. Particularly those societies that aspire to develop into 'knowledge societies' should be expected to give priority to the acquisition of knowledge over the accumulation of money. Knowledge is part of the common heritage of humankind and cannot be the exclusive property of a few members of the community. This, however, is precisely what is happening: the kind of knowledge to produce and disseminate and be made accessible follows the choices which the leading commercial producers make.

It is often argued that creative production and artistic expression would stop if there were no adequate protection of economic interests. This presupposes that technicians, artists and scientists would not create without the guarantee of monetary remuneration. There is no real substantiation for this argument and it would seem to be inspired more by people who know about money than by those who know about science and arts.

What today is called a violation of copyright has been in most of the world's cultural history merely the use of the common heritage of humankind. Bach copied and reworked music made by others and did this with great respect, creativity and innovation. Many of his choral melodies were taken from other composers. If copyrights were indeed very strictly enforced, jazz musicians would be in deep trouble. Any time a pianist used someone else's left hand 'voicings' copyright would have to be paid. In line with the current regime jazz legend Bill Evans should have copyrighted his brilliant harmonic discoveries and any time somewhere in the world a pianist used his way of playing a B flat chord, money would have to be paid to Evans' publisher or record company.

The realization of an international human right to knowledge would need a balance between a set of rival claims:

The claim to the rightful protection of intellectual property rights should be balanced against the claims to global welfare. Intellectual property rights should not only benefit the industrial nations, but should also stimulate free innovation in poorer nations. Rather than strengthening the control of TNCs over technology and reinforcing the monopolistic rights of technology providers, the technological capabilities in the developing countries should be strengthened. The pressure to create a uniform global system of IPR protection constrains the flexibility that developing countries need in order to adapt the IPR system to their specific needs and interests.

The claims to property rights should be balanced against the obligations of rights holders. The emphasis in the emerging system would seem to be rather exclusively on the rights of knowledge producers, and would almost completely bypass the duties of rights holders. Such obligations could include the duty of disclosure, the obligation to provide information and supporting documents concerning corresponding foreign applications and grants. The rights holder could be obliged to work a patent in the country where the patent was granted and could be required to refrain from engaging in abusive, restrictive or anti-competitive practices.

The claims to property rights should be balanced against rules on liability. A right to knowledge implies that claims to ownership of immaterial products should be acknowledged and respected. These claims provide a right to control and exploit knowledge as property. The law of property commonly recognizes these claims as absolute; they are valid vis-à-vis all other legal subjects. A proper balance recognizes the claim to protection of products of the mind and as such provides incentives, rewards and recognition for individual producers of knowledge. However, it also demands that the control of knowledge is restricted by rules and norms adopted by the community in which ownership is practised. The liberty of ownership does not imply the right to damage others. Owners abuse their rights in case the disadvantage they cause to others (by withholding knowledge) is greater than the benefits that may accrue to them (by not working a patent, for example). Property rights should be restricted in the sense that their use may not damage someone else's property rights. This happens whenever intellectual property protection has monopolistic effects. Property implies liability for its use and a proper balance implies that the governance of intellectual property rights includes both property rules and liability rules.

The claims to the protection of private property should be balanced against the claims to the protection of community interests. This would imply among others the following policy decisions:

- The notion of 'fair use' should be maintained and a global consensus should be achieved on a liberal interpretation. Meaning that non-commercial use by non-profit users should be exempt from copyright protection.

- The scope of 'works in the public domain' should be extended and efforts to bring such works under copyright protection should be discouraged.
- The legal rules on intellectual property protection should not exclusively focus on the individual inventor but should also recognize the communal production of knowledge and protect this accordingly.
- Movements towards alternative practices in the innovation of knowledge should be encouraged. 'Copyleft' is an example of a global movement in which developers of software freely share ideas and experiences, reject tight control of copyright laws over computer programs and accept no secret source codes.
- As the corporate copyright holders extensively profit from the use of materials from the public domain, they should be taxed for this. Tax revenues could be used to promote the creation of artistic expression and scientific knowledge.

Basic to all these considerations is obviously the realization that the right to knowledge is too important to be left to commercial forces only. The much heralded 'knowledge societies' are not likely to be more than paper tigers if their governance is delegated to the marketplace. The market will produce and distribute knowledge according to people's purchasing capacities. A human rights-inspired system of governance will favour the availability of knowledge according to people's needs and aspirations.

Notes

1. The website for the campaign is at http:// www.eff.org/blueribbon.html.
2. The leading companies are all involved in various joint ventures. Disney produces TV programmes that Time-Warner (Warner Brothers) broadcasts. Sony produces TV programmes that News Corp. (Fox Broadcasting) broadcasts. Viacom (Paramount) makes a film (*Face/Off*) for which Disney produces the music (Hollywood Records) and News Corp. (HarperCollins) publishes the book on which the film is based. News Corp. (Twentieth Century Fox) and Viacom (Paramount) jointly produce the *Titanic* film for which Sony (Sony Classical) delivers the music, News Corp. (HarperCollins) publishes the book and Time-Warner (HBO) signs for the distribution of the film.
3. It is questionable whether the notion of a protection against the copying of materials is still adequate now that in the digital environment all forms of consultation, browsing and so on, imply making copies, however temporary.
4. Data from the International Federation of the Phonographic Industry, 1996 Report, *Pirate Sales 1995*, IFPI, London.

5. Data from International Intellectual Property Alliance, 1996, Washington DC.
6. WIPO is the UN specialized agency for intellectual property rights.
7. The European Commission wants to leave only those temporary copies free which have no independent economic significance.

The Democratization of Technology Choice   7

Everyone has the right to take part in the government of his country. . . .
The will of the people shall be the basis of the authority of government.
                          Universal Declaration of Human Rights, Article 21

The conclusion of the earlier chapters is that current practices and rules
of global governance in CyberSpace militate against the standards of
a human rights-based social morality. This morality proposes a social
and international order in which the rights and freedoms of the Universal
Declaration of Human Rights can be fully realized (Article 28). The
governance of this order requires certain institutional standards. Of crucial
significance are the requirements of democratic participation and public
accountability. The institutions of global governance for CyberSpace
should facilitate broadly-based civic participation and public accountability in their decision-making processes.

Democratic participation

Taking the classical democracy literature (for instance by Dahl, 1956,
1989; Dworkin, 1977, 1985; Pateman, 1970, or Schumpeter, 1942) and
common political practice in democratic states as point of reference, there
is a broad consensus about a definition of the 'democratic ideal' as a
political decision-making procedure that enables all those concerned to
participate on the basis of equality. This minimalist definition proposes
that the fundamental principle of democracy is political equality. This basic
procedural definition needs, however, considerable qualification if we want
to secure the egalitarian nature of democratic arrangements. When political
equality is conceived in a narrow sense there is no guarantee that the
democratic procedure enables the widest possible participation of all people
in public decision-making.

Actually, in most conceptions of democracy only a limited interpretation
of people's participation is foreseen. One could argue though that political

equality has meaning only if it goes beyond the right to vote and to be elected and encompasses civil rights such as freedom of speech, but also extends to institutions through which political equality should be secured. To promote the freedom that is basic to political equality democratic participation has to extend into areas where ordinary people do not normally participate. For Pateman, who represents against such 'realists' as Schumpeter and Dahl a normative approach, participation is 'a process where each individual member of a decision-making body has equal power to define the outcome of decisions' (Pateman, 1970: 71).

Following this reasoning we should extend the standard of political equality to mean the broadest possible participation of all people in processes of public decision-making. In addition, the democratic process should be moved beyond the political sphere and extend the requirement of participatory institutional arrangements to other social domains. Forms of participatory democracy have therefore to be designed for policy-making in the sphere of the production, development and dissemination of information and communication technologies. This conflicts with the observation that there is presently a widening gap between the domains of technological development and political decision-making (Winner, 1993: 61). As Ulrich Beck notes, 'Faith in progress replaces voting' (1992: 214). The development of biotechnology provides a good illustration. Scientists and investors cooperate to produce artificial tissue, blood vessels and organs such as hearts and livers. Charles Vacanti, top scientist in the field of 'regenerative' medicine thinks enough experimentation has been carried out with animals. It is time to begin the renovation of human beings. *Business Week* expects that the bio-industry will soon bring a veritable 'body shop' with human spare parts on the market (*Business Week*, 27 July 1998: 44). Irrespective of possible advantages versus disadvantages, the whole process evolves outside any form of social control. The German sociologist Beck points out that social concerns and anxieties about developments in genetic technology have no impact on the real decisions in this domain. These decisions have already been taken because the question whether certain developments were socially desirable was never posed: 'One can say "no" to progress, but that does not change its course at all' (Beck, 1992: 203). This course is determined outside the political domain. Policies on technology are not made by the political system:

> No votes are taken in parliament on the employment and development of microelectronics, genetic technology or the like; at most it might vote on supporting them in order to protect the country's economic future (and jobs). It is precisely the intimate connection between decisions on technological development and those on investment which forces the industries to forge their plans in secret for reasons of competition. Consequently,

decisions only reach the desks of politicians and the public sphere after being taken. (Beck, 1992: 213)

There is today a worldwide trend for governments to delegate the responsibility for basic social choices to the marketplace. The democratic control of important social domains is thus increasingly eroded without any major societal debate. Following their desire to deregulate, liberalize and privatize, many governments are leaving the governance of the new ICTs in the hands of private entrepreneurs. The European Commission's Action Plan *Europe's Way to the Information Society* (17 July 1994) – for example – states that European regulation must promote the mechanisms of the marketplace. The Commission proposes that through liberalization a competitive climate can be created within which the forces of the market can freely operate: 'The creation of the information society will be entrusted to the private sector'.

One implication is that the realization of social potential of ICTs comes to depend more on investment decisions than on considerations of common welfare. For anyone who cherishes the democratic ideal, this is a regrettably short-sighted position that demonstrates a basic lack of democratic sensitivity. If democracy represents the notion that all people should participate in those decisions that shape their future welfare, such social forces as the ICTs cannot just be left to the interests and stakes of commercial parties on the market. If we are serious about the democratic nature of our societies, there is a public responsibility in such a crucial domain as the design, development, and deployment of ICTs. Since the choices that are made in this domain have a far-reaching impact on societies, the political process requires the broadest possible participation of all those concerned. In other words, there is an urgent need for an extensive public dialogue about 'our common digital future'.

Public accountability

There is a strong tendency in most democracies to let a small élite decide on behalf of others. Particularly in large and complex societies, it becomes difficult to avoid forms of delegation of power to politicians, experts or entrepreneurs. There may be nothing wrong with delegating decisions, but those entrusted with deciding for others should provide a full and transparent account to those on whose behalf they are invited to act. This implies that a democratic arrangement should have rules, procedures and institutional mechanisms to secure public accountability. The principle of accountability logically implies the possibility of remedial action by those whose rights to participation and equality may be violated. Only through effective recourse to remedial measures can fundamental standards be implemented. If those who take decisions engage in harmful acts, those affected should have access to procedures of complaint, arbitration, adjudication and compensation. The process of establishing the responsibility for decisions taken and demanding compensation for wrongs inflicted, secures the egalitarian nature of the democratic arrangement.

If the principle of public accountability makes all key players accountable for their decision-making on behalf of others it applies to both public and private power holders. This has important implications for domains such as CyberSpace where the decision-makers are increasingly private parties which are neither elected nor held accountable. The global corporations that control ever more facets of people's daily lives have become less accountable to public authorities everywhere in the world: 'Most corporate leaders, while proudly exercising their constitutionally protected right to influence elections and legislation, deny that they are making public policy merely by doing business. They do not accept responsibility for the social consequences of what they make or how they make it' (Barnet and Cavanagh, 1994: 422).

Shifts in global governance institutions

The key requirements of democratic participation and public accountability are challenged by the major changes that over the past decade took place in the arena of global ICT-governance. Among the most important ones are the following:

The international governance system for communication operated during the past hundred years was mainly to coordinate national policies that were independently shaped by sovereign governments. Today's global governance system to a large extent determines supra-nationally the space that national governments have for independent policy-making.

World communication politics is increasingly defined by trade and market standards and ever less by political considerations. There is a noticeable shift from a predominantly political discourse to a largely economic/trade discourse. Evidence of this can be found in the growing emphasis on the economic importance of intellectual property and the related priority of providing protection for investors and corporate producers. In the telecommunications field the standards of universal public service and cross-subsidization have given way to cost-based tariff structures. In the area of transborder electronic data flows, politics changed from political arguments about national sovereignty and cultural autonomy to such notions as trade barriers and market access.

The most powerful private players have become more overtly significant. The 'invisible' hand of the economic interests that have all along guided political decision-making became in recent years increasingly visible. Transnational corporations became very prominent players in the arena and began to play their role very explicitly in the foreground. Actually the locus of much policy-making shifted from governments to associations of private business actors.

World communication politics was traditionally made in such intergovernmental fora as UNESCO, the World Intellectual Property Organization, and the International Telecommunication Union. These organizations were relatively open to the sociocultural dimension of developments in the field of information and communication technologies. Moreover, they offered a platform where also the interests of developing nations could be voiced. They also provided, at least in principle and not always very effectively, a possibility for the non-governmental community to provide an input in international negotiations. In recent years the position of these intergovernmental organizations was considerably weakened as the major players began to prefer the forum of the World Trade Organization. The WTO is generally more favourable to the trading interests of the major industrial countries than other intergovernmental bodies. Most of its economic and financial rules are made by self-selected policy groups that exclude the majority of national governments and that consult with only a select number of developing countries. The decision-making processes in these élite groups lack transparency, formal mechanisms of civil representation or procedures for public accountability. Among the main policy principles that guide the WTO are the worldwide liberalization of markets, and the non-discrimination principle that provides for national treatment of foreign competitors in national markets. A consequence of this orientation is that the WTO accepts that the interests of world trade supersede local political and economic interests. The implication is that the interests of the main traders (the world's leading transnational corporations) are considered more important than the interests of ordinary local people.

In its basic mandate the WTO violates the core of the human rights system: the recognition that all people should be treated equitably. The organization sets international standards for, among others, the safety of products. These are minimal standards and national legislation of member states has to be brought into line with these minimal requirements. If a country refuses it risks sanctions in terms of fines or retaliatory measures:

'The fact that its citizens simply do not want to be exposed to the higher level of risk accepted by the lower WTO standards isn't acceptable to the WTO as a valid justification' (Korten, 1995: 174). Against this there are no democratic procedures for appeal and remedy. The procedure by which violations of WTO rules are established is largely secretive. Cases are presented in secret hearings to panels of trade experts (usually corporate lawyers) with the use of secret documents. Decisions of the panels are adopted by the WTO unless within a period of sixty days there is a unanimous rejection of the recommendations by the member states. A basic feature of 'good governance' that appeals procedures are in principle effective and not by definition useless, is herewith violated. As Korten summarizes, 'The WTO is, in effect, a global parliament composed of unelected bureaucrats with the power to amend its own charter without referral to national legislative bodies' (Korten, 1995: 177).

Although there is formal representation of poor countries in the WTO decision-making processes, this means little since not all these countries have diplomatic missions for their participation in negotiations, and those that do are usually understaffed, underfunded and overworked. The decision-making mechanism that favours consensus and work in committees with select membership benefits mainly the rich countries. The mode of operation is largely such that agreements are worked out between the more powerful players and then negotiated with other parties. In the process usually a great deal of pressure is exercised on them. The main threat is that the violation of adopted agreements leads to heavy sanctions. If countries contest this, they can refer to the WTO dispute settlement system, but this mechanism is an expensive proposition for most countries as it involves the services of highly specialized trade lawyers. In conclusion one can say that at present the WTO does not measure up against the institutional standards of 'good governance'.

Next to the WTO an important new forum has emerged in recent years, the Global Business Dialogue. During the Interactive Conference of the ITU in September 1997 European Commissioner Martin Bangemann proposed the idea of a Charter with key principles for the information society. The Charter was to be a non-binding agreement on a framework for global communications in the twenty-first century. The idea was further elaborated during a G-7 meeting in Brussels in October 1997. On 29 June 1998 Commissioner Bangemann invited some 50 board chairmen and corporate presidents from 15 countries to a round-table discussion on global communications. Among the companies invited were Microsoft, Bertelsmann, Reuters, Polygram, IBM, Siemens, Deutsche Telekom, Sony, Toshiba and VISA. On the agenda were questions such as: 'What are the most urgent obstacles to global communications and what are the most effective means to remove them?' As urgent issues, intellectual property rights, taxation, tariffs, encryption, authentication, data protection and liability were identified.

The invitation was part of a plan to launch an International Charter on Communications as a political declaration which would launch a process of dialogue between governments and companies on the global electronic marketplace (I-Ways, 1998: 11). Commissioner Bangemann had suggested that the goal would be a market-led approach 'whereby the private sector can participate actively in a consultative process with governments and international organizations in the shaping of global communications policy' (I-Ways, 1998: 11).

Even before the round-table session began some American corporations had expressed reservations about the usefulness of a Charter. During the round-table session the business participants proposed that regulation must be kept to a minimum since the global nature of the online economy makes it impossible for any single government or body to regulate. The industry expressed a clear preference for self-regulation. The meeting proposed to set up a Business Steering Committee to ensure that the initiative would be business-led. The industrialists announced the start of a new Global Business Dialogue to which governments and international organizations will be invited. Ironically, the initial Bangemann plan aimed at a political declaration which would launch a dialogue between governments and companies on the global electronic marketplace. The process is now taken over by the private sector that will – when it sees fit – invite governments and international organizations in the shaping of a self-regulatory regime.

On 13 September 1999 the Global Business Dialogue on Electronic Commerce was convened in Paris. Some 500 top executives from media and IT industries (among them CEOs from Time-Warner, Bertelsmann, Nokia, AOL and Japanese NTT) discussed policy topics such as taxation, data protection, intellectual property rights, tariffs, information security and authentication. Government representatives (some 100, among them the Secretary General of the ITU) were invited but only as observers. Basically global business leaders told governments what to do in the governance of CyberSpace. Their main message was that the shaping of the Global Information Society should be driven by the market and led by the industry. The business executives recommended among other actions a moratorium on Internet taxes, lifting restrictions on the exports of encryption software, and third-party arbitration in e-commerce disputes. Against the strict rules of the European Union on the protection of privacy, the Global Business Dialogue promotes a relaxation of these rules as in the interest of global trading. The strategies and policy proposals are prepared by a 29-member steering committee with representatives from the private sector only.

Citizens and consumers

It is no surprise that CyberSpace governance is shifting to a global trade forum given the increasing economic value of communication networks and information services. In 1997 the global info-com market generated revenues of more than US$1.5 billion. Together with the fact that the major communication and information corporations provide the essential support structures for commodity and financial markets, the governance of communication issue areas is now largely destined to be subjected to a global trade regime. Global governance of CyberSpace is thus largely committed to minimizing public intervention and maximizing freedom for market forces. As a general trend people are increasingly seen as 'consumers' for whom ICTs provide commercial services and not as 'citizens' for whom ICTs offer a political forum for exchange and interaction. The 1997 European Commission *Greenbook on Convergence in Telecommunications, Media and IT* (of 3 December, for example, presents the users of ICTs almost exclusively as purchasers of goods and services on a market. There is little interest in ICTs as vehicles for people's political interactions and exchanges.[1]

Obstacles to good global governance

The enemies of the egalitarian democratic ideal are those forces that actively shape the 'new world order' that currently emerges largely in response to the collapse of Communism. The new world order poses a serious threat to the project of an egalitarian democracy since it exacerbates existing inequalities and results in a deep erosion of people's liberty to achieve self-empowerment. Since the new world order is not welcome everywhere, it also provokes a fierce opposition in forms of national, ethnic and religious fundamentalism that – ironically – equally threaten the prospect of an egalitarian democratic arrangement of world communication.

The new world order is characterized by the following features. It is driven by a 'globalization-from-above' (Falk, 1993: 39) which is controlled by the world's largest business corporations, the most powerful industrial states and their political and intellectual élites often with the generous support of the media moguls of the late twentieth century. The global reach of these forces is not matched by their acceptance of global responsibility. In fact, the most salient characteristic of the new world order is an ever wider ranging control over people's daily lives without even minimal public accountability.

The proponents of the new order readily claim that the process is democratic and supports global harmony and prosperity. The promotional language suggests that a free global market represents people's best interests. The promise that global trading in a deregulated global market leads to unprecedented prosperity to all, does not explain why in the real world the development of prosperity is highly uneven; why in fact poverty and inequality are worsening; why of the 5.6 billion people in the world at the end of 1994 over 1 billion try to survive on less than US$370 per year; why one billion adults are illiterate; why for over 500 million children there are no schools; why of the 2.8 billion labour force over 30 per cent is unemployed. A significant characteristic of the new world order is that: 'Far from producing a solution to the gap between the world's "haves" and "have-nots", the changing structures of international business and investment may exacerbate them' (Kennedy, 1993: 47).

The globalization of the new world order is characterized by social Darwinism and fragmentation. The leading economic theory suggests that poor countries 'only become relevant when they learn the lessons of the marketplace and possess those features which allow them to compete in the borderless world' (Kennedy, 1993: 61). This is corroborated by a social Darwinism that suggests that those who cannot make it in the marketplace are basically to blame themselves for their own inadequacies.

In several parts of the world the globalization-from-above has already led to aggressive forms of rejection of this imposition of modernity. The new world order is based upon the assumption that the poor will emulate the example of the rich and that they are eager to learn how to consume. It does not cater for the very real possibility that the poor may entrench into forms of national and religious fundamentalism and reject a world order that teaches them to want more material possessions or that they move in large numbers to the places of prosperity.

The new world order combines an unprecedented concentration of power with a stunning parochialism:

> The G-7, the group of the seven most powerful countries, dictate global affairs, but they remain narrow, local, and parochial in terms of the interests of all the world's communities. The World Bank is not really a bank that serves the interest of all the world's communities. (Shiva, 1993: 54)

The emergence of the new world order is greatly facilitated by a conservative libertarian belief system that is broadcast widely across the globe by the world's largest communication conglomerates. Among the essential beliefs that legitimize the opposition to the democratic ideal are the following.

A key belief is the gospel of privatization. It declares that the world's resources are basically private property, that public affairs should be regulated by private parties on free markets, and that the state should retreat from most if not all domains that affect people's daily lives. This conventional belief is that a free market guarantees the optimal delivery of ideas and information which 'has recently enjoyed a spirited revival as the unquestioned creed of the new fundamentalists of privatisation' (Murdock, 1994: 3).

An equally important belief is that 'the very essence of the democratic process' is 'the freedom to persuade and suggest' (Chomsky, 1989: 16). This freedom to 'engineer consent' may be concentrated in the hands of a few social actors only, but this should not be a concern in a free society and certainly no rationale for interfering in any way with the activities of the small oligarchies of business that control the provision of information and production of culture.

Very helpful to the enemies of the democratic ideal is also the widespread belief that people cannot be trusted to make sound and sensible decisions about their own lives. People can be left free to select what they eat and wear, but their choice for the system of governance is better left to those in control and their allies in engineering consent.

Prospects for change

The inevitable question that still needs to be addressed concerns the realistic prospect of an egalitarian democratic arrangement for the governance of CyberSpace. Given the formidable power of the driving forces of the new world order and the supporting belief system, this prospect would seem rather dim, to put it generously. The forces behind the new world order and their fundamentalist opponents divide our planet in endless repetitions of 'us' versus 'them' conflicts. Against this the most effective remedy is to achieve a level of distance from our own sectional interests that allows us to see 'everyone's life as of equal worth and everyone's well-being and freedom as equally valuable' (Lukes, 1993: 36). World political reality is not very encouraging for those who adopt this egalitarian perspective.

It seems unlikely that we could mobilize counterforces against a world order which provides an uneven access to the world's communication resources and which reinforces a growing gap between knowledge-rich and knowledge-poor nations and individuals. Even so, one could argue in support of this mobilization that the current arrangement can only continue as long as most people believe that a social and international order which is inegalitarian, insecure and undemocratic is in their best interest. Can we, however, bank upon the realization of a 'globalization-from-below' against the 'globalization-from-above' (Falk, 1993: 39)? The key component of an egalitarian and democratic social and international order is a vibrant, active, self-mobilizing world civil society. This is today no longer a chimera:

> Twenty years ago many despaired that global problems were spinning out of control. But slowly, inexorably, communities have shown that global change is within their power. They have cut the world's problem down to manageable size and exerted influence far in excess of their numbers. They have ended wars, freed political prisoners, cleaned up the global environment, rebuilt villages, and restored hope. (Shuman, 1994: 91)

Today millions of people around the world are involved with forms of local community-based activities that focus on global problems. A new type of world politics is emerging through these initiatives. They represent a shift from conventional international relations mainly conducted by the national foreign affairs élites of statesmen, diplomats and politicians towards a world political arena in which people in local communities involve themselves directly in the world's problems, often bypassing their national officials. As these local communities begin to network and cooperate, a new formidable force in the shaping of world politics develops. Local communities no longer depend upon the national leadership to make the world a safer place to live. In this process, globalization of the local is countered by local communities going global! Local communities have begun to recognize responsibility for problems outside their boundaries and have put world problems on their policy agenda. Local initiatives provide people with the opportunity to address this responsibility and increase people's contribution to political life. People in local communities accept that the fundamental obligation to take the future in their own hands is inherent in the democratic ideal. As local communities around the world are presently engaged in such areas of activity as development, environment and human rights, it could be argued that the achievement of a democratic world communication order should equally be put on their agenda as a decisive contribution to the quality of life in the third millennium.

Participation

Participation by representatives of non-governmental sectors (NGOs) has been an important asset of the UN system from its inception. Intergovernmental organizations such as UNESCO and WIPO have, throughout the years, benefited from the contributions made by institutional and individual members of civil society. In the forum of the ITU the active participation of NGOs has so far been mainly restricted to private commercial parties. The 1994 Kyoto ITU Plenipotentiary conference, for example, adopted a resolution that recognized the rights of the private sector to be included in the decision-making process of ITU study groups. In September 1998 the ITU decided to allow more participation in its deliberations by public interest NGOs.

During the May 1998 Ministerial Conference (at Geneva) the 132 WTO member states declared that the WTO must seek to involve NGOs more in its activities. In his speech to this Conference, US President Clinton stated 'We must modernize the WTO by opening its doors to the scrutiny and participation of the public'. In fact he proposed 'that all hearings by the WTO be open to the public'. In Clinton's view private citizens should be able to present their views before the WTO.

The requirement of more active civic participation in the global policy fora raises complex substantial and logistical questions. It seems obvious enough to call for the mobilization of civil society in order that the public interest is effectively represented. However, in much of the literature and debates one finds the tendency to 'romanticize' civil society by viewing it as inherently good and homogeneous. In reality, civil society is neither. A realistic historical assessment provides sobering observations such as the fact that the pervasive crime of genocide is often committed by ordinary members of civil society, and that the fastest growing sector of civil society is organized crime. The civic sector of most societies is composed of a heterogeneous collection of – often mutually exclusive – interests. There are divisions and antagonisms among the members of civil society. Moreover, the civil institutions that represent the public interest are not necessarily paragons of democratic governance.

As a result, it may be unrealistic to hope for public interest intervention in the global fora by a permanent, homogeneously-orientated entity that represents civil society. It seems more useful to adopt the position that public interest intervention in IPR negotiations may need a different coalition from the intervention in the proceedings of the ITU plenipotentiary when the organization deals with tariffs and accounting rates. Different fora and different issues require different modalities of intervention. It will be necessary to establish changing ad hoc coalitions that focus on specific issues and that put pressures on the decision-makers to take public interest motives into account. These ad hoc coalitions should be cross-border in nature. Not only in the geographical sense, but also in terms of discipline and orientation. They should involve not only civil movements that are active in the info-com field but stretch beyond this community to include public interest groups in fields such as human rights, environmental concerns, peace and security matters, and so on. And since the political and business domains are divided, there could also be alliances – on certain issues – with representatives from business and diplomatic communities.

An interesting model for public interest intervention is the opposition that since 1996 – to a large extent through the use of the Internet – has been mobilized against the Multilateral Agreement on Investment (MAI). The Agreement has been prepared since 1995 in secret negotiations under the umbrella of the Organization for Economic Co-operation and Development (OECD) held in Paris. The text of the Agreement followed a draft that was presented in 1996 by the International Chamber of Commerce. The main elements of the proposed Agreement are the full freedom of mobility for global capital flows and the far-reaching rights of international investors. The MAI denies national governments the right to impose restrictions on international investments and grants private corporations the right to bring charges against governments before an international tribunal of experts. The tribunal can impose fines and rule that governments pay immediate compensations to corporations if they violate the MAI rules. The MAI was supposed to be concluded in April 1998 at the OECD annual ministerial meeting. By that time so much public opposition had been mobilized by NGO activists that the process of negotiations could not be completed. As a result of the NGO campaign questions were asked in several national Parliaments as the parliamentarians began to realize that they were being left out of the MAI deliberations. Interesting in the MAI case is also that the public opposition caused the governments to announce in their 1998 Ministerial Statement that there will be consultations with civil society.

The MAI negotiations were not only affected by the NGO opposition but also by divisions among the negotiating parties. The French government, for example, in fact withdrew from the negotiations (by decision of October 1998). There is disagreement between European governments and the US government about the continuation of the negotiations. The European Union prefers to shift the negotiations to the WTO, but the USA prefers to stay with the OECD. An important component in the anti-MAI activism is the emphasis on constructive alternative proposals. The opponents not only criticize the deregulatory approach the negotiators have taken but also work towards the proposal of alternative forms of investment regulation. The most important features of the MAI model are the formation of an ad hoc coalition, a very precise target for public interest intervention and the proposal of alternative governance measures.

Similar to the MAI campaign the global governance of CyberSpace needs the active intervention by civic coalitions that represent the voices of those whose lives are deeply affected by the ICT-related choices that are made in global fora.

The intervention by public interest coalitions, the presentation of alternative policy proposals, and the effective publicity around such action, will not come about spontaneously. This demands organization and mobilization. A modest beginning has been made to achieve this through the Platform for Cooperation on Communication and Democratization. The platform that was established in 1995 is at present made up of AMARC, APC, Article 19, Cencos, Cultural Environment Movement, GreenNet, Grupo de los Ocho, IDOC, IFJ, IPAL, International Women's Tribune Centre, MacBride Round Table, MedTV, One World Online, Panos, People's Communication Charter, UNDA, Vidéazimut, WACC, WETV, and Worldview International Foundation. Members of the platform have agreed to work for the formal recognition of the right to communicate to be recognized. Members also emphasize the need to defend and deepen an open public space for debate and actions that build critical understanding of the ethics of communication, democratic policy and equitable and effective access.

Voices 21

Currently several Platform members are engaged in an initiative that was developed in 1998 during a meeting of the MacBride Round Table at Amman, Jordan and was baptized 'Voices 21'. The central focus of Voices 21 is to address problems and show solutions to one of the greatest challenges of our time: that the voices and concerns of ordinary people around the world are no longer excluded. In spite of all the solemn declarations about information societies and communication revolutions, most of the world's voices are not heard. In today's reality most people have neither the tools nor skills to participate in social communication or in communication politics. The preamble of the People's Communication Charter states, 'All people are entitled to participate in communication and in making decisions about communication within and between societies'.[2] In spite of all the developments and innovations in the field of information and communication, this standard has not yet been realized. Around this basic focus several campaigns are projected that focus on the following themes.

Access and accessibility

The main concern here is that participation in social communication presupposes access to big media, to community media, to computer networks, to information sources and to other tools. However, physical access is currently for many people around the globe neither sufficient nor affordable. Most people in the world are denied access to such basic tools as a telephone. As a result, a social gap grows between those who can afford access to information and those who will be excluded. Possible actions to address this concern include:

- the development of new forms of media and communication access, for example through telecentres and low-cost radiowires;
- the use of modern techniques where local infrastructure does not exist, such as solar energy, satellite and radio communications, and so on.

The right to communicate

The main concern here is that around the world old and new forms of statal and commercial censorship are rampant; they not only threaten the independence of conventional mass media but also the right to communicate through new channels like the Internet. Universal access to media and networks means little in the absence of adequate public space where information, opinions and ideas can be freely exchanged and debated. State censorship and providers' self-censoring of social debate, copyright rules, laws on business defamation, are all complex matters where rules need to be defined not to hinder, but to support political debate and exchange on socially important matters. Possible actions to address this concern include:

- to support and facilitate distribution of censored voices and material;
- to provide support to various anti-censorship campaigns around the world;
- to widely publicize examples of commercial censorship;
- to lobby at forthcoming meetings of WTO, WIPO, and the EU Commission.

Diversity of expressions

The main concern here is that the commercialization of media and concentration of media ownership erode the public sphere and fail to provide for cultural and information needs, including the plurality of opinions and the diversity of cultural expressions and languages necessary for democracy. This occurs not only in the conventional media business but is beginning also to affect the Internet. Possible actions to address this concern include:

- to build independent media and communication channels for civil society;
- to create a civil society media economy to make non-profit media channels sustainable;
- to develop concrete proposals for anti-cartel regulation;
- to mobilize local consumer actions against media mergers;
- to promote alternatives where they exist.

Security and privacy

The main concern here is that electronic communications through such media as the Internet have become targets for the surveillance by governments without public debate on the social consequences. Across the world, 24-hour ubiquitous electronic surveillance is expanding (for example through the Echelon programme of the US National Security Agency), employee monitoring, and widespread commercial data-mining. Internet Service Providers are made liable for contents they carry, and the bigger ones have begun collaborating with the security police. This forces forms of self-censorship upon the ISPs, and makes the Internet an unsafe place for people living under dictatorships or political oppression. Possible actions to address this concern include:

- developing legislative proposals for effective protective measures against various forms of privacy intrusion;
- educating people to the risks of widespread electronic surveillance.

The Voices 21 project proposes international and national campaigns around these themes as concrete manifestations of the provisions embedded in the so-called People's Communication Charter (PCC). A very encouraging and inspiring concrete example of implementing the PCC was the First International Public Hearing on Violations of the Charter that took place in early May 1999 at the Hague in The Netherlands. The theme of the Hearing 'Languages and Human Rights' focused on Article 9 of the PCC which claims the people's right to a diversity of languages. The Hearing was organized in response to the prediction made by language experts that 90 per cent of the world's languages are in danger of dying out within a century. Control over someone's language has become one of the primary means of exerting power over other aspects of people's life. At the end of the twentieth century the world's languages are disappearing faster than ever before in human history. During the Hearing a panel of five independent judges heard witnesses that made cases in support of Creole language, Kurdish language, Sign languages, Bilingual education in California, and Berber language. Among their recommendations and opinions the judges stated that: 'There is an urgent need for international bodies and national governments to be more energetic in guaranteeing that clauses in international covenants and in the PCC relating to language rights, to elaborate strategies for monitoring violations and for preventive diplomacy' (Hamelink, 1999b: 14). The recommendations of the Public Hearing will be put to intergovernmental bodies such as UNESCO and to the national governments involved in the five cases examined by the judges.

The organizers of this first Hearing (the PCC Amsterdam chapter, the World Association for Christian Communication, the Institute of Social Studies and the Organization of Local Broadcasters in The Netherlands) have agreed to explore the feasibility of holding hearings annually on different articles of the Charter. Eventually these Hearings could develop into a permanent institution for the enforcement of the PCC. This could take the form of an Ombudsoffice for communication and cultural rights.

This idea largely follows a recommendation made by the UNESCO World Commission on Culture and Development chaired by Javier Pérez de Cuéllar in its 1995 report, *Our Creative Diversity*. The Commission recommended the drawing up of an International Code of Conduct on Culture and – under the auspices of the UN International Law Commission – the setting up of an 'International Office of the Ombudsperson for Cultural Rights' (World Commission, 1995: 282). As the Commission writes:

> Such an independent, free-standing entity could hear pleas from aggrieved or oppressed individuals or groups, act on their behalf and mediate with governments for the peaceful settlement of disputes. It could fully investigate and document cases, encourage a dialogue between parties and suggest a process of arbitration and negotiated settlement leading to the effective redress of wrongs, including, wherever appropriate, recommendations for legal or legislative remedies as well as compensatory damages. (1995: 283)

The PCC initiative supports this, albeit with some hesitation as far as the governmental standing of the new institution is concerned. Full independence from statal interests would have to be secured as well as adequate financing. Both are difficult to achieve. Obviously, an Office that operates from a non-governmental background would have no possibilities for effective remedies in the sense of compensation or other sanctions. But the question is whether this is the most important feature. Amnesty International cannot hand out prison sentences to those who violate human rights. However, its politics of shame and exposure is certainly effective and provides a good deal of protection for victims of human rights violations. Ideally one would like to see the establishment of an institution that is fully independent, receives funding from both governments and industries and that develops a strong moral authority on the basis of its expertise, its track record and the quality of the people and the organizations that form its constituency. Building this new global institution constitutes one of the most exciting challenges for the twenty-first century!

Socratic education

Civic intervention is obviously rather meaningless if people are inadequately informed. Crucial for the democratization of technology choices is 'the education, in a major way, of the scientific and technical understanding of the public to the extent that some forms of democratic participation in scientific-technical policy-making becomes feasible and useful, and not simply an empty populist piety' (Wartofsky, 1992: 18). Against the argument that the public might make unwise decisions, it is far from certain that this is indeed the case when the public has access to full and undistorted information about matters of choice. Moreover, the expertise needed can be learnt: the capacity for informed and balanced public decision-making is not part of the human constitution. As Dewey has argued, 'effective intelligence is not an original, innate endowment, . . . the actuality of mind is dependent upon the education which social conditions effect' (quoted in Hickman, 1992: 101).

Therefore there is worldwide an urgent need for well-designed programmes of ICT education. There is a growing interest in this, but usually the resources are insufficient and the dominant approach tends to focus on the development of functional ICT skills. These are certainly important but they have to be complemented by the training of reflexive ICT skills. Critical thinking about the ICT potential and the balance of social risks versus benefits is essential. Educational systems around the world need well-designed curricula for in-depth courses on the social and ethical implications of the deployment of ICTs in societies.

In 1994 the International Baccalaureate (IB) introduced a course on Information Technology in a Global Society (ITGS) as a 'pilot' programme. By 1998 ITGS was taught in more than 80 schools worldwide. The syllabus of the course (designed for use in international schools for the age category of 16 to 19) provides an exemplary model of teaching that addresses the most important social and moral implications of ICT-developments. It is very encouraging to establish that this new topic is received by so many schools with great enthusiasm.[3]

The ITGS syllabus begins with an introduction to the nature of ICTs, then discusses social implications in a global society, the process of ethical decision-making, areas of social impact and problem-solving in a social context. Attention is given to the analysis of ICT tools, hardware, software and services. Specific areas of impact are studied such as security, reliability, teleworking, telebanking, freedom of expression, intellectual property rights, democracy and cultural homogenization. Among the aims of the programme are to promote an understanding and appreciation of the social significance of information technology and networking for individuals, communities and institutions; to analyse and evaluate in a critical manner the ethical considerations arising from the widespread use of information technology and networking; to appreciate the key elements of continuity and change in the development of information technology and networking leading from the past, through the present and into the future, and to assess their impact; to develop an understanding of new technologies as methods of enhancing and expanding our knowledge of the world, and of meeting the needs of society.

With the ITGS programme, the IB has developed a very appropriate curriculum to contribute to its larger mission which places a strong emphasis on the ideal of responsible citizenship. The IB aspires for its students to become critical and compassionate thinkers, lifelong learners and informed participants in local and world affairs. The present programme can obviously be further refined and improved. Most important is, however, to ensure that this approach finds a much broader application – beyond the IB schools – into all kinds of primary and secondary education. Teaching courses on 'ICTs and Society' should be a permanent feature of education worldwide. Only in this way can we hope that future generations are empowered to participate in those choices that will determine the quality of their lives.

The essence of Socratic thought is found in a statement Socrates makes during his defence before the Athenian judges. He proposes that the unexamined life is not worth living. This should form the main source of inspiration for educational programmes as proposed above. They should in essence prepare people for the 'culture of dialogue' that the democratic process requires. This means that citizens deliberate and reflect on the choices that optimally serve the common interest. This implies that they should be able to distance themselves from their own assumptions. They need the capacity to reason through their own positions and justify their preferences. This requires 'Socratic qualities' of all participants in the dialogue. The American philosopher Martha Nussbaum argues this in her book *Cultivating Humanity*. She writes, 'In order to foster a democracy that is reflective and deliberative, rather than simply a marketplace of competing interest groups, a democracy that genuinely takes thought for the common good, we must produce citizens who have the Socratic capacity to reason about their beliefs' (Nussbaum, 1997: 19).

For Socrates the critical investigation of our own assumptions is the essence of all serious reflection. Socrates establishes that our positions are often more determined by beliefs than by knowledge and we often fail to explain these beliefs. The Socratic approach does not ignore the significance of factual knowledge, but wants to explore its meaning. Socrates is in search of wisdom and therefore he asks whether we know what our knowledge represents. His investigations reveal in a merciless manner that we often talk about many matters we have little understanding of and that frequently we do not even understand our own thinking. This sceptical attitude is very useful in relation to the domain of the ICTs. With regard to our digital futures there are many more beliefs than serious explanations. There is an abundance of dogmatic propaganda by 'digiphiles' about revolutions and new societies. The problem-solving magic of ICTs tends to be exaggerated and the possible risks are belittled. There are also the unfounded fears of the 'digiphobes' about the uncontrollable nature of technological development and their unproductive all-out refusal to get involved with the new possibilities of the ICTs. Socratic education provides the future citizens of CyberSpace with a techno-scepsis that empowers them against both the frivolous declaration of the 'digiphiles' and the desperate scenarios of the 'digiphobes'.

Notes

1. In line with this thinking most national ICT policy plans neglect the provision of non-commercial services through ICTs. A very important exception to this trend is, however, provided in the Protocol on Public Service Broadcasting to the European Union, Amsterdam Treaty of June 1997. The EU has agreed that

public service broadcasting is related to democratic, social and cultural needs and to the need to preserve media pluralism. The social and cultural significance of public broadcasting is acknowledged by allowing it to function outside the regime of free market funding.
2. The web site with the current text of the People's Communication Charter and background information about the PCC is: www.pccharter.net.
3. The International Baccalaureate is a non-profit organization that provides primary and advanced education in over 750 schools in more than 90 countries. The IB 'mission statement' states among others, 'Beyond intellectual rigour and high academic standards strong emphasis is placed on the ideals of international understanding and responsible citizenship, to the end that IB students may become critical and compassionate thinkers, lifelong learners and informed participants in local and world affairs.'

Bibliography

Abramson, J.B., Aterton, C. and Orren, G.R. (1988) *The Electronic Commonwealth: The Impact of New Media Technologies on Democratic Politics.* New York: Basic Books.

Achterhuis, H. (ed.) (1992) *De Maat van de Techniek.* Amsterdam: Ambo.

Akthar, S. (1994) *Building North–South Bridges on the Information Superhighway: Toward a Global Agenda for Collaborative Research and Action.* Ottawa: IDRC.

Albert, S.A. (1998) 'Health Care Information: Access, Confidentiality and Good Practice', in K.W. Goodman (ed.), *Ethics, Computing and Medicine.* Cambridge: Cambridge University Press. pp. 75–101.

Alderman, E. and Kennedy, C. (1995) *The Right to Privacy.* New York: Vintage Books.

Almond, B. (1995) 'Introduction: Ethical Theory and Ethical Practice', in B. Almond (ed.), *Introducing Applied Ethics.* Oxford: Blackwell. pp. 1–14.

Alston, P. (ed.) (1992) *The United Nations and Human Rights: A Critical Appraisal.* Oxford: Clarendon Press.

An-Na'im, A.A., Gort, J.D., Jansen, H. and Vroom, H.M. (eds) (1995) *Human Rights and Religious Values.* Amsterdam: Editions Rodopi.

Apel, K.-A. (1988) *Diskurs und Verantwortung.* Frankfurt: Suhrkamp.

Aristotle (1995) *Politics.* Trans. Ernest Barker. Oxford: Oxford University Press.

Armstrong, J.E. and Haman, W.W. (1980) *Strategies for Conducting Technology Assessment.* Boulder, CO: Westview Press.

Arnbak, J.C. (1997) 'Managing the Radio Spectrum in the New Environment', in W.H. Melody (ed.), *Telecom Reform: Principles, Policies and Regulatory Practices.* Lyngby: Technical University of Denmark. pp. 139–47.

Aronson, J.D. and Cowhey, P.F. (1988) *When Countries Talk: International Trade in Telecommunications Services.* Cambridge, MA: Ballinger.

Ashley, D. (1990) 'Habermas and the completion of "The Project of Modernity"', in B.S. Turner (ed.), *Theories of Modernity and Postmodernity.* London: Sage. pp. 88–107.

Association for Computing Machinery (1991) *Software Engineering Notes,* 11 (1).

Association for Computing Machinery (1994) *Ethics in the Computer Age,* ACM Conference Proceedings of November 1994.

Baase, S. (1997) *A Gift of Fire: Social, Legal and Ethical Issues in Computing.* London, Prentice Hall.

Bagdikian, B.H. (1989) 'The Lords of the Global Village', *The Nation,* 12 June: 805–20.

Baker, J. (1987) *Arguing for Equality.* London: Verso.

Bangemann, M. (1994) *Europe and the Global Information Society*, Recommendations to the European Council, Report of the Bangemann Commission, May.

Barbour, I. (1992) *Ethics in an Age of Technology*. London: SCM Press.

Baresch, D. and Schlechter, R. (1998) 'Secure Electronic Communication – The European Community Approach', in D.L. Goldman and R. Winsbury (eds), *Digital Signatures and Cryptography*, IIC Special Report, 26 (6): 6–11.

Barnet, R.J. and Cavanagh, J. (1994) *Global Dreams: Imperial Corporations and the New World Order*. New York: Simon & Schuster.

Barrett, N. (1996) *The State of the Cybernation*. London: Kogan Page.

Barron, I. and Curnow, R. (1979) *The Future with Microelectronics*. London: Frances Pinter.

Basque, G. (1995) 'Introduction to the Internet', in E. Mackaay, D. Poulin and P. Trudel (eds), *The Electronic Superhighway*. The Hague: Kluwer. pp. 7–20.

Beauchamp, T.L. (ed.) (1991) *Philosophical Ethics*. New York: McGraw-Hill.

Beck, U. (1992) *Risk Society: Towards a New Modernity*. London: Sage.

Beekman, G. (1994) *Computer Currents: Navigating Tomorrow's Technology*. Redwood City: Benjamin/Cummings Publishing.

Behar, R. (1997) 'Who's reading your E-mail?', *Fortune*, 3 February: 29–36.

Bekkers, V., Koops, B.J., and Nouwt, S. (1996) *Emerging Electronic Highways: New Challenges for Politics and Law*. The Hague: Kluwer Law International.

Bell, D. (1976) *The Coming of Post-Industrial Society: A Venture in Social Formation*, Harmondsworth, Penguin.

Beniger, J.R. (1986) *The Control Revolution: Technological and Economic Origins of the Information Society*. Cambridge, MA: Harvard University Press.

Benson, I. and Lloyd, J. (1983a) *Employment, Economics and Technology*. London: Kogan Page.

Benson, I. and Lloyd, J. (1983b) *New Technology and Industrial Change*. London: Kogan Page.

Berendt, A. (1995) 'Universal Service: What is it, and How?, *Intermedia*, 23 (2): 42–4.

Bertin, G.Y. and Wyatt, S. (1988) *Multinationals and Industrial Property: The Control of the World's Technology*. Atlantic Highlands, NJ: Humanities Press.

Berting, J. (ed.) (1990) *Human Rights in a Pluralist World*. Westport, CT: Meckler.

Bijker, W.E. (1997) *Of Bicycles, Bakelites, and Bulbs: Toward a Theory of Sociotechnical Change*. Cambridge, MA: MIT Press.

Bijker, W.E., Hughes, Th.P. and Pinch, T. (eds) (1987) *The Social Construction of Technological Systems: New Directions in the History and Sociology of Technology*. Cambridge, MA: MIT Press.

Bodington, S. (1973) *Computers and Socialism*. Nottingham: Spokesman Books.

Bourdieu, P. (1985) Reprint of 'Social Space and Genesis of Classes', *Theory and Society*, 14: 723–44.

Bowyer, K.W. (1996) *Ethics and Computing: Living Responsibly in a Computerized World*. Los Alamitos, CA: IEEE Computer Society Press.

Brown, D. (1997) *Cybertrends: Chaos, Power and Accountability in the Information Age*. New York: Penguin Books.

Brownlie, I. (ed.) (1981) *Basic Documents on Human Rights*. Oxford: Oxford University Press.

Brunner, J. (1975) *The Shockwave Rider*. New York: Harper & Row.

Buchan, J. (1998) *Frozen Desire: An Inquiry into the Meaning of Money*. London: Picador.

Buergenthal, T. (ed.) (1977) *Human Rights, International Law and the Helsinki Accords*, New York: Allanbeld/Osmun.

Burnham, D. (1980) *The Rise of the Computer State*. New York: Random House.

Burstein, D. and Kline, D. (1995) *Road Warriors: Dreams and Nightmares along the Information Highway*. New York: Plume.

Business Week (1998) 'Biotech Bodies', 27 July: 42–9.

Bynum, T.W. and Fodor, J.L. (1998) 'Medical Information and Human Values', in K.W. Goodman (ed.), *Ethics, Computing and Medicine*. Cambridge: Cambridge University Press. pp. 32–56.

Campbell, T., Goldberg, D., McLean, S. and Mullen, T. (eds) (1986) *Human Rights: From Rhetoric to Reality*. Oxford: Basil Blackwell.

Carey, J. (1998) 'Human Clones: It's Decision Time', *Business Week*, 10 August: 37.

Cassese, A. (1990) *Human Rights in A Changing World*. Cambridge: Polity Press.

Chapman, A.R. (1995) 'A New Approach to Monitoring the International Covenant on Economic, Social and Cultural Rights', in *The Review*, International Commission of Jurists, 55: 23–37.

Chomsky, N. (1989) *Necessary Illusions*. Boston: South End Press.

Christians, C.G. (1999) 'Ethics, Economics and Innovation: The Future of Accountability', *Media Development*, 46 (2): 12–15.

Clynes, M.E. and Kline, N.S. (1960) 'Cyborgs and Space'. *Astronautics* (13): 26–75.

Cogburn, D.L. (1996) *Information and Communications for Development: Nationalism, Regionalism, and Globalism in Building the Global Information Society*. Report by the Global Information Infrastructure Commission, Washington DC.

Collingridge, D. (1980) *The Social Control of Technology*. Milton Keynes: The Open University.

Collingridge, D. (1982) *Critical Decision Making*. London: Frances Pinter.

Compaine, B.M. and Weinraub, M.J. (1997) 'Universal Access to Online Services: An Examination of the Issue', *Telecommunications Policy*, 21 (1): 15–33.

Connor, J.A. (ed.) (1998) 'Privacy in International Data Flow', *Communication Research Trends*, 18 (1).

Conway, F. and Siegelman, J. (1984) *Holy Terror: The Fundamentalist War on America's Freedom in Religion, Politics and our Private Lives*. New York: Dell Publishing.

Council of Europe (1995) *Concerning Problems of Criminal Procedure Law Connected with Information Technology*. Strasbourg: Council of Europe.

Cuéllar, J.P. de (1995) *Our Creative Diversity*. Report of the World Commission on Culture and Development. Paris: UNESCO.

Curran, J. (1991) 'Mass Media and Democracy: A Reappraisal', in J. Curran and M. Gurevitch, *Mass Media and Society*. London: Edward Arnold. pp. 82–117.

Daes, E.I.A. (1983) *The Individual's Duties to the Community and the Limitations on Human Rights and Freedoms under Article 29 of the Universal Declaration of Human Rights*. New York: United Nations.

Dahl, R.A. (1956) *A Preface to Democratic Theory*. Chicago: University of Chicago Press.

Dahl, R.A. (1989) *Democracy and its Critics*. New Haven, CT: Yale University Press.

Dahlgren, P. and Sparks, C. (eds) (1991) *Communication and Citizenship*. London: Routledge.

Davies, C. (1997) 'WIPO Treaties: The New Framework for the Protection of Digital Works', *Communications Law*, 2 (2): 46–8.

Der Derian, J. and Shapiro, M.J. (eds), (1989) *International/Intertextual Relations: Postmodern Readings of World Politics*. Lexington, MA: Lexington Books.

Dertouzos, M. (1997) *What Will Be: How the New World of Information will Change our Lives*. London: Piatkus Publishers.

Dery, M. (1996) *Escape Velocity: Cyberculture at the End of the Century*. London: Hodder & Stoughton.

Dinstein, Y. (1981) 'The Right to Life, Physical Integrity, and Liberty', in L. Henkin (ed.), *The International Bill of Rights*. New York: Columbia University Press. pp. 114–37.

Doheny-Farina, S. (1996) *The Wired Neighborhood*. New Haven, CT: Yale University Press.

Donnelly, D.F. (1999) 'Selling on, Not Out, the Internet', in S.J. Drucker and G. Gumpert (eds), *Real Law@Virtual Space: Communication Regulation in Cyberspace*. Cresskill, NJ: Hampton Press. pp. 287–302.

Donnelly, J. (1993) *International Human Rights*. Boulder, CO: Westview Press.

Donnelly, J. and Howard, R.E. (1988) 'Assessing National Human Rights Performance: A Theoretical Framework', *Human Rights Quarterly*, 10 (2), 214–48.

Drucker, S.J. and Gumpert, G. (1999a) 'Freedom and Liability in Cyberspace: Media, Metaphors, and Paths of Regulation', in S.J. Drucker and G. Gumpert (eds), *Real Law@Virtual Space: Communication Regulation in Cyberspace*. Cresskill, NJ: Hampton Press. pp. 71–94.

Drucker, S.J. and Gumpert, G. (1999b) 'Of Firewalls and Unlocked Doors: Expectations of Privacy', in S.J. Drucker and G. Gumpert (eds), *Real Law@Virtual Space: Communication Regulation in Cyberspace*. Cresskill, NJ: Hampton Press. pp. 325–47.

Dryden, J. (1999) 'Policies for Global E-Commerce: The Role of the OECD', *I-Ways*, 22 (2): 25–9.

Duchrow, U. (1995) *Alternatives to Global Capitalism*. Utrecht: International Books.

Dutton, W.H. (ed.) (1996) *Information and Communication Technologies: Visions and Realities*. Oxford: Oxford University Press.

Dutton, W.H., Blumler, J.G., Garnham. N., Mansell, R., Cornford, J. and Peltu, M. (1996) 'The Politics of Information and Communication Policy: The Information Superhighway', in W.H. Dutton (ed.), *Information and Communication Technologies: Visions and Realities*. Oxford: Oxford University Press. pp. 387–405.

Dworkin, R. (1977) *Taking Rights Seriously*. London: Duckhart.

Dworkin, R. (1985) *A Matter of Principle*. Cambridge, MA: Harvard University Press.

Edel, A., Flower, E. and O'Connor, F.W. (1994) *Critique of Applied Ethics*. Philadelphia, PA: Temple University Press.

Edge, D. (1995) 'The Social Shaping of Technology', in H. Heap, R. Tomas, G. Einon, R. Mason and H. Mackay (eds), *Information Technology and Society*. London: Sage. pp. 14–32.

Eide, A. (1993) (ed.) *The Universal Declaration of Human Rights: A Commentary*. Oslo: Scandinavian University Press.

Electronic Privacy Information Center (1999) *Cryptography and Liberty 1999: An International Survey on Encryption Policy*. URL: www.epic.org/

Electronic Privacy Information Center & Privacy International (1999) *Privacy and Human Rights 1999: An International Survey of Privacy Laws and Development*. URL: www.privacyinternational.org/survey

Ellul, J. (1964) *The Technological Society*. New York: Vintage Books.

Ellul, J. (1980) *The Technological System*. New York: Continuum.

Elster, J. (1983) *Explaining Technical Change*. Cambridge: Cambridge University Press.

Ermann, M.D., Williams, M.B. and Gutierrez, C. (eds) (1990) *Computers, Ethics and Society*. Oxford: Oxford University Press.

European Commission (1994) *Europe's Way to the Information Society*. Brussels: European Commission. p. 10.

European Commission (1996a) 'The Common Position (EC) 7/97', *Official Journal of the EC*, 10.2.1997.

European Commission (1996b) *Communication to the European Parliament, the Council, the Economic and Social Committee and the Committee of the Regions on Universal Service for Telecommunications in a Perspective of a Fully Liberalised Environment*. Brussels, COM (96) 73.

European Commission (1996c) *Building the European Information Society for us all*. Brussels: European Commission, DG V.

European Commission (1997a) *Towards a European Framework for Digital Signatures and Encryption*. Brussels: European Commission.

European Commission (1997b) Greenbook on Convergence in Telecommunications, Media and IT. Brussels: European Commission.

European Commission (1998a) *Proposal for a European Parliament and Council Directive on Certain Legal Aspects of Electronic Commerce in the Internal Market*. Brussels: COM (1998), 586 final.

European Commission (1998b) *Proposal for a Directive on 'A Common Framework for Electronic Signature*. Brussels: COM (98) 197/2.

European Parliament and Council of the European Union (1995) *Directive on the Protection of Individuals with Regard to the Processing of Personal Data and on the Free Movement of Data*. Strasbourg, Brussels.

Falk, R.A. (1981) *Human Rights and State Sovereignty*. New York: Holms and Meier.

Falk, R.A. (1983) *The End of World Order: Essays on Normative International Relations*. New York: Holms and Meier.

Falk, R.A. (1993) 'The Making of Global Citizenship', in J. Brecher, J.B. Childs and J. Cutler (eds), *Global Visions: Beyond the New World Order*. Boston: South End Press. pp. 39–50.

Ferné, G. (1996) 'Information Technology', in *World Science Report*. Paris: UNESCO. pp. 269–80.

Flichy, P. (1995) *Dynamics of Modern Communication: The Shaping and Impact of New Communication Technologies*. London: Sage.

Forester, T. (1985) *The Information Technology Revolution*. Oxford: Basil Blackwell.

Forester, T. (1987) *The High-Tech Society: The Story of the Information Technology Revolution*. Cambridge, MA: MIT Press.

Forester, T. and Morrison, P. (1995) *Computer Ethics*. Cambridge, MA: MIT Press.

Forsythe, D.P. (1989) *Human Rights and World Politics*. Lincoln and London: University of Nebraska Press.

Foucault, M. (1984) *Le Souci de soi*. Paris: Gallimard.

Foucault, M. (1992) 'What is Enlightenment?', in P. Waugh (ed.), *Postmodernism*. London: Edward Arnold. pp. 96–108.

Fox, J. (1998) 'Europe is Heading for a Wild Ride', *Fortune*, 138 (4): 27–31.

Freeman, C. (1995) *Information Highways and Social Change*. Ottawa: IDRC.

Frost, M. (1986) *Towards a Normative Theory of International Relations*. Cambridge: Cambridge University Press.

Fuchs, G. and Koch, A.M. (1996) 'The Globalization of Telecommunications and the Issue of Regulatory Reform', in E. Kofman and G. Youngs (eds), *Globalization: Theory and Practice*. London: Pinter. pp. 163–74.

Galtung, J. (1994) *Human Rights in Another Key*. Oxford: Polity Press.

Garcia-Sayan, D. (1995) New Path for Economic, Social and Cultural Rights, *The Review*, International Commission of Jurist, 55: 75–80.

Garnham, N. (1997) 'Universal Service', in W.H. Melody (ed.), *Telecom Reform: Principles, Policies and Regulatory Practices*. Lyngby: Technical University of Denmark. pp. 207–13.

Gauthier, D. (1986) *Morals by Agreement*. Oxford: Oxford University Press.

Gavaghan, H. (1998) 'Satellites: A New Reading of Earth', *Sources*, 105: 10–11.

Gay, P. (1973) *The Enlightenment: An Interpretation. Part 2: The Science of Freedom*. London: Wildwood House.

Gershon, R.A. (1997) *The Transnational Media Corporation*. Mahwah, NJ: Lawrence Erlbaum Associates.

Geuna, A. (1997) *Joining the Information Society: Internet Access Issues for Europeans*. Working Paper No. 17. Science Policy Research Unit, University of Sussex.

Gibson, W. (1984) *Neuromancer*. New York: Ace Books.

Giddens, A. (1991a) *The Consequences of Modernity*. Oxford: Polity Press.

Giddens, A. (1991b) *Modernity and Self-Identity: Self and Society in the Late Modern Age*. Oxford: Polity Press.

Glaser, J.W. (1994) *Three Realms of Ethics*. Kansas City: Sheed & Ward.

Global Information Infrastructure Commission (1995) *Assessing Data Privacy in the 1990s and Beyond*. Washington DC: Center for Strategic and International Studies.

Golding, P. (1990) 'Political Communication and Citizenship: The Media and Democracy in an Inegalitarian Social Order', in M. Ferguson (ed.), *Public Communication: The New Imperatives*. London: Sage. pp. 84–100.

Golding, P. (1994) 'The Communications Paradox: Inequality at the National and International Levels', *Media Development*, 41 (4): 7–9.

Goldman, D.L. and Winsbury, R. (eds) (1998) 'Digital Signatures and Cryptography', *IIC Special Report*, 26 (6).

Goodman, K.W. (ed.) (1998a) *Ethics, Computing and Medicine*. Cambridge: Cambridge University Press.

Goodman, K.W. (1998b) 'Bioethics and Health Informatics: An Introduction', in K.W. Goodman (ed.), *Ethics, Computing and Medicine*. Cambridge: Cambridge University Press. pp. 1–31.

Gould, C.C. (1988) *Rethinking Democracy: Freedom and Social Cooperation in Politics, Economy and Society*. Cambridge: Cambridge University Press.

Graber, M.A. (1991) *Transforming Free Speech*. Berkeley: University of California Press.

Gray, C.H. (1997) *Postmodern War*. London: Routledge.

Gray, J. (1998) *False Dawn: The Delusions of Global Capitalism*. London: Granta Books.

Greider, W. (1998) *One World, Ready or Not: The Manic Logic of Capitalism*. New York: Simon & Schuster.

Griffioen, S. (ed.) (1990) *What Right does Ethics have? Public Philosophy in a Pluralistic Culture*. Amsterdam: VU University Press.

Gumpert, G. and Drucker, S. (1998) 'The Demise of Privacy in a Private World: From Front Porches to Chat Rooms', *Communication Theory*, 8 (4): 408–25.

Habermas, J. (1993) *Moral Consciousness and Communicative Action*. Cambridge, MA: MIT Press.

Hamelink, C.J. (1983) *Cultural Autonomy in Global Communications*. New York: Longman.

Hamelink, C.J. (1986) *Militarization in the Information Age*. Geneva: World Council of Churches.

Hamelink, C.J. (1988) *The Technology Gamble*. Norwood, NJ: Ablex Publishing.

Hamelink, C.J. (1994) *The Politics of World Communication*. London: Sage.

Hamelink, C.J. (1995) *World Communication*. London: Zed Books.

Hamelink, C.J. (1996) 'Globalisation and Human Dignity: The Case of the Information Superhighway', *Media Development*, (1): 18–21.

Hamelink, C.J. (1997a) *Information-Communication Technologies for Social Development*. Geneva: UNRISD.

Hamelink, C.J. (1997b) 'Making Moral Choices in Development Cooperation: The Agenda for Ethics', in C.J. Hamelink (ed.), *Ethics and Development: On Making Moral Choices in Development Cooperation*. Kampen, Kok. pp. 8–24.

Hamelink, C.J. (1999a) 'The Elusive Concept of Globalisation', *Global Dialogue*, 1 (1): 1–9.

Hamelink, C.J. (1999b) 'The Right to Communicate: the PCC beyond 2000'. *IDOC Internazionale*, (30) 1–2: 10–14.

Hannikainen, L. (1988) *Peremptory Norms in International Law*. Helsinki: Finnish Lawyers' Publishing Company.

Haraway, D. (1985) 'Manifesto for Cyborgs: Science, Technology, and Socialist Feminism'. *Socialist Review* (80): 85–108.

Harris, P. (1997) 'Communication and Global Security: The Challenge for the Next Millennium', in P. Golding and P. Harris (eds), *Beyond Cultural Imperialism*. London: Sage. pp. 147–62.

Hartmann, C.J. (1995) 'The Emergence of a Statutory Right to Privacy in England', *Media Law & Practice*, 16 (1): 10–20.

Haywood, T. (1995) *Info-Rich Info-Poor: Access and Exchange in the Global Information Society*. London: Bowker-Saur.

Heap, H., Tomas, R., Einon, G., Mason, R. and Mackay, H., (eds) (1995) *Information Technology and Society*. London: Sage.

Herman, E.S. and McChesney, R.W. (1997) *The Global Media: The New Missionaries of Global Capitalism*. London: Cassell.

Hickman, L.A. (1992) 'Populism and the Cult of the Expert' in: Winner, L. (ed.) (1992) *Democracy in a Technological Society*. Dordrecht: Kluwer, pp. 91–103.

Hills, J. (1984) *Information Technology and Industrial Policy*. Beckenham: Croom Helm.

Hills, J. (1989) 'Universal Service: Liberalization and Privatization of Telecommunications', *Telecommunications Policy*, 13 (2): 129–44.

Hills, J. and Papathanassopoulos, S. (1991) *The Democracy Gap: The Politics of Information and Communication Technologies in the United States and Europe*. New York: Greenwood Press.

Hinman, L.M. (1994) *Ethics: A Pluralistic Approach to Moral Theory*. New York: Harcourt, Brace, Jovanovich.

Hirst, P. and Thompson, G. (1996) *Globalization in Question*. Oxford: Polity Press.

Hoboken, R. van (1998) 'Consult Risk Management', Volkskrant, 22 May: 9.

Holland, K. and Cortese, A. (1995) 'The Future of Money', *Business Week*, 12 June: 36–46.

Holmes, P., Kempton, J. and McGowan, F. (1996) 'International Competition Policy and Telecommunications: Lessons from the EU and Prospects for the WTO', *Telecommunications Policy*, 20 (10): 755–67.

Hossain, K. (1997) *Promoting Human Rights in the Global Market Place*. Amsterdam: Vrije Universiteit.

Hoven, M.J. van den (1995) *Information Technology and Moral Philosophy: Philosophical Explorations in Computer Ethics*. Dissertation, Erasmus Universiteit Rotterdam.

Howkins, J. and Valantin, R. (eds) (1997) *Development and the Information Age*. Ottawa: IDRC.

Hudson, H.E. (1997) 'Converging Technologies and Changing Realities: Toward Universal Access to Telecom in the Developing World', in W.H. Melody (ed.), *Telecom Reform: Principles, Policies and Regulatory Practices*. Lyngby: Technical University of Denmark. pp. 395–404.

Independent Commission for World Wide Telecommunications Development (1984) *The Missing Link*. Geneva: International Telecommunication Union.

Information Highway Advisory Council (1997) *Preparing Canada for a Digital World*. Final Report. Ottawa: IHAC.

International Chamber of Commerce (1998) *Revised Guidelines on Advertising and Marketing on the Internet*. Paris: I.C.C.

ITU (1997) *World Telecommunication Development Report 1996/97: Trade in Telecommunications*. Geneva: International Telecommunication Union.

ITU (1998a) *World Telecommunication Development Report: Universal Access*. Geneva: International Telecommunication Union.

ITU (1998b) *General Trends in Telecommunication Reform 1998 – World*, Volume 1. Geneva: International Telecommunication Union.

ITU (1998c) *Valetta Declaration and Action Plan*, adopted by the Second World Telecommunication Development Conference held at Valetta, Malta, March 1998.

I-Ways (1996) *Digest of Electronic Commerce Policy and Regulation*. Fairfax Station: Transnational Data Reporting Service, 19 (2).

I-Ways (1998) *Digest of Electronic Commerce Policy and Regulation*. Fairfax Station: Transnational Data Reporting Service, 21 (2).

Jackson, J. (1993) 'Reconciling Business Imperatives and Moral Virtues', in E.R. Winkler and J.R. Coombs (eds), *Applied Ethics*. Oxford: Basil Blackwell. pp. 104–17.

Jager, P. de and Bergeon, R. (1997) *Managing 00: Surviving the Year 2000 Computing Crisis*. New York: John Wiley.

Jaggar, A. (1993), 'Taking Consent Seriously', in E.R. Winkler and J.R. Coombs (eds), *Applied Ethics*. Oxford: Basil Blackwell. pp. 69–86.

James, J. (1996) *Thinking in the Future Tense*. New York: Simon & Schuster.

Johnson, D.G. (1994) *Computer Ethics*. London: Prentice Hall.

Jokinen, P. (1996). *The Promise of the Information Society for Sustainable Development*. Paper for the Telecommunications and Sustainability Workshop at the Conference on Challenges of Sustainable Development, Amsterdam, 22–25 August 1996.

Jongman, J.J. and Schmidt, A.P. (1994) *Monitoring Human Rights*. Leiden: PIOOM.

Kallman, E.A. and Grillo, J.P. (1996) *Ethical Decision Making and Information Technology*. New York: McGraw-Hill.

Katz, J. (1997) 'The Digital Citizen', *Wired*, 5 December: 68–82, 274–5.

Kelly, K. (1994) *Out of Control*. New York: Addison-Wesley.

Kennedy, P. (1993) *Preparing for the Twenty-First Century*. New York: Vintage Books.

Khor, M. (1995) *Globalization and the Need for Coordinated Southern Policy Response: Cooperation South*. New York: UNDP TCDC.

Khor, M. (1998) 'WTO partly marred by anti-globalisation protests', *Third World Network Features*.

Kimman, E.J.J.M. (1991) *Organisatie Ethiek*. Assen: Van Gorcum.

Kizza, J.M. (ed.) (1994) *Ethics in the Computer Age*. ACM Conference Proceedings of November, New York.

Kleinwächter, W. (1998) 'The People's Right to Communicate and a Global Communication Charter: How Does Cyberspace Change the Legal Concepts of Human Rights and Participation?', *The Journal of International Communication*, 5 (1/2), 105–21.

Kleinwächter, W. (1999) 'The Cyberright to Communicate: A Human Rights of the fourth Generation?', in R.C. Vincent, K. Nordenstreng and M. Traber (eds), *Towards Equity in Global Communication: MacBride Update*. Cresskill, NJ: Hampton Press. pp. 91–101.

Kling, R. (ed.) (1996) *Computerization and Controversy: Value Conflicts and Social Choices*. New York: Academic Press.

Korten, D.C. (1995) *When Corporations Rule the World*. West Hartford, CT: Kumarian Press.

Korten, D.C. (1998) *Globalizing Civil Society: Reclaiming our Right to Power*. New York: Seven Stories Press.

Kramer, R.C., Jaksa, J.A. and Pritchard, M.S. (1996) 'Ethics in Organizations: The Challenger Explosion', in J.A. Jaksa and M.S. Pritchard (eds), *Responsible Communication*. Cresskill, NJ: Hampton Press. pp. 53–73.

Kuitenbrouwer, F. (1996) 'Dutch Experiences with Privacy Self-Regulation', *I-Ways*, 4: 17–21.

Kurzweil, R. (1999) *The Age of Spiritual Machines*. New York: Viking.

Kuttner, R. (1998) *Everything for Sale: The Virtues and Limits of Markets*. New York: Alfred A. Knopff.

Landauer, Th. K. (1995) *The Trouble with Computers*. Cambridge, MA: MIT Press.

Laudon, K.C., Traver, C.G. and Laudon, J.P. (1995) *Information Technology: Concepts and Issues*. London: International Thompson Publishing.

Lee, J.A.N. and Berleur, J. (1994) 'Progress towards a World-Wide Code of Conduct', in J.M. Kizza (ed.), *Ethics in the Computer Age*. ACM Conference Proceedings, New York, pp. 100–94.

Leslie, J. (1996) *The End of the World*. London: Routledge.

Leveson, G. and Turner, C.S. (1993) 'An Investigation into the Therac-25 Accidents', *Computer*, 26 (7): 18–41.

Lindblom, C.E. (1977) *Politics and Markets: The World's Political-Economic Systems*. New York: Basic Books.

Loader, B.D. (ed.) (1997) *The Governance of Cyberspace*. London: Routledge.

Lohr, S. (1994) 'Data Highway Ignoring Poor, Study Charges', *New York Times*, 24 May: A1, D3.

Lukes, S. (1993) 'Five Fables about Human Rights', in S. Shute and S. Hurley (eds) *On Human Rights*. New York: Basic Books. pp. 19–40.

Lyon, D. (1988) *The Information Society: Issues and Illusions*. Cambridge: Polity Press.

Lyon, D. (1994) *Postmodernity*. Buckingham: Open University Press.

Lyon, D. (1995), 'The Roots of the Information Society Idea', in H. Heap, R. Tomas, G. Einon, R. Mason and H. Mackay (eds), *Information Technology and Society*. London: Sage. pp. 54–73.

Lyotard, J.-F. (1979) *La Condition Postmoderne*. Paris: Les Éditions de Minuit.

Lyotard, J.-F. (1985) *The Postmodern Condition*. Manchester: Manchester University Press.

MacIntyre, A. (1988) *Whose Justice? Which Rationality?* Notre Dame, IL: Notre Dame University Press.

Mackaay, E., Poulin, D. and Trudel, P. (eds) (1995) *The Electronic Superhighway: The Shape of Technology and Law to Come*. The Hague: Kluwer Law International.

Mackie, J.L. (1977) *Ethics: Inventing Right and Wrong*. Harmondsworth: Penguin.

Madsen, W. (1999) 'World Encryption Regulation Down, Report Shows', *I-Ways*, 22 (2): 9–13.

Maitland, D. (1986) *The Missing Link: World Telecommunications Forum Report*. Geneva, ITU.

Makridakis, S. (1995) 'The Forthcoming Information Revolution: Its Impact on Society and Firms', *Futures*, 27 August: 799–821.

Malley, J. (1996) *Introductory Paper*. Telecommunications and Sustainability Workshop at the Conference on Challenges of Sustainable Development, Amsterdam, 22–25 August 1996.

Mansell, R. (1997a) 'Designing Networks to Capture Customers: Policy and Regulation Issues for the New Telecom Environment', in W.H. Melody (ed.),

Telecom Reform: Principles, Policies and Regulatory Practices. Lyngby: Technical University of Denmark. pp. 83–96.

Mansell, R. (1997b) *Consumer and Citizen Rights and Expectations: Commercialising Advanced Communication Services in the Information Society.* Working Paper No. 25. Science Policy Research Unit, University of Sussex.

Mansell, R. (1998) 'Citizen Expectations: The Internet and the Universal Service Challenge', *Intermedia*, 26 (1): 4–7.

Mansell, R. (1999) 'The Politics of Designing Information Networks', *Media Development*, 46 (2): 7–11.

Mansell, R. and Wehn, U. (1998) *Knowledge Societies: Information Technology for Sustainable Development.* Oxford: Oxford University Press.

Margalit, A. (1996) *The Decent Society.* Cambridge, MA: Harvard University Press.

Masuda, Y. (1980) *The Information Society as Post-Industrial Society.* Washington DC: World Future Society.

Mattelart, A. (1999) 'Against Global Inevitability', *Media Development*, 46 (2): 3–6.

M'Bayo, R. (1997) 'Africa and the Global Information Infrastructure', *Gazette*, 59 (4/5): 345–64.

Melody, W.H. (1996) 'Toward a Framework for Designing Information Society Policies', *Telecommunications Policy*, 20 (4), 243–59.

Meyer, T. (1989) 'Philosophie, Pädagogik, Politik – Ihr Zusammenhang im Werk Leonard Nelsons', in D. Krohn (ed.), *Das Sokratische Gespräch.* Hannover: Junius Verlag. pp. 33–54.

Michael, D.N. (1984) 'Too Much of a Good Thing? Dilemmas of an Information Society', *Technological Forecasting and Social Change*, 25: 347–54.

Michael, J. (1994) *Privacy and Human Rights.* Paris: UNESCO.

Millard, C. (1997) 'Local Content Filters and the "Inherent Risk" of the Internet', *Intermedia*, 25 (1): 21–2.

Miller, S.E. (1996) *Civilizing Cyberspace: Policy, Power, and the Information Superhighway.* New York: Addison-Wesley.

Miller, T. (1996) 'Law, Privacy and Cyberspace', *Communications Law*, 1 (4): 143–8.

Mitchell, J. (1997) 'Convergent Communications, Fragmented Regulation and Consumer Needs', in W.H. Melody (ed.), *Telecom Reform: Principles, Policies and Regulatory Practices.* Lyngby: Technical University of Denmark. pp. 441–51.

Mody, B., Tsui, L.-S., and McCormick, P. (1993) 'Telecommunication Privatization in the Periphery: Adjusting the Private–Public Balance', *International Review of Comparative Public Policy*, 5: 257–74.

Murdock, G. (1994) 'The New Mogul Empires: Media Concentration and Control in the Age of Divergence', *Media Development*, 41 (4): 3–6.

Muto, I. (1993) 'For an Alliance of Hope', in J. Brecher, J.B. Childs and J. Cutler (eds), *Global Visions: Beyond the New World Order.* Boston, MA: South End Press. pp. 147–62.

Nederveen Pieterse, J. (1996), 'Globalisation and Culture', *Perspectives*, 8 June: 1389–93.

Negrine, R. (1997), 'Communication Technologies: An Overview', in A. Mohammadi (ed.), *International Communication and Globalization.* London: Sage. pp. 50–66.

Negroponte, N. (1995) *Being Digital*. London: Hodder & Stoughton.

Neumann, P.G. (1995) *Computer Related Risks*. New York: Addison-Wesley.

Nilsson, N.J. (1990) 'Artificial Intelligence, Employment, and Income', in M.D. Ermann, M.B. Williams and C. Gutierrez (eds), *Computers, Ethics and Society*. Oxford: Oxford University Press. pp. 248–62.

Nino, C.S. (1993) *The Ethics of Human Rights*. Oxford: Clarendon Press.

Noeding, T. (1998) 'Distance Selling in a Digital Age', *Communications Law*, 3 (3): 85–93.

Nussbaum, M.C. (1997) *Cultivating Humanity: A Classical Defense of Reform in Liberal Education*. Cambridge, MA: Harvard University Press.

OECD (1995a) *Satellite Communication: Structural Change and Competition*, OECD/GD(95)109. Paris: OECD.

OECD (1995b) *International Telecommunications: A review of issues and developments*, Committee for Information, Computer and Communications Policy. Paris: OECD.

OECD (1997a) *Measuring Electronic Commerce*, OECD/GD(97)183. Paris: OECD.

OECD (1997b) *The Economic and Social Impacts of Electronic Commerce: Preliminary Findings and Research Agenda*. Paris: OECD.

OECD (1997c) *Communications Outlook 1997*, Volumes 1 and 2. Paris: OECD.

OECD (1997d), *Guidelines for Cryptography Policy*, Paris: OECD.

OECD (1998a) *Internet Infrastructure Indicators*, DSTI/ICCP/TISP(98)/Final. Paris: OECD.

OECD (1998b) *Cross-Ownership and Convergence: Policy Issues*, DSTI/ICCP/TISP (98)3/Final. Paris: OECD.

Ogden, M. (1996) 'Electronic Power to the People: Who is Technology's Keeper on the Cyberspace Frontier?', *Technological Forecasting and Social Change*, 52 (2/3): 119–33.

Ogden, M. (1999) 'Catching Up to Our Digital Future? Cyberdemocracy versus Virtual Mercantilism', in R.C. Vincent, K. Nordenstreng and M. Traber (eds), *Towards Equity in Global Communication: MacBride Update*. Cresskill, NJ, Hampton Press. pp. 103–38.

Oliner, S.P. and Oliner, P.M. (1988) *The Altruistic Personality: Rescuers of Jews in Nazi Europe*. New York: The Free Press.

Olliges, R. (1996) 'The Social Impact of Computer-Based Communications', *Communication Research Trends*, 16 (2).

Omega Foundation (1998) *An Appraisal of the Technologies of Political Control*. Report to the European Commission, February. Manchester: Omega Foundation.

PANOS (1998) *The Internet and Poverty*, Panos Media Briefing No. 28. London: PANOS.

Parker, D., Swope, S. and Baker, B. (1990) *Ethical Conflicts in Information and Computer Science, Technology and Business*. Wellesley: QED Information Sciences.

Pateman, C. (1970) *Participation and Democratic Theory*. Cambridge: Cambridge University Press.

Petersen, J.L., Wheatley, M. and Kellner-Rogers, M. (1998) 'The Y2K Problem: Social Chaos or Social Transformation?', *The Futurist*, October 1998: 21–8.

Pipe, G.R. (ed.) (1995) *Assessing Data Privacy in the 1990s and Beyond*. Washington DC: The Global Information Infrastructure Commission.

Plato (1955) *The Republic*. Trans. Desmond Lee. London: Penguin.

Pool, I. de Sola (1983) *Forecasting the Telephone: A Retrospective Technology Assessment of the Telephone*. Norwood, NJ: Ablex Publishing.

Porter, V. (1995) 'Wanted: A New International Law on Intellectual Property Rights on the GII', *Intermedia*, 23 (4): 31–6.

Postman, N. (1993) *Technopoly*. New York: Vintage Books.

Postmes, T. (1996) *Social Influence in Computer-Mediated Groups*. Ph.D Dissertation, University of Amsterdam.

Punch, M. (1996) *Dirty Business: Exploring Corporate Misconduct*. London: Sage.

Quittner, J. (1997a) 'No Privacy on the Web', *Time*, 2 June: 62–3.

Quittner, J. (1997b) 'Invasion of Privacy', *Time*, 25 August: 34–9.

Raboy, M. (1998) 'Global Communication Policy and the Realisation of Human Rights, *The Journal of International Communication*, 5 (1/2): 83–104.

Ramcharan, B.G. (1981) 'Equality and Nondiscrimination', in L. Henkin (ed.), *The International Bill of Rights*. New York: Columbia University Press. pp. 246–69.

Ramcharan, B.G. (1994) 'The Universality of Human Rights', *The Review*, 53: 105–17.

Rawls, J. (1973) *A Theory of Justice*. Oxford: Oxford University Press.

RAWOO (1998) *Information and Communication Technology and Development*, RAWOO lectures and seminar, Publication no. 18. The Hague: Netherlands Development Assistance Research Council.

Raz, J. (1984) 'Right-Based Moralities', in J. Waldron (ed.), *Theories of Rights*. Oxford: Oxford University Press. pp. 182–200.

Raz, J. (1994) *Ethics in the Public Domain*. Oxford: Clarendon Press.

Reijne, Z., Kouwenberg, R.F. and Keizer, M.P. (1996) *Tappen in Nederland*. Gouda: Quint.

Reinders, J.S. (1995) 'Human Rights from the Perspective of a Narrow Conception of Religious Morality', in A.A. An-Na'im, J.D. Gort, H. Jansen and H.M. Vroom (eds), *Human Rights and Religious Values*. Grand Rapids, MI: William B. Eerdmans. pp. 3–23.

Renteln, A.D. (1990) *International Human Rights: Universalism versus Relativism*. London: Sage.

Rescher, N. (1993) *Pluralism*. Oxford: Oxford University Press.

Rheingold, H. (1995) *The Virtual Community*. London: Mandarin Paperbacks.

Rogers Commission (1986) *Report to the President by the Presidential Commission on the Space Shuttle Challenger Accident*. Washington DC.

Rorty, R. (1996) 'Putting Your Money Where Your Mouth Is', *UNESCO Sources*, 79, May. Paris: UNESCO.

Rose, L. (1995) *NetLaw: Your Rights in the Online World*. New York: McGraw-Hill.

Rosenberg, R.S. (1992) *The Social Impact of Computers*. San Diego: Academic Press.

Roszak, T. (1986) *The Cult of Information*. New York: Pantheon Books.

Sale, K. (1995) *Rebels Against the Future: The Luddites and Their War on the Industrial Revolution*. New York: Addison-Wesley.

Sampson, C.I. (1996) 'Liberalisation of Trade in Telecommunications Services and the Implication of GATS/WTO for Developing Countries', *InterMedia*, 24 (5): 19–30.

Sayers, D. (1997) *Name-linked Data Legislation: Current Practice and Enforcement Issues for the Information Society*, Working Paper No. 15. Science Policy Research Unit, University of Sussex.

Schiller, H.I. (1993) *Mass Communications and American Empire* (revised edition). Boulder, CO: Westview.

Schumpeter, J.A. (1942) *Capitalism, Socialism and Democracy*. London: Allen & Unwin.

Schwartau, W. (1996) *Information Warfare*. New York: Thunder's Mouth Press.

Seeskin, K. (1987) *Dialogue and Discovery*. Albany: State University of New York.

Shapiro, N.Z. and Anderson, R.H. (1985) *Toward an Ethics and Etiquette for Electronic Mail*. Santa Monica (CA): RAND.

Shelley, M. (1818) *Frankenstein*. Penguin Classics edition of 1985.

Shenk, D. (1997) *Data Smog: Surviving the Information Glut*. London: Abacus.

Shields, R. (1996) *Cultures of InterNet: Virtual Spaces, Real Histories, Living Bodies*. London: Sage.

Shiva, V. (1993) 'The Greening of the Global Reach', in J. Brecher, J.B Childs and J. Cutler (eds), *Global Visions: Beyond the New World Order*. Boston, MA: South End Press. pp. 53–60.

Shiva, V. (1999) 'Diversity and Democracy: Resisting the Global Economy', *Global Dialogue*, 1 (1): 19–30.

Shuman, M. (1994) *Towards a Global Village: International Community Development Initiatives*. London: Pluto Press.

Shutt, H. 1998) *The Trouble with Capitalism*. London: Zed Books.

Singer, P. (1979) *Practical Ethics*. Cambridge: Cambridge University Press.

Singer, P. (1997) *How are We to Live? Ethics in an Age of Self-Interest*. Oxford: Oxford University Press.

Slouka, M. (1995) *War of the Worlds: Cyberspace and the High-Tech Assault on Reality*. New York: Basic Books.

Snapper, J.W. (1998) 'Responsibility for Computer-based Decisions in Health Care', in K.W. Goodman (ed.), *Ethics, Computing and Medicine*. Cambridge: Cambridge University Press. pp. 43–56.

Soete, L. and Kamp, K. (1997) 'Taxing Consumption in the Electronic Age', *Intermedia*, 25 (4): 19–22.

Sogolo, G. (1994) 'Continuity-in-Change: Alternative Scenarios for the Futures of African Cultures', in *The Futures of Cultures*, Paris, UNESCO: 123–37.

Sreberny-Mohammadi, A. (1997) 'The Many Cultural Faces of Imperialism', in P. Golding and P. Harris (eds), *Beyond Cultural Imperialism*. London: Sage. pp. 49–68.

Standen, I. (1996) *'Porning' Privacy in Cyberspace*. Working Paper No. 11. Science Policy Research Unit, University of Sussex.

Stephens, G. (1995) 'Crime in Cyberspace', *The Futurist*, September–October: 24–8.

Stoll, C. (1991) *The Cuckoo's Egg*. London: Pan Books.

Stoll, C. (1995) *Silicon Snake Oil: Second Thoughts on the Information Highway*. New York: Doubleday.

Stout, J. (1990) *Ethics After Babel: The Languages of Morals and Their Discontents*. Cambridge: James Clark & Co.

Sussman, G. (1997) *Communication, Technology and Politics in the Information Age*. London: Sage.

Sutherland, P. and Sewell, J.W. (1998) *The Challenges of Globalization*. Washington DC: Overseas Development Council.

Szafran, E. (1998) 'Regulatory Issues Raised by Cryptography on the Internet', *Communications Law*, 3 (2): 38–50.

Szanton, M.C.B. (1972) *A Right to Survive: Subsistence Marketing in a Lowland Philipine Town*. Philadelphia: The Pennsylvania State University Press.

Talbott, S.L. (1995) *The Future does not Compute*. Sebastopol, CA: O'Reilly & Associates.

Tang, P. (1995) 'Intellectual Property Right and the Internet: The Future Needs Work', *Intermedia*, 23 (4): 22–5.

Tapscott, D. (1995) *The Digital Economy*. New York: McGraw-Hill.

Tenner, E. (1997) *Why Things Bite Back: Predicting the Problems of Progress*. London: Fourth Estate.

Toffler, A. (1971) *Future Shock*. New York: Bantam Books.

Toffler, A. and Toffler, H. (1998) 'Preparing for Conflict in the Information Age', *The Futurist*, June–July: 26–9.

Tuchman, B.W. (1984) *The March of Folly: From Troy to Vietnam*. London: Sphere Books.

Tumber, H. and Bromley, M. (1998) 'Virtual Soundbites: Political Communication in Cyberspace', *Media, Culture & Society*, 20 (1): 159–67.

Turkle, S. (1995) *Life on the Screen*. New York: Simon & Schuster.

UNCITRAL (1996) *Model Law on Electronic Commerce*. New York: United Nations.

UNDP (United Nations Development Program) (1997) *Human Development Report 1997*. New York: Oxford University Press.

UNDP (United Nations Development Program) (1998) *Human Development Report 1998*. New York: Oxford University Press.

UNDP (United Nations Development Program) (1999) *Human Development Report 1999*. New York: Oxford University Press.

UNESCO (1994) *The Futures of Cultures*. Paris: UNESCO.

UNESCO (1996) *UNESCO and an Information Society for All*. Paris: UNESCO.

UNESCO (1997) *World Communication Report: The Media and the Challenge of the New Technologies*. Paris: UNESCO.

UNESCO (1998) *World Education Report*. Paris: UNESCO.

UNICEF (1999) *State of the World's Children*. New York: United Nations.

United Nations (1948) Universal Declaration of Human Rights. URL: www.hrweb.org/legal/udhr.html

United Nations (1993) Vienna Declaration and Programme of Action. United Nations General Assembly. A/CONF. 157/23.

United Nations Administrative Committee on Coordination (1997) 'Universal Access to Basic Communications and Information Services', *I-Ways*, 20 (2): 19–25.

United Nations (1998) *World Economic and Social Survey*. New York. United Nations.

Venturelli, S. (1998a) 'Cultural Rights and World Trade Agreements in the Information Society', *Gazette*, 60 (1): 47–76.

Venturelli, S. (1998b) *Liberalizing the European Media: Politics, Regulation and the Public Sphere*. Oxford: Clarendon Press.

Walch, J. (1999) *In The Net: Computer Support for Social Action*. London: Zed Books.

Walters, M. (1995) *Globalization*. London: Routledge.

Wartofsky, M.W. (1992) 'Technology, Power and Truth: Political and Epistemological Reflections on the Fourth Revolution' in: Winner, L. (ed.) (1992) *Democracy in a Technological Society*. Dordrecht, Kluwer, pp. 5–34.

Waugh, P. (ed.) (1992) *Postmodernism*. London: Edward Arnold.

Webster, F. (1995) *Theories of the Information Society*. London: Routledge.

Weeramantry, C.G. (1983) *The Slumbering Sentinels: Law and Human Rights in the Wake of Technology*. Harmondsworth: Penguin Books.

Weeramantry, C.G. (ed.) (1990) *Human Rights and Scientific and Technological Development*. Tokyo: The United Nations University Press.

Weeramantry, C.G. (ed.) (1993) *The Impact of Technology on Human Rights: Global Case Studies*. Tokyo: The United Nations University Press.

Weizenbaum, J. (1976) *Computer Power and Human Reason*. San Francisco, CA: W.H. Freeman and Company.

Went, R. (1996) *Grenzen aan de Globalisering?* Amsterdam: Het Spinhuis.

Wertheimer, R. (1993) 'Socratic Skepticism', in E.R. Winkler and J.R. Coombs (eds), *Applied Ethics*. Oxford: Basil Blackwell. pp. 143–63.

Whittle, D.B. (1997) *Cyberspace: The Human Dimension*. New York: W.B. Freeman and Company.

Wildstrom, S.H. (1996) 'They're Watching you Online', *Business Week*, 11 November.

Williams, B. (1985) *Ethics and the Limits of Philosophy*. Cambridge, MA: Harvard University Press.

Williams, R. and Edge, D. (1996), 'The Social Shaping of Technology', in W.H. Dutton (ed.), *Information and Communication Technologies: Visions and Realities*. Oxford: Oxford University Press. pp. 53–67.

Winkler, E.R. and Coombs, J.R. (eds) (1993) *Applied Ethics*. Oxford: Basil Blackwell.

Winner, L. (1986) *The Whale and the Reactor: A Search for Limits in an Age of High Technology*. Chicago, IL: Chicago University Press.

Winner, L. (1993) 'Citizen Virtues in a Technological Order', in E.R. Winkler and J.R. Coombs (eds), *Applied Ethics*. Oxford: Basil Blackwell. pp. 46–68.

Winseck, D. and Cuthbert, M. (1997) 'From Communication to Democratic Norms: Reflections on the Normative Dimensions of International Communication Policy', in A. Sreberny-Mohammadi, D. Winseck, J. McKennan and O. Boyd-Barrett (eds), *Media in Global Context*. London: Edward Arnold. pp. 162–76.

Wissema, J.G. (1997) *Rijden managers door rood licht?* Assen: Van Gorcum.

Woodhull, N.J. and Snyder, R.W. (eds) (1998) *Media Mergers*. London: Transaction Publishers.

World Bank (1995) *Workers in an Integrating World*. Washington: World Bank.

World Commission on Culture and Development (1995) *Our Creative Diversity*. Paris: UNESCO.

Yourdon, E. and Yourdon, J. (1998) *Time Bomb 2000*. New York: Prentice-Hall.

Yu, H., Xiaoming, H. and Kewen, Z. (1997) 'Challenges to Government Control of Information in China', *Media Development*, 44 (2): 17–22.

Index